Aama
in
America

Aama
in
America

A Pilgrimage
of the Heart

BROUGHTON
COBURN

ANCHOR BOOKS
DOUBLEDAY
New York London Toronto Sydney Auckland

AN ANCHOR BOOK
PUBLISHED BY DOUBLEDAY
a division of Bantam Doubleday Dell Publishing Group, Inc.
1540 Broadway, New York, New York 10036

ANCHOR BOOKS, DOUBLEDAY, and the portrayal
of an anchor are trademarks of Doubleday, a division of
Bantam Doubleday Dell Publishing Group, Inc.

All photos except top photo on p. iv (William
Thompson), p. 19 (Eric Valli), and p. 300 (Russell
Johnson) are by the author and are reprinted by
permission of the author.

Aama in America: A Pilgrimage of the Heart was
originally published in hardcover by Anchor Books in 1995.

Book Design by Gretchen Achilles

The Library of Congress has cataloged the hardcover
edition as follows:

Coburn, Broughton, 1951–
   Aama in America : a pilgrimage of the heart /
Broughton Coburn. —
1st ed.
      p.   cm.
   1. United States—Social life and customs—1971–
2. United States—Description and travel.   3. Gurung,
Vishnu Maya—Journeys—United States.   4. Nepalese—
Travel—United States.   I. Title.
   E169.04.C64   1995
   917.304'92—dc20   94-38806
                                                CIP

ISBN 0-385-47418-0
Printed in the United States of America
First Anchor Books Trade Paperback Edition: April 1996

10 9 8 7 6 5 4 3

For Alex and Lu.

In the most general terms a pilgrimage represents a person's journey from the world of the profane, or ordinary, to the world of the sacred, and as such is often marked by the characteristics of a rite of passage in which the participant undergoes a process of separation, threshold, and incorporation.

—David R. Kinsey, *Hinduism*

Haré Om, *please bless me and my dharma son and daughter-in-law and the drivers of the airplane and all the people joining us on this long journey, for I am going in ignorance of what will befall me. . . .*

—*Aama*

Acknowledgments

The extraordinary and unanticipated generosity of Vishnu Maya Gurung ("Aama"), her relatives, and the Gurung people of their village in the hills of Syangja District, Nepal, formed the early inspiration for this book. To return their rich hospitality and friendship would be difficult. Taking Aama to America could represent only a perfunctory thank you.

Before my girlfriend Didi and I left Nepal with Aama for the United States, I had thought of documenting Aama's reactions to America. Privately, I worried that Aama might register little beyond shock and displeasure at the fleeting, contorted circus acts of our nation. Initially Didi and I had only the skeleton of an agenda, and Aama had none. The West Coast was our sole destination, and we were prepared at any point to return to Nepal with Aama, if she desired. We never imagined this would occur after three months, twelve thousand car miles, and the kind of physical and mental obstacles that Hindu and Buddhist pilgrims have come to expect.

We had elected ourselves—or, rather, I had chosen myself and dragged Didi along—as Aama's driver and attendant. Tethered together like Apollo astronauts in the front seat of a station wagon, the three of us swept over the continent. Lying beneath the uniform, commercial, man-made epidermis of our country, Aama found a culture and landscape that was alive and sacred, and she steered us toward it.

Didi and I ended up taking a backseat to Aama's search, sharing in her discovery and her frustration, witnessing her ancient worldview draw up short before our modern one, and then leap over it. I had lived in Aama's home and village long enough to sense her moods, but America constantly challenged me to bridge the sizable cultural and age gaps, to unravel her sometimes obscure associations, and to fulfill her expectations about Americans as people.

Eventually I gave up trying to define or interpret what Aama was seeing clearly for herself, and simply began to record. I missed a lot. I assumed that the camera, pen, and tape machine would document it all adequately. But what meets the eye or ear only selectively emerges as thought and analysis. Memory, seasoned by time, will often recall events with greater depth than the best efforts of description during their original occurrences. The journey had become a process, and that process a catalyst—for uncovering more than we had bargained for.

I had presumed that including Aama on our road trip would cost only nominally more than her plane ticket to the States. We continued to live in our accustomed low-budget manner, while I watched my bank balance leak away. I shot 380 rolls of film with three older-model Nikon single-lens reflex cameras, and recorded more than fifty hours of conversation on a series of cheap microcassette recorders that each ran at different speeds.

I am indebted to Aama's daughter, Sun Maya Gurung. To those who generously advised, guided, and encouraged us during our journey across the United States, and to those who extended gifts and hospitality, I express my sincere gratitude. The list is too long to include them all, but I'll begin by thanking Randy Bell, Chad and Darlene Broughton, Anita Byock, Kanak Dixit, Ronnie Egan, Deborah Flanders, Lisette Gunther and the late Kurt Gunther, Nar Bahadur and Kushi Gurung, Raine Hall, the Hanuman Ashram of Taos, Nancy Hawver, Bill Kite, Jeff Long, Efale McFarland, Tom McMackin, Don and Kareen Messerschmidt, the Milford Colony of Hutterian Brethren, Stephanie and Michael Nadeau, Kathleen Peterson, Cecilia Pleshakov, Chuck and Joan Pratt, Tom Pritzker, Geoff and Janet Rockwell, Dan Rotrosen and Liz Dugan, David Sassoon, David Shlim, Larry Shlim, Florence and Lawrence Singer, Minu Singh, Todd Stuart, Christian Swenson and Abigail Halperin, the people of the Taos Pueblo, Caroline Tawangyma, Hilda and the late Austin Two Moons, Mary Ellen Valyo, Thekla von Hagke, Nevada Wier,

Maria Wilhelm, and Richard Wiswall. I apologize to those I've missed.

While the manuscript and photographs were being prepared, the following friends offered invaluable assistance: Scott Andrews, Dick Dorworth, John Frederick, Paul Gallagher, Jeff Greenwald, Mary Gurdy, Ashok Gurung, Chandra Prasad Gurung, Dil Bahadur Gurung, Jagman Gurung, Nancy Jo Johnson, Ella Laub, Lobsang Lhalungpa, Hemanta and Sushma Mishra, Laura Nolan, Stephen Olsson, Gajendra Nath Regmi, Jamuna Gurung Shrestha, Eric Valli, and Melissa Walia. I would like to specially thank Misty Haley, Sandra Lambert, and Dotty and Palmer Smith for their careful proofreading, advice, warmth, and refuge.

My agent, Sarah Lazin, provided an expert balance of criticism and encouragement. She recognized the end of the story at the time it occurred—well after Aama had returned to Nepal and before it had been written down. The lessons that ordeals teach us sometimes are learned only later, and unexpectedly.

Charlie Conrad, my editor at Anchor Books, followed the book into its present form with faith and patience; Jon Furay and Kevin Lang tended to important details, and did much careful, tedious footwork.

In particular, I want to thank my parents, Alex and Lunette Coburn, for their love, assistance, and good cheer. Also, many thanks to Doug and Karen Chadwick, David Larkin and Susan Cochran, Ann and Greg Lyle, William Thompson and Tori Withington, Genna Thunder, Barbara Thunder, and Betsy Withington, who gladly offered their homes and hearts well beyond any conventional welcome period. They, too, are like family.

Most important, I am grateful to Didi Thunder, a placid reservoir of love and compassion. Didi made the journey, along with its halting conclusions and blessed commencements, possible.

Perhaps, as travel with Aama suggested, initial misperception can be a painful, and often comical, stepping-stone to understanding.

Aama
in
America

Chapter 1

I was prepared to hear Aama's daughter Sun Maya say, "We took her up there," referring to the site where I had last seen several of Aama's relatives: the cremation ground.

The gnarled roots of a banyan fig tree formed a natural stairway leading upward to a grassy terrace. I stopped climbing to rest and to wait for my girlfriend, Didi. My head was throbbing, swollen with blood searching for oxygen, though we were less than six thousand feet above sea level.

A village woman in a vivid print sarong walked by, hunched beneath a rustling basketload of corn leaves and fodder grass, her line of sight fixed to the trail by a tumpline. Health illuminated her burnished red face. She prodded a cow with a willow switch, her glass bangles jingling, then paused. The dried cow pies at the edge of the terrace would be good fuel for her fire pit, and she tucked them in with her fodder. Had she noticed my jeans and foreign sneakers? She rolled her head upward and observed me quickly, speculating. Was I hiking up to the hamlet on the ridge to inoculate children for the Nepalese government? Perhaps I was the schoolteacher who years ago lived with the old woman in the village on the far side of the hill; or maybe a recruiter for the Gurkha regiments of the British Army, joined by a wife following dutifully several paces behind.

"Oounhh," she said softly, a sound that asked as well as answered her question, whatever it was. She pivoted and resumed her pace, upper body smooth and stable out of respect for the load, her feet controlling the descent by shuffling from side to side of the hollowed path, rubber sandals flapping. She negotiated the hillside as casually as Didi or I would a sidewalk.

Didi settled onto the landing. In the banyan's shade we drank water and shared a package of crackers while we scanned the cool profile of the Annapurna range of Nepal's Himalayas. A fluted ridge of over twenty thousand feet tethered three lesser summits to Annapurna I, the planet's tenth highest mountain. To the northwest, the five peaks of Dhaulagiri lay stacked and rumpled in a frozen wave train. Macchapucchare, the Fish's Tail, stood downstage of this white curtain like an announcement, its pyramidal form conveying a hopeful message of permanence and of release. Riding on updrafts from the scorching plains of India, my imagination soared northward beyond the Himalayas to embrace the dry, pastel features and crystalline air of the Tibetan plateau.

We were grateful to be away from Kathmandu, the frenetic and polluted capital where we worked, retreating to the middle hills, the country's geographic center. Around us, terraces of dark soil had been sculpted into topographic map contours that cradled small hamlets of grass-thatched, earthen houses. The subtropical scene was peaceful and motionless, the distant chatter of mynahs and staticky buzz of cicadas the only sounds.

For Didi especially, getting here had been a long trip. Impatient to shake off her six years at the Convent of the Sacred Heart, near San Diego, she set out for Europe in the early seventies with her sister Teddi. They landed on an island in the Mediterranean, then kept going—across the Middle East to Asia on the sixties' silk route, the Hashish Trail. When their microbus broke down in Afghanistan, they hitchhiked to India and Nepal.

Didi and I had each lived in the foothills of the Himalayas for more than a decade before we were introduced. Through the expatriate grapevine, she had heard about my illegal crossing of a snowbound pass from Tibet to Nepal, and told a mutual friend that she'd like to meet me.

"So, what have you been up to all these years?" I asked Didi as I stood beside her at a party, intently swirling my drink.

"Studying the culture, and Buddhism." She smiled ironically. "And I ran a trekking company called Humpayeti Tours with my boyfriend. We led treks to remote areas. Actually, he's my *ex*-boyfriend now." Yes, she was the woman in boots and a beret I had seen weaving around town on a red motorcycle, buying jewelry and rugs for export.

"That's gotta be more rewarding than working for the government," I said stiffly, trying to conceal my attraction to her soft features and demure manner, not what I expected of a woman biker. Sounding dull by comparison, I told her that I had spent the seventies and early eighties in the hills teaching school and working with international aid agencies on rural development projects.

That was four years ago. Since then we had lived together in Didi's house in Kathmandu and recently agreed to travel the U.S. together—as Didi put it, to determine how serious about each other we really were. For me, it would be a summer's trial run, to see if our relationship would weather the sea change of cultures.

But there was someone else I wanted to see before we left Nepal.

Another hour of hiking separated us from our destination, a village of twenty houses inhabited by subsistence farmers of the Gurung tribe. The Gurung migrated from Tibet several centuries ago and settled over a hundred villages across the southern flanks of the Annapurnas. They are Mongoloids by race and Hindu-Buddhists by birth, but live in symmetry with the Brahmins and untouchable castes, the thinner-profiled Hindu Caucasians who moved into adjacent villages centuries later. Among themselves, the Gurung speak largely in their own tribal language, but they are bilingual in Nepali, the medium of education and government that Didi and I had learned.

I knew the region well. Fresh from college in the early seventies, I had taught science for the Peace Corps in the high school on a nearby ridge. My home was the hayloft of a water buffalo shed attached to the house of a sixty-nine-year-old woman. My landlady, Vishnu Maya, was known to most villagers as Aama, the Nepali term for mother. She cooked for the two of us, when not climbing trees to cut fodder for the buffalo or carrying crops from the valley floor far below, alongside her daughter and granddaughters.

Aama had been widowed for many years, and lived alone. Frustrated but not bitter, she had given up trying to claim the pension that relatives said was due following her husband's death during service in the Indian Army. Even if his pension was rightfully allotted to her, she rationalized, her son-in-law or other relative would surely intercept the monthly payments before she could reach the local remittance office to sign for them.

Aama had one daughter, Sun Maya, but had never given birth to a son, a stigma in Hindu society that branded her as only partially fertile and sentenced her to old age with no one to support her.

Sun Maya was married off within the village in order to remain close by and help her with the heavy chores. When not teaching, I tried to assist with the more repetitive but surprisingly difficult tasks, such as carrying water and splitting wood. This resulted in amusement for the villagers and protests from Aama, who was convinced that manual labor would tarnish my "master-sah'b"—schoolteacher —dignity. I suspected that it may have been *her* dignity at stake, if someone were to see her houseguest working. But she recognized in me a dharma son, the male offspring she had never given birth to, sent from the heavens by the deities to be spiritually adopted, she had said, as was written long ago on her fate.

And, as it transpired, on mine. My own mother had died unexpectedly when I was nineteen, three years before I arrived at Aama's village.

Didi and I sat on the terrace without speaking, and I admitted to myself that I felt closer to Aama than I did to Didi. Life in Aama's village had been my second youth; without trying to, Aama had guided me out of the loss I felt following my mother's death and into the nonindulgent rhythm of her family and village. I was returning to my second home.

But was Aama still alive? It had been two years since I had last trekked up this hill to see her, and I had not received a letter from Sun Maya, who knew how to write, in over a year. The expression on the face of the woman carrying fodder on the trail didn't tell us, though she would have known. People of the middle hills, interlinked by a web of gossip and intuition, become aware of nearby events at the moment they occur.

The Gurung don't usually write with bad news and often won't announce it to visitors even after they arrive. I pictured Aama's relatives greeting Didi and me. They would say she was traveling or fetching water from the spring. When she failed to appear, they would gaze downward and continue to cook or split bamboo strips for a basket or sweep up drying grains until someone, Sun Maya perhaps, would lift her head and point with extended lips to the outline of the small Shiva shrine on the peak of the ridge. I was prepared to hear her say "We took her up there," referring to the place just beyond the shrine where I had last seen several of Aama's relatives. The cremation ground.

I swallowed the rest of the crackers with difficulty as Aama's words of hope sprung to mind—her desire that she die promptly when no longer able to support herself, to avoid burdening her family. She would be approaching her mid-eighties, and a relative would have sharecropped her fields. Her youngest granddaughter would be married off by now, severing Aama's last helping hand.

We continued climbing. Miniature dust clouds arose with our footsteps, which we timed to our breaths. Didi knew of Aama from my descriptions of village life, and she was eager to meet her. I told her that I regretted not having offered to take Aama to America when she was younger, to share with her my country and kin, as she had with me.

Mercifully, the trail leveled out near the ridgeline, where it merged with a track worn as deep as a man's height from centuries of barefooted heavy loads. As if impelled forward by the scenery, we strolled beneath oak and poplar and giant poinsettias bordering fields newly planted with millet seedlings. Sunset colors cast a glow of antiquity on the weathered hillsides and the faces of the farmers we passed.

Tired, we arrived at the overlook above Aama's village, three thousand feet higher than the valley we had left in the morning. Groves of tall bamboos arched like fountains, framing a timeless cluster of modest stone houses. Children playing in raucous circles on nearby fallow terraces didn't see us. I didn't stop to watch or join them in play, as I often had.

I climbed onto the stone stile behind Aama's house. The sweat bathing my spine and sunburned neck had begun to cool. I shivered.

"Aama?" I called, hoarse and restrained, like a survivor warily invoking the departed.

Curls of smoke sifted through the roof thatch.

"Nani?" she answered expectantly from inside, using the affectionate title for a young child. She sounded healthy. I released the breath I was holding, then stepped into her narrow kitchen. She sat as she had years before on her carved wooden block, fire tongs in one hand. Instinctively she reached for the teakettle, placed it atop the trivet, and blew on a handful of smoldering cornstalks beneath it.

"You know, I haven't kept chickens in some time now," she said as if continuing a conversation of two years earlier. Again she blew on the fire. I smiled and set down my rucksack.

"I don't have the energy to chase after them anymore, and the hawks flew off with most of the chicks from the last brood. But we can get a rooster for tonight's dinner from my niece who lives in the house below here. I'm glad you didn't come late. . . . Who's this?" Tilting her head to the side, she faced Didi, who stood silhouetted in the kitchen doorway. Shiny bronze skin crinkled around Aama's eyes.

"You've brought me a daughter-in-law."

Didi laughed as she pulled off her scarf, then placed her hands together prayer-fashion and said "Namasté." Aama returned the greeting.

Bent from years of field work and load carrying, and osteoporosis, Aama laid out vegetables from her garden on the floor of the kitchen. As she carefully sectioned a squash, she described the spring hailstones that had ripped leaves from trees and the drought that nearly prevented the ears of corn from emerging. She recalled dreams where she heard my voice calling from the trail, dreams stirred to life by the schoolchildren who, as they giggled and scampered off, would announce that I was at the entrance of the village. She wiped tears from her eyes, remembering her memories and her relatives, worrying. She was alone now. All three granddaughters who took turns helping her had married and moved away. One of them had a new son, Aama's first great-grandson.

Aama poured us glasses of tea lightly spiced with black pepper, the way it was served decades ago, before sugar was widely available. Sun Maya arrived with a few ears of corn and a large copper urn filled with water. Her face was wrinkled from the dry sun, perpetual work, and a difficult husband; she was now in her fifties. Taking over from Aama in the kitchen, Sun Maya unassumingly prepared the evening meal. Quiet and trusting, she reminded me of Didi. Both of them spoke as if uncomfortable with speech, yet their faces clearly expressed their thoughts. I wondered if Didi had picked up her passive but solid nature from Asian women.

We ate sitting cross-legged in the room adjoining the kitchen. Aama gathered the plates, settled onto the mat beside us, and repositioned the brass kerosene lamp to take a prolonged look at Didi and me. She laughed congenially and toothlessly at my changed appearance—older, mostly, she said—then lingered on Didi's features, smiling openly at Didi's plain coral necklace, light-colored hair, and angular profile. At least she didn't visibly disapprove of my selection of a woman from outside the village, as I had assumed she might. A Gurung daughter-in-law would help Aama with the chores, providing relief that might even allow her to live longer.

From my rucksack I pulled gifts of printed cloth and a pint of rum, standard offerings expected of a son returning from a tour of duty with the British or Indian armies, the Gurkha regiments of which were composed largely of Gurung and other Mongoloid hill tribes from Nepal. I had often tried to rival the stories of adventure told by the village's sons on leave from barracks in London, Hong Kong, Malaysia, and northern India, tales that formed much of the Gurung's view of the outside world.

But now Aama had stories to tell.

"I think someone wrote you that Tyauré Aapa, my cousin, died last year. We held his funerary ceremony last month. Relatives came from two days' walk away, dressed in new clothes made of what they call *poly-ster*. But that's not the latest death—my other cousin, your aunt Chyaurey, passed on. My generation are dying ahead of me and dying around me, and I haven't had a chance to bid them farewell.

Work in the fields gives us no time to visit, and I can't climb hills as I used to. In our village, there are now four fully ripened, ready-to-die old people, and I'm the next in line!"

Aama examined the rum bottle at arm's length as if she were reading the label, then delicately opened it. She told me that Sun Maya had read my letters aloud to her, and each year they had hoped I would arrive in time for their fall festival. I explained that development work had kept me in Kathmandu and America, and that I had tried to get basic rural improvements directed to her district. If a source of water could be found on the hillside above their houses, I had told the village leaders, we could install a gravity-flow drinking-water system. Aama looked at me skeptically, amused by the shameless claim that I might be able to alter their legacy of neglect by the government, which they had now accepted as destiny.

Leaning against the wall, she straightened her legs and lifted the pint bottle well above her opened mouth, deftly pouring in small cascades of neat rum, her jaw seeming to dislocate to receive it, lips stretched and bowed inward where teeth had once been.

"This can be good medicine, but you shouldn't drink too much of it," she cautioned with a smile. She licked her lips, then retracted and slowly savored her tongue. Youthful energy illuminated her wrinkles, which hung and moved like strangely attractive adornments.

"In the early spring of this year, seven Brahmin priests came to officiate at my eighty-four-year long-life ritual, the *nwaran*. So from now on, I'm living on free time—hah! And if we live to one hundred, the priests tell us, the aging process reverses and we will become younger, grow new teeth, and then should remarry; our reincarnation begins again in this lifetime."

Indeed, aspects of the eighty-four-year ritual are identical to the Hindu christening, also called the *nwaran,* which is done for an infant eleven days after birth. Aama reveled in recounting the ceremony—the music, incense, offerings, flower garlands, goat sacrifice, and arrival of relatives bringing gifts, for which she must reciprocate.

"I gave one cow to my daughter and one to my brother-in-law, and presented gifts of cooking oil and incense and money to each of my grandchildren. We cooked nearly ten gallons of rice, and there were lentils, chutneys, and fried breads for everyone, and distilled spirits for the drinkers."

On the day of the ritual, the priests had told her, she might view 1,008 full moons, the sacred number of lunar months she had been alive, and would then acquire the blessings that such a vision brings. After eighty-four, the elderly are considered to be elevated to the level of deities, and it is propitious for younger people to have a *darshan,* an appearance before them, to touch upon these blessings.

The Brahmins had dug a small furrow in the front courtyard, symbolizing the river of eternity. While the priests chanted and recited, Aama grasped the tail of a calf and was pulled to the far side of the furrow, initiating and preparing her for the last crossing of the final river of this lifetime.

The eighty-four-year watershed marks the completion of one's present life of worldly responsibilities. Following the ceremony, Hindu custom prescribes retreat to a cottage in the forest for meditation. Alternatively, one can undertake a religious pilgrimage. Just as a child gains nourishment from breast-feeding, the pilgrim gains a sacred kind of sustenance and spiritual union from sacred places. By touring power spots, the devout Hindu can begin to settle the debt that the priests say we acquire from consuming our mothers' milk. Aama had often spoken of her desire to undertake such a pilgrimage during her final years, to roam as a mendicant on a circuit of holy sites.

Bujay, Aama's gravel-voiced, aging cousin, climbed the stairs from her house on the terrace below. She was followed by other relatives, and they sprawled onto straw mats and vied for cigarettes and the chance to question me about Didi and where I had been. Like a large communal home, the village overflowed with people sharing in group tasks and teamwork. There were few personal boundaries, and attempts to defend one's privacy only made people more curious. Bujay drew noisily on a cigarette stuffed into a short bamboo holder, and to better hear she adjusted her saucerlike gilded ear ornaments, aiming them to work like crude ear trumpets. Not only was Aama lucky to be alive, Bujay said, but she had been blessed by a son and now a daughter-in-law. Two of Bujay's four children had died in infancy.

"Uhnnh," Aama agreed. She took another taste of the rum and began to recall my arrival in the village nearly a generation ago, conveying the fresh enthusiasm that accompanied each of her well-told tales. Aama and the other Gurung women had sharpened their wits during years of work in the fields, singing and conversing and building upon each other's conjured, fanciful anecdotes. For them, fact and legend were much the same, both equally dependent upon a good story line to endure and thrive. We settled in.

"One year, in the month of January, I had just returned from fetching a load of water at the spring. My son-in-law—our village headman and head scoundrel—had brought this foreigner to my house, and they were sitting on the porch, awaiting me. The foreigner had been posted to teach school in the nearby village, and my son-in-law proposed that he stay at my house and that I cook for him. I thought: 'I hope he's not like some of the ungracious Nepalese travelers who come through here asking for the headman and who then get unloaded on me.' Apparently he didn't want to live in the bazaar town and get stuck teaching English to all the merchants' children in the evenings after school. He wouldn't be a devious sort, I figured, because people who are lazy or want to cause trouble prefer the bazaar towns. The white schoolmaster then said 'Namasté' to me and placed his hands together in the Nepalese form of greeting. It looked funny to see a foreigner do that; normally we Gurung don't say 'Namasté' even to each other, only to Brahmins and other Nepalese, so I couldn't help but laugh."

Didi and I found ourselves appreciating as much as listening. Aama's voice resonated with the diction and cadence of her ancestors. Bujay's eyelids sagged into their accustomed after-dinner repose, and Aama looked at her sympathetically. I recalled a Nepalese friend's advice: "Gurung mothers tell stories as if they are being told for the first time, so we must listen as if hearing them for the first time. Sometimes they'll catch you. They'll ask a question that can't be answered with a long, soothing 'uhhhn . . .' then they'll scold you, saying you're the type that sits around and daydreams." A pre-rogative of old age, I guessed. Relaxed but attentive, I looked at Aama as she continued.

"My son-in-law said that the schoolmaster could sleep in the loft above my water buffalo and walk to school each morning. But who would do the work to support him? Sun Maya tilled the fields and tended her livestock all day, and I could barely carry the water or split the firewood needed to sustain myself. 'The foreigner will pay you to cook his food, so you can hire someone to help. You might earn a few extra rupees that way, too,' my son-in-law suggested, clearly hoping that *he* could acquire a few extra rupees from the bargain, somehow. He had already gotten into my house and poured a glass of alcohol for the new schoolmaster, and for himself, of course, so I knew he was up to something."

Renewed by the flush of attention and the rum, Aama looked even younger and more alert than when I had last seen her. The old-age ritual had granted her life a new lease, and a new leisure. She set down the rum delicately and observed it.

"I was unsure of the idea. I asked my son-in-law, 'What kind of food does the schoolmaster eat? Certainly nothing that I could make for him.' I would have been embarrassed to have even my relatives come and stay, mainly because the buffalo wasn't giving milk at the time. 'And I don't own any tables or chairs,' I added, 'and I don't know how to speak English.' Then the schoolmaster—Nani here—spoke up in Nepali, and he enunciated slowly, so I could understand him. He stated that eating whatever I eat would be fine. 'I can see that you are a very cultured woman,' he said. 'Where have you trav-eled and what have you experienced such that you know about tables and chairs and the habits of foreigners?' Ha! I laughed at that. I told him, 'In the army in India, more than fifty years ago, I lived in barracks with my husband.' Imagine my surprise; sitting here on my porch was a foreigner—the caste of people who, I have heard, sleep in big sacks filled with dead chicken skins, feathers and all. . . .''

I had heard that one before. Didi glanced at our sleeping bags and laughed, which roused Bujay, who looked up and refocused her earpieces in time to join in with genuine-sounding laughter.

"Yes, he lived here two years. When he first came, he would lean back and rest on one arm while he ate, unable to sit squarely on a straw mat. And when he picked up a handful of rice he'd rotate his wrist as if he didn't know where to put the food. Oh, we've laughed so much at the way he ate and did things. He had a distinctive smell, too, when he first moved here. Not a bad smell, just different. And he was always misplacing and forgetting things, like his books or his flashlight, and would walk around in circles looking for them. Once, Sun Maya and I silently watched him look for a pencil that was behind his ear."

Aama smiled at me innocently. I recalled the nickname tagged on me in college, "Slow, but Chaotic." The title had long ago expired, I thought, but was now reviving in another country and language. I looked at Didi and nodded in begrudging confirmation of Aama's account. Didi smiled knowingly, picturing the awkward, naive, overly polite boy she had suspected I had been and might still partly be.

"But then he began to carry water and split firewood. He was very helpful. This is the son I gave birth to in a previous life, come to live with me in this life. He was a motherless son, and I was a sonless mother."

Sun Maya poured tea into brass cups for each of us and quietly substituted a cup for Aama's rum bottle. I felt a surge of gratitude and affection, and plainly saw why I had returned to the village. To see Aama was to glimpse my own mother—the mother who had suddenly abandoned my sister and me when she died. Here she was, reborn as an eighty-four-year-old, ritually liberated Gurung hill woman. The image was vicarious, perhaps fabricated to supply the missing parts for a young man's personal world, a world that had been disassembled and refashioned during a long period of living alone in a foreign culture. But Aama's warmth and my feeling for her could not have been invented.

A longing for my deceased mother gripped me. In my youth, I shared my secrets with her. This changed as I aged, as sports, girls, and my peers induced me to contrive and conceal. By the time I left home for college, rebellious and cocky and on the threshold of freedom, I was too distracted to appreciate my mother as I had before. That's when she died unexpectedly in her sleep.

Now, long after her death, a contortion of guilt, dormant but tenacious, had kept me locked in a malingering adolescence. I felt a need to unload the burden of debt I owed to my mother, or *thought* I owed her: the indebtedness of her years of love and nurturing, the indebtedness from consuming her milk. But I couldn't fully describe this feeling, this need, and saw no tangible means to deal with it.

Until now. What had begun as a notion in Kathmandu and developed into a premature regret on the trail now looked like a wild possibility. I looked at Didi. She raised her eyebrows, anticipating another of my impulsive thoughts. Should we assist Aama on her end-of-life pilgrimage? Would she like to join us in the U.S.? Could she travel? We tested it out on each other, exploring the implications and hazards.

We agreed that if Aama wanted to, she probably could. She was clearly restless, and had long been curious about where I had come from and who my relatives were. She would list her common excuses, complaining of pain and age and her needy livestock, and of not wanting to impose on us any more than she would want to encumber her daughters or granddaughters. But a tour of the U.S. might rejuvenate her even more. And I might learn something, as well. I had aimlessly explored America on college road trips, but the value of these wanderings was questionable; I was thankful simply not to have been arrested.

"We should discuss it more," Didi said. "I just think we should be aware of what we're getting into here, don't you?" I didn't reply. I was busy conjecturing that, after a trip to the U.S., Aama might also be able to tell me what I should do about Didi, whether to stay with her or move on.

Aama was in the middle of an endless-loop description of my antics. I decided to simply ask her. "Aama, how would you like to go to America with us?" My words sounded strangely clear, but reckless, and I alarmed myself at the level of commitment I was extending —more than I had offered before to anyone.

From the kitchen, Sun Maya was the first to react. She glanced over at us and laughed, envisioning the comical scenes her mother might cause in a developed, foreign land. Didi might have been right in suggesting that we discuss it further.

Fortified by her medicine, Aama responded at once. "Why wouldn't I want to go? Why wouldn't I want to see my dharma son's and daughter-in-law's home and meet their relatives?" she implored, as if my question were expected and her answer obvious. Indeed, our relatives might comprise the only feature of America that she could begin to visualize.

"Just look at me and you can see why." Her hands opened as they spiraled upward, articulating her sincerity. The kinked outermost joints of her fingers pointed wildly. "I'm no longer able to do heavy work or take care of myself, and am a bother for my daughter. I'm useless here. Also, I've completed the eighty-four-year long-life ceremony. People are warned not to eat, drink, urinate, or defecate during the totality of a solar eclipse, but after the old-age rite even these serious things don't matter—they say that we are protected from accumulating further bad karma."

Despite the deitylike status conferred by the longevity ceremony, Aama knew well that in daily life elderly people are often neglected.

For subsistence farmers, supporting the needs of a deity, especially one who is weak or incapacitated, can be a routine nuisance. The long-life ritual contains elements of a retirement banquet in which the faithful retiree is toasted heartily, though partly out of an unspoken gratitude for his departure.

Sun Maya collected the teacups as Didi and I tried to picture the maze of details. Bujay cackled and held her shoulders back and head up primly, parodying the queenly posture adopted by some Gurung mothers of British Army recruits. Joining a son at his foreign post heightened the social status of a returning mother, and every Gurkha longed for the tenure needed to call his family to join him at his barracks. Going to America fit just right. Finally, a son in foreign service.

Aama normally ate coarsely ground millet mush. I ruminated about American food, which Didi and I considered too rich and soft even for our tastes. For someone without teeth, on the other hand, American cuisine might be a delight. When I told Aama that sugar was cheap and fish available most places in America, she assured us that she would have no trouble adjusting.

"But what if you were to get homesick, Aama—or even die—in a foreign place?" I asked, aware that a death in America might hinder a favorable rebirth if relatives and Buddhist lamas and Hindu priests were not present to bless the body properly and protect it from contamination before cremation.

"It's good to die quickly when you get old, but I already tried to die and couldn't, so why not go with you to Amrita?" she retorted, laughing. *Amrita,* she called our country, the religious term for the legendary holy elixir that, if found, confers immortality.

But Aama didn't seem to need *amrita.* She had never broken a bone, though she had nearly died from malaria and intestinal complaints, sicknesses that were diagnosed and treated by her cousin, the shaman. In a trance, he would journey to the underworld to encounter and identify the demons afflicting her, then allow them to manifest in his own body, sometimes brutally. In these late-night treatment sessions, relatives would watch calmly as the doctor-shaman, called to effect a cure, would attack and attempt to strangle the patient, offering Aama a window of chance in the immediate, physical world to fight off the normally unapproachable demons. Provoked, she would resist, and either be relieved of her sickness in the process or relapse. Aama partly attributed her longevity to this cousin, whose ability was first recognized when he spontaneously went into a trance one day while plowing a field. He was a *bhuiphatta*, a self-emanated shaman, a natural. He saw that her constitution would allow for a long life, but that she would face many obstacles.

A pilgrimage to America would present some of those, I predicted, although the hope of encountering truly sacred sites should help overcome them. But Didi and I wondered if America's holy places would sufficiently reward the devout. Then I recalled Hindu priests saying that merit can be gained simply by undertaking a spiritual journey, especially if it is prolonged and hazardous.

Chortling and hacking, Bujay slowly stood, straightened her creaking body as much as she could, and borrowed a flashlight to find the trail to her house. I suggested that she use her ear ornaments as candle reflectors. She barked a laugh, then waggled her cane at me.

Aama retired to her wooden bed on the porch. Long before daylight, she would be up grinding or winnowing grains. Didi and I found our way through the luxuriant night air to the water buffalo shed. In its straw-filled loft, we unstuffed our sleeping bags and stretched out, at home in the remoteness of the hills. Our shivering and giggles gave way to sighs and yawns.

Absently Didi's failing flashlight traced the curves of bamboo strips that secured the bundles of thatch to the rafters. Speaking softly, she mulled over her new title of daughter-in-law. She decided that it sounded all right.

"It's worth talking about," I mouthed audibly, "but in the morning when we've had some sleep."

At first light, Aama called us down for tea and parched corn. We sat on the porch, absorbing the sunrise and watching life come to a village that had not changed in generations. Squatting at the edge of the courtyard, Aama performed her morning ablution. From a brass urn she poured water into her cupped right hand and massaged the liquid forcefully into her wrinkles, chanting.

". . . Haré Om, ye Iswar Bhagwan, Krishna Bhagwan, Kailaspati, Baigundanath, Jagganath, Pasupatinath, Rameswor, Muktinath. . . ."

The names of deities and sacred places of the Indian subcontinent came to her mouth each morning, she had said, when she took her place on the far side of the terrace, and the words flowed spontaneously in a sequence that she could not recall during the day. She concluded her mantra with a definitive *"Om, Om, Om,"* then rose slowly and turned. In a brief, quiet moment that felt solid yet light, the day was consecrated.

At the least, Aama's vitality and perpetual curiosity would make her an engaging, if unpredictable, tour companion. "How do you feel about traveling with Aama?" I asked Didi. "What do you think might happen?"

Didi tightened her lips as if unsure, then she nodded slowly. "Like Aama's life, it will be enjoyable and heartfelt and humorous, but also difficult."

Chapter 2

"Why do you always drive the motorcycle in places where the wind blows?"

A woman known in the village as Tutay's Mother was returning to her house nearby when she looked down from the trail and spotted Aama puttering in her kitchen garden. *"Phursaailiiii,"* she called, using Aama's kinship name, father's third eldest sister; she stretched the last syllable into the high musical note used to hail someone from a long distance. Tutay's Mother slipped off her tumpline, lowered her basket of branches and grass fodder, and leaned over the wall. A gold nose pin sat loosely in its hole through her left nostril, accenting her smooth, tan features, lustrous from field work and woodsmoke.

"Ohhn," Aama acknowledged, standing upright. "My garden is disappointing. The beans and cucumbers are producing fewer fruits than they did last year. But Nani and my daughter-in-law here have offered to take me to their country." Aama smiled whimsically at the ironic image of an old village woman recast as world traveler. Tutay's Mother darted her tongue out a half inch and clenched it between her teeth in amazement and disbelief. Didi and I watched from the porch.

"When my dharma son calls me, I have to go," Aama continued. "But where will I find someone to look after my buffalo? Your children and all the other village kids go to school nowadays. There's so much work—the house needs new thatch, the chicken shed is falling apart, and the hay needs to be restacked to keep rain from leaking into the pile and rotting it. The buffalo should be giving birth any day now, too. I have long wished to travel, to head southward on pilgrimage across India, but am afraid that when I leave it will be for the last time, because I'd have to sell everything I own to pay for my wanderings. It may be best to sell it all, anyway—I don't want worries about my possessions always drawing me back."

Perhaps the holy sites of India were on the way to America. "Nani?" Aama asked me familiarly. "In which direction do you travel to get to Amrita?" *Amrita,* the mythical nectar of immortality, the semen of the gods. Some villagers say that *amrita* issues forth from the ocean, and then usually admit they have never seen the ocean. Aama smiled at the wild prospect of bathing in the precious ambrosia of her dharma son's country.

"We can go east *or* west," I said. "We'd get there going in either direction." Aama laughed deeply. Tutay's Mother looked even more curious; her tongue came out and again lodged between her teeth.

I stooped beneath the porch's low eave and stepped onto the courtyard, then spoke loudly so that both of them could hear.

"Aama, the earth is shaped like a ball, like the moon or the sun." I rummaged for universal images and examples from nature, something that might work better than my attempt of several years ago, but nothing came through the fuzz of my hangover. "Here the sun rises in the east and sets in the west, right?" Aama nodded expectantly as if the punchline of a joke were imminent. "In America it does, too, except that the sun doesn't actually go around us, it stays in one place while our whole earth turns. America is on the opposite side of the world, and that's why when it's daytime here, they have nighttime in America."

"How do people there work in the dark all the time?" Aama said, and turned to share a cackle with Tutay's Mother. They didn't bother to look back for an answer. I waved an arm in an effort to salvage their attention.

"No, in America right now, people are sleeping. When the sun sets here, it rises in America, and they wake up and begin their day." My arms described grand circles and small objects, clumsily assembling a diagram of the universe. Tutay's Mother's eyebrows shot upward. She had never traveled farther than a few hours' walk from the village. "It all makes sense if our world is *round,* like a ball. The stars pass across the sky in perfect formation, night after night, east to west, in the same direction as the sun and the moon, right? So, it makes sense that we're the ones moving, and not they, doesn't it?"

"Well, I haven't heard that story before," Tutay's Mother said, her laughter now directed at my hand gestures. Aama's terrace had become a courtroom arena, and I felt silly and vulnerable. Didi's face reflected Aama's and Tutay's Mother's skepticism, and she nodded as she perused my appearance and stance. My offer to take Aama to America was beginning to sound capricious, if not daunting and improbable.

"But if you say so, we'll believe you," Aama offered. "You're my dharma son and are smart—that's why you were sent here to teach school. You know about these sorts of things, probably from learning them in books, so it could be true." The operation of a mystical universe where deities flew, shamans diverted hail, and an elephant's head had been transplanted onto a man's body was fully explained in the Hindu texts they had heard readings from, but my account was sounding akin to the outlandish theories that children were now bringing home from school.

"Unnnh." Tutay's Mother sighed, in laconic appreciation that someone may have figured all this out. She turned to Aama. "He really is a son from a previous life."

While the old women continued to chat, Didi reminded me that getting the government of Nepal to issue Aama a passport would be a long process, probably requiring a personal contact in the government just to make sure the application worked its way through the pile.

In the end, it might not be possible. Sun Maya told me that a government team of clerks and photographers had recently passed through the village during a nationwide campaign to issue citizenship papers to every villager in the country. These papers would expedite approval of passport applications, which were frequently turned down. Aama surely would have been photographed and finger-printed. I asked Sun Maya if I could see the documents. No, she had none. The officials had figured that an eighty-four-year-old woman would never need such papers, and within a radius of several hamlets Aama was the only villager they had skipped. Logically, the ritual which marks 1,008 moons of life should release the elderly from bureaucratic as well as worldly duties.

Didi and I needed to return to Kathmandu. I had taken time off work, and Didi had her house and export business to attend to. Sun Maya assured us that she would help compile Aama's papers at the district center. I told them to come directly to Kathmandu once the documents were processed, privately wondering if they would ever make it. The district center had one external phone line. I wrote Didi's phone number on a slip of paper and gave it to Sun Maya.

Before Didi and I left, Aama and Sun Maya discussed the future. The cow wasn't giving milk and would fetch a poor price, but Sun

Maya should try to sell it anyway, Aama said, in order to pay off her debt to another relative, the village moneylender. "With all the energy and work we put into them, the cattle and water buffalos seem to benefit more from us than the other way around," Sun Maya said, smiling. I had never heard her complain before nor seen concern show on her face.

"Also, you can sell most of the thatch grass from my plot in the forest," Aama told her quietly, "but save a few of the drier bundles for patching the hole in the roof where it leaked last monsoon. I'll repair it when I return." Sun Maya smiled at Aama's self-assurance.

Didi and I devoured a meal of leftover chicken, rice, and chilies, fried in buffalo butter. Before allowing us to head down the trail, Aama loaded our rucksacks with fruits and vegetables from her garden, though we had no porter to help carry it all. At the edge of town we glanced back at the village, then passed off most of the produce to the untouchable blacksmith caste family living in a small house above the trail. Aama would have approved, but not if we had asked her in advance.

A few days later, Aama departed her village in the tradition of the mother of a Gurkha recruit. Signifying the beginning of a new venture, thin blades of *dubo* grass, the hair of Vishnu, hung from the corners of her mouth, clamped in her teeth, which prevented her from speaking. Parting words could only be inadequate. Custom said that she must not prolong the farewell nor gaze homeward once she walked from the doors of her house for the last time.

Sun Maya remained in the village to work and do chores, as I expected she would. In her place, Aama's eldest grandson, Tagu, an introverted sixteen-year-old, accompanied Aama the several hours' walk to the district center. For nearly a week they camped there in the apartment of a distant nephew. Each day they submitted her appeal to the district officials.

At six o'clock in the morning near the end of the following week, Didi's phone rang. She reached from the bed to answer it, and I could overhear the voice of a young man unaccustomed to speaking on the telephone say that he and Aama had arrived in Kathmandu and needed to be picked up. It was Tagu. He mumbled, then hung up before he could tell Didi where they were, but a rickshaw horn and the background street sounds clearly indicated they were downtown, probably at the bus station. I rolled out of bed, gagged down a cup of instant coffee, and jogged out to the road to grab a taxi.

The taxi careered into Kathmandu's International Bus Park, barely missing pushcart vendors and sleep-deprived villagers trying to recover their bindles and their bearings. A woman carrying an infant on her hip casually dodged our fender. Weary and disoriented, Aama and Tagu stood near a tea stall, awash in a confusion of people and pavement and power lines. They had taken one of the night buses, described on the roof carriage as a Deluxe Mini Super Express Night Coach, the kind that race over mountain roads packed with jostled, vomiting passengers on padded platforms that seat six across, interior lights glaring, radio cranked on high.

Aama's four-foot ten-inch height matched the scale of the cottage where she lived, but with the city as backdrop she appeared tiny. "Unh, you're here, Nani," she quietly confirmed when I stepped from the taxi. Tagu wore a gold-colored wristwatch and immaculate white high-top sneakers. The rupees I had left for Aama in the village had been passed around, apparently, as I had guessed would happen. We squeezed into the backseat of the rusting taxi and lurched into the boisterous city traffic. I assured Aama that we were still planning to go to America and that plane reservations had been made.

Aama pulled from her shoulder bag a sheaf of jumbled rice-paper documents held together with a straight pin. "All the official questions and paper shuffling in the district center annoyed Tagu and my nephew," Aama said, "and I told them several times to forget the whole thing."

Didi had restored and landscaped her house into a quiet refuge that reflected her patient temperament. She greeted Aama and Tagu and, just as Aama would have, turned to make a breakfast of tea and fried breads, plus a large cheese omelette. Aama and Tagu ate hungrily, then stretched out on the rug in the living room. Tagu admired his new shoes, neatly paired in a corner. Aama's free hand burrowed into her hair, targeting a head louse as she spoke.

"Now that my brothers and sisters are dead, I've become the mother hen for the brood of nieces and nephews, and I need to nurture and provide for them. They urged me to go to Amrita to see how it is, then return to the village in time for the fall Dasain festival to give them all the *tika* blessing. I told them I would." Aama inspected her fingernails for parasite parts. Didi observed her with equal parts amazement, humor, and compassion, and said to me that she had lice shampoo and would delouse her in the sink.

"The morning I left the village," Aama continued, "I didn't have a rooster to sacrifice in order to view the position and the lines and color of its liver. This would have helped determine the course of my future, and my daughter's future."

In a nebulous way, I felt that fate had already joined us there in Didi's living room, and it was kicking in, favorably, protecting us. I was about to speak, to share this sensation, but Aama looked as if she had a question.

"Anyway, the Brahmin who came to check the planetary alignment for the day I wanted to depart said that the journey looked auspicious. But I wanted to consult my cousin the shaman, as well, because I am closer to him, of course. I wanted to ask him whether I would die in Amrita. If he foresaw that I might, then I wouldn't have come. But then I decided that it doesn't matter, that it would be all right to die in Amrita if the planets and gods desired it, so I didn't call him over. I forgot to ask you, though: If this were to happen, how would my body be treated? Could it be defiled on the way to the cremation ground? What do your people do?" She tilted her head back and peered at me as if through a pair of spectacles perched well down on her nose. "You probably just have your bodies hauled away or buried underground or something, like the Muslims do." She laughed at the brazen irreverence of her suggestion. "The Muslims even dig their graves before they die, as if hoping that death will come along quickly." She looked at me calmly, and her voice softened. "Nani, are there any Gurung lamas in Amrita, or shamans, or Brahmins, even?" She was speaking on my account, addressing her concern to the practical matter of whether I would be able to fulfill the ritual obligations of a son at the time of a mother's death. The actual prospect of dying seemed less important.

"Uh, well, shamans and Gurung lamas might be hard to find in America, but there are Brahmins," I said, trying to think of where we would begin to look. "We would have to get a good one because, as you know, many Brahmins don't obey the Hindu rules of prohibition as they used to—and especially the Brahmins living in America, I suspect." A devout Brahmin should not drink alcohol or eat chicken, pork, or beef, especially beef, the sacred cow.

"Nothing will happen to you, Aama, but we'll find a Brahmin if we need one, or perhaps a Tibetan lama," I said sincerely.

"Mainly I'm worried about falling over. I've fallen down three times in the past few years. I didn't think I would ever arise from that last fall." As Aama spoke, she reached for her bamboo cane, lifted herself from the rug and looked for the door. Enough unproductive time had been spent inside for the day; there must be work to attend to outside, as always.

In a rustic Zen sort of randomness, Didi's garden flourished with vegetables, medicinal herbs, and exotic flowers. Aama padded about observing the plants as if they were photographs of lost friends, noting how the climate or food had changed them after leaving the village. She paused every few feet to probe the ornamental rocks with the fingertips of her right hand, then brought her fingers to her forehead to take blessing from them, mouthing her mantra. When sanctified by a village lama or shaman, rocks like these would qualify as representations of deities, and would be placed in a ridge-top shrine or be nested together at the base of a clump of mountain bamboo.

The papers Aama had brought with her from the district were merely the beginning. I had one friend with connections at a high enough level to arrange approval of a passport, and he agreed to place a call to a relative in the Home Ministry, to make a personal reference.

The only vehicle I owned was a motorcycle, the most efficient means of negotiating Kathmandu traffic. I rolled it from the shed and showed it to Aama.

"In the old days, people didn't ride these. Does it take fodder or kerosene?"

"Petrol—it's like kerosene," I said, sitting astride it. I indicated the pillion and the footrest on the left side, cocked my right hand up as if scratching the back of my neck, and told her to grab my right hand with her right. She pivoted up and over using near-effortless leverage, the kind of slow fluidity and economy of motion that older people develop out of necessity. After the third or fourth time, I didn't need to watch; she climbed onto the cycle like a biker's old lady.

We weaved into the clamor of central Kathmandu, stopped first at a street-side photo stall for passport photos, then rode to the Home Ministry to drop the application. We bought a new shoulder bag—her village one was frayed—and some necklaces, coins, and other souvenirs to take to America. In the afternoon, we pulled out onto the Ring Road and headed home, cruising in fourth gear, savoring the clear air that followed a brief but heavy rain shower. From the corner of my eye I could see her squinting into the wind behind me, trying to speak.

"Why do you always drive the motorcycle in places where the wind blows?" she shouted weakly over the roar of the wind. I swung over to the shoulder and stopped the bike, then turned to look at her.

"Is it windy now?" I asked.

"No. The wind stopped."

I dropped Aama at home and returned to town to tie up some loose ends at work and go to the bank.

The central bank accepts revenue for the government, and passport applicants must deposit the passport fee in person unless exempted. I had no excuse for not bringing Aama with me other than being swept up in a routine day full of hurry, the kind of rush that had often backed me into a corner. The last thing we needed now was a bureaucrat attempting to slow the paperwork down in order to apply resistance and up the stakes—"pressurizing," as it is referred to jocularly in local English.

Through an opening in the cyclone fence that formed the teller's cage, I submitted a pocketful of rupees and the deposit form, marveling that cash deposits must be approved. The teller reflexively passed the form to the section officer sitting at a desk behind him. After several minutes of scrutinizing the filled-in sheet, the section head abruptly rubber-stamped it and jotted what looked like comments in the margin, then motioned me to step through the plywood door leading to his desk, inside the teller's area, in order to accept the receipt, which would save him from getting up. About to hand it to me, he first asked in Nepali whom the passport was for. He had undoubtedly read the name of the depositor on the application and was wondering where the person was.

"A Nepalese," I said.

"Yes. A Nepalese woman, right?"

"Yes."

"Oh ho!—a woman," he said loudly, delighting in the confirmation. The staff of the Treasury section looked up from their newspapers and the viscera of oversized current account registers spilling over with columns of figures. There wasn't a calculator to be seen.

"How old is this woman?"

"Eighty-four," I said.

The section head turned to the token taker on his left and said coolly, "He must mean forty-eight." He turned back to me. "You

need to work on your Nepali," he voiced even more loudly, garru-
lously, as if trying to break through a language barrier. " 'Forty-
eight' is what you must be trying to say. 'For-tee-*eight*,' " he enunciated again in proper, Sanskritized Nepali, in the manner my language
instructor had, exaggerating the articulation of his lips and tongue
while raising his eyebrows and bulging his eyes, as additional aids to
more effective communication. "But are you sure she isn't *twenty-
four?*" He paused dramatically to allow an atmosphere of scandal to
build among the dozen or so staff of the department, now fully distracted. Before I could respond, he said "Hmmmmm . . . ?" in a
drawn-out, rising tone, protracting my hesitation for me. I knew
what they were thinking. Civil servants in Nepal subscribed to a kind
of nationally shared view of the world, replete with common sense,
tradition, and double standard. It was clear that I had found a wife,
and unfortunate that a Nepalese woman was betraying her heritage
and religion to marry a foreign man—she was probably a low-caste
girl or one who had gotten into trouble. This reflected poorly on me,
but foreigners wouldn't know better, of course.

Yet each of the bank staff likely coveted the chance to visit or
find work in America, the country still considered more than any the
land of unlimited wealth and opportunity, where money might be
picked up from the airport tarmac upon arrival, but in any event
would be found lying on the streets in town. They knew that if
Vishnu Maya was my bride, we would have to live overseas forever,
because Nepal provided long-term visas only to foreign women—not
to foreign men—who married Nepalese. Passport approval was not
exactly under the bank's authority, but the gravity of this breach of
tradition justified insinuation into the approval process.

"No. She's eighty-four," I said. Returning the dramatic pause, I
opened my briefcase with deliberation, rustled about inside and withdrew a passport photo, looked at it for a moment, then handed it to
the section head. The department staff rose simultaneously, like a
grade school class at recess, and moved into a huddle behind the
officer. They froze, silent, studying the image.

"He's right! She must be *at least* eighty-four," the section head exclaimed. "Maybe a *hundred* and eighty-four!" The entire staff looked up at me, and we laughed in unison. The intrigue of this new situation instantly transcended the game of correctness in pronunciation, or of culture.

"Must be for medical treatment," one of the clerks suggested dourly. The others didn't speak. The women clerks softened, as if viewing a baby picture, dreaming that one day someone would take their mother, or maybe them, to America. The section head handed me the receipt with formal politeness, placing one hand beneath the other and bowing his head slightly, an amiable closure to our impromptu gathering.

The bank receipt was the last of the paperwork needed for a passport. I telephoned Didi, and she said that the call to the ministry had gone through. I motored into the Parliament building complex, picked up Aama's passport, and confirmed our plane tickets. But Aama needed still one more approval.

The consul of the U.S. Embassy in Kathmandu was notorious for denying visa requests from Nepalese. The stainless steel drawer beneath the bulletproof window in the reception area of the consular section was, indeed, the gateway to America, and a lineup of applicants concentrated on it with a palpable intensity.

The assistant called me in to speak with the consul. Damn, I thought, it always works this way. We already had the plane tickets, and now my own government was going to throttle the process. But when I shook the consul's hand, I instantly felt a kind of sympathy. He wanted only to relax and talk, to take a break from the endless chain of decisions he constructed from the broad, gray area of U.S. immigration policy. The relentless deluge of pleading and cleverness and hope, born out of desperation, had worn lines in his forehead, like gully erosion.

"Vishnu Maya Gurung's visa will be taken care of by this afternoon," he said, up front and anticlimactically. "It's improbable that she would seek work or take a job away from an American while in the U.S., and if she's a holy woman or something, the U.S. might benefit by her being there."

Coated with a sooty layer of the city's pollution, I returned to Didi's house. Aama and Didi sensed my tiredness and triumph.

"Everything would have been easier," Aama offered, smiling shyly, "if only I had died some time ago. My daughter Sun Maya wouldn't have to see me through my old age, and you wouldn't have this bent-over old charge to take care of." It was not an appeal for pity or attention, nor an apology. She was simply remarking on the way things looked.

Aama's query about death reminded me of health insurance, which would be difficult to get for a foreign woman of her age, especially for a brief trip and on short notice. But we had already decided, or rather, Aama had. She had prepared for and embarked on a final odyssey, to seek out and uncover, as she said, whatever was meant to befall a woman waiting for fate to take its course. Didi and I would simply have to hang on to her and hope she hung on to us, too.

Aama and Tagu had slept in the living room, and were now sitting up in a swirl of blankets in the middle of the floor, sipping tea. Didi was gone. She had taken an early-morning flight to Hong Kong, where her sister Teddi lived. Aama and I would leave that afternoon for Bangkok, then rendezvous with Didi in Tokyo the next day to take the same flight to Seattle.

Aama asked me for some water to pour over her gold jewelry, a means of purifying wash water for her face, essential on a morning of worship. Before leaving Nepal, she wanted to make offerings. If fate had sealed the events of this life, worship and devotion might favorably influence her rebirth and the events of the next one.

Only Hindus are allowed inside Kathmandu's Pasupatinath, one of the subcontinent's holiest Shiva shrines, situated relative to Benares, cosmologically, as a head is to a tail. A police officer ambled

back and forth in front of the entrance, guarding it with the dual
authority of a Hindu government. I released Aama at the tunnellike
gateway and peered inside. Shiva's golden ox Nandiné sat on its
haunches, draped ethereally in morning mist and smoldering incense,
poised to spring into a frolic of fertility around a magical realm I
would never see. As exclusive as they are, I wondered why someone
would choose to be a Hindu. But Hinduism is not something you
choose. You are born that way. At the same time, all humans are
sentient beings of the realm of Brahma the Creator, and of Bhagwan,
the formless but omniscient vitality of God—pure existence, consciousness, and bliss.

Hinduism is the ancestor and ally of Buddhism, and by many
accounts they are the same. Aama had never flaunted her Hinduism
or Buddhism, nor forgotten them, because she didn't distinguish her
faith from her daily actions and the unfolding drama of life around
her. Her brand of religion is not incompatible with other beliefs, it is
simply a description of life as it has been and will be. Dharma. The
universal way, or path.

I stood at the exit, near the bathing and funeral ghats of the
Bagmati River. Aama emerged calm and rejuvenated. She poured
into my open hand some rice grains brilliant with vermilion, for
placing a *tika* blessing in the middle of my forehead. Without speaking, she handed me her shoulder bag and headed for the ghats.

She paused to give coins to the Ahgori Babas, naked yogis of a
Shivaite sect sitting in yoga asanas. Some were smoking hashish,
waiting for something, it seemed. Their bodies were smeared in ashes
swept from the funeral ghats, to protect them from ghosts and to
help retain body heat, though they don't tend to get cold, even in
winter. As part of a tantric Hindu practice, the Aghoris occasionally
eat human flesh from the pyres. But when meditating, Aama had
said, Aghoris require no food, for they have no hunger. They gain
sustenance from their devotion: They are nourished by the gods.

Angling her body sideways for stability, she descended the stairs
to water level, and kept going. Still wearing her saree like the women

around her, she immersed herself and bathed. Knee deep in the river, she faced southeast and three times lifted and held her cupped palms at face level to drip water from the tips of her fingers in an offering to Surya, the sun, which was assertively cauterizing a hole in the fog. Again she scooped, lifted, and released her water libation, this time to the sacred River Ganges, into which the Bagmati flows. Gods and goddesses spoke almost audibly to her of life, suffering, karma, and fate, and she muttered back humbly. A few yards downstream, the trees and pagoda-roofed temples swayed and shimmied through the flames of a funeral pyre. A charred foot and an arm reached out, starkly beckoning to its relatives tending the pyre, while starlike embers soared erratically skyward like fairy sprites, searching for the heavens.

Chapter 3

"You think it's funny that we don't have this sort of thing in our village." Didi gave her a mother's look, wondering where that small item would end up, and in what condition.

Two of Aama's grandnephews were waiting at the Kathmandu airport for us when we climbed from our taxi. Feeling out of place in such a large building, they shuffled their feet, hands in their pockets. Proud to see Aama off and gracious toward her, they were visibly disappointed; with their military background in the Police Marching Band they would be of more use in America, certainly, than their great-aunt, long since discharged from active life. Tagu had wanted to go, too, though he said nothing. His shoes and wristwatch now seemed meager consolation.

The loader tagged my overweight luggage, three handmade sheet metal trunks from the tinsmith's bazaar that can endure only a couple of international flights. Aama gripped my hand as her bamboo cane explored the smooth floor, searching for traction. We're in trouble already, I feared; she could fall over right here.

The trunks passed customs inspection, barely, getting a slash of white chalk like a check mark on a school test, and the loaders hefted them onto a battered cart behind them. "Why are these lights on during the daytime?" Aama asked, studying the translucent panels embedded in the ceiling. "Where are all these people from and where are they going? Everywhere I look I see beautiful bags like the ones the young army recruits bring with them to the village when they are on leave. How is it all sorted out?"

I held out my hand to take hers.

At the women's security check, a policewoman took Aama's shoulder bag and told me to pass through the men's side and retrieve her from inside the lounge. I circled around as Aama issued from the curtained booth, grinning.

"The woman dressed like a soldier checked my pockets and sash to see if I had put any heavy things in them after we were weighed. We were weighed, weren't we? No? Then how do they know how much to charge us?" The ten-kilogram baggage weight limit for internal flights was legend. In the grittier domestic wing of the airport, I had seen passengers bound for remote areas respond to the baggage rules by wearing all of their clothes, every pocket filled with stone-cutting chisels, hammers, and hardware.

I frisked myself in case I had misplaced our passports or tickets, as I was prone to do. The crush and noise of immigration and customs subsided as we proceeded to the transit lounge. We were an odd pair, absurdly mismatched in size, color, and age. Bystanders may have suspected I was absconding with her, but it didn't matter now.

Our flight had been announced and technically, we had departed Nepal.

We squeezed through the narrow terminal door and onto the runway skirt, our carry-on cases, cameras, and Aama's bamboo cane swinging about embarrassingly like prosthetic devices gone haywire. Anticipation and curiosity gleamed in her eyes. She pressed her lips together, then moved them slightly, ready to verbalize the moment a scene captured her attention long enough to form a complete thought. I guided her to a seat on the transit bus. She asked why the airplane was so small, and if I would have to remain standing next to her the entire trip.

"This isn't the airplane," I said, feeling her grip tighten. "It's the bus that takes us *to* the airplane."

"Did we buy a ticket for the bus ride?"

"No." I detected a trend in the questioning.

We stepped onto the tarmac in front of a long metal flight of stairs leading up to the rear of a Thai Airlines Airbus. The plane dwarfed us. This was the jet that first flew into Kathmandu before the airport owned a stairway tall enough to reach its door. Arriving passengers backed outward from the doorway onto a wooden step-ladder positioned on the top landing of the old hand-pushed stairway, the whole contrivance stabilized by three runway crew.

Wait. Aama stopped at the foot of the stairway. Nepalese businessmen, bureaucrats, tourists, and sunburned trekkers still in climbing boots and rucksacks were lined up tightly behind us; they stepped to the side and peered over shoulders to see Aama. Freeing her hand from mine, she bent over and placed her fingers on the bottom step of the stairway, palms down, then rotated her wrists and touched her fingertips to her forehead. She repeated this twice while intoning a mantra barely audible over the engines, which were whining at us to hurry up. Then she recited an invocation of blessing.

"*Haré Om,* please bless me and my dharma son and daughter-in-law and the drivers of the airplane and all the people joining us on this long journey, for I am going in ignorance of what will befall me. If I should die while in a foreign place, may arrangements be made for the proper ceremonies for my body and departing soul, and may all my relatives and acquaintances find peace, in the names of my ancestors, *Haré Om.*"

Sincerity and resolve tingled in her grip as we climbed the steel stairs. As a young woman, she grew aware that industrialization, somewhere, was affecting people profoundly. She and her friends at first believed that airplanes were forms of Garuda, the eagle with the humanlike head, the sacred winged vehicle of Vishnu, Aama's namesake. Later they learned that planes were operated by humans and were designed to carry people, without attendant miracles other than the astonishing fact of flight itself.

Aama was entering another realm. I was just going home, or at least thought I was. The interior of the plane felt strangely like a holding area, a synthetic limbo between cultures and continents. At our row, I placed Aama at the window seat, a good place to be, Aama remarked, because we would get a cool breeze.

She looked at me curiously. "When you handed our tickets to the woman plane driver standing in the doorway, she returned them to you—are they no good?"

Aama analyzed the features and movements of the cabin, while I took a moment to close my eyes and drift within our state of transition, bracketing the past and future, mentally resigning from the stressful job with the foreign aid agency that I would have to return to.

The plane backed up slowly, and I told Aama that we were departing.

"What happened? Why would the plane leave before it is full of people?" She must have been picturing a Nepali bus, packed well beyond capacity yet still awaiting more paying passengers.

As if in slow motion, the Airbus gathered speed, tilted back, and became airborne. The city fell away behind us as uncountable neatly cropped terraces of the valley's hillsides came into view. I envisioned the labor that went into creating and irrigating and plowing each miniature field, then sowing and harvesting them, and maintaining their fertility. Using only hand tools and draft animals, humans had transformed the face of the earth. Perhaps the West would arrive here some day on a quest for the living cultural and agricultural roots of mankind, to learn how to dig and grow as these hill people do.

In Thailand, Aama was awakened by the stillness that followed the engines shutting down. Lethargically we traversed the machine-buffed floor of the immigration lounge as if floating in a rubber raft, and ominously approached the waterfall-like top of a down escalator. The edge came closer. It was too late to explain now.

"This stairway here is moving, and we're going to get on and ride it," I said hastily, trying to sound perfectly sensible. "Standing up," I added, in case she got other ideas. "Give me your cane, and I'll hold this hand while you put the other one on that moving red rail." I stepped onto the escalator and turned to face her, then gripped her arms. She resisted, unable to figure out what was going on. Still holding her, I walked quickly up the stairs, taking care not to trip and bring us both crashing down onto the flashing metal teeth.

"Okay, let's go, *walk,*" I said firmly, knowing that if anything else, she wouldn't be afraid. I had yet to see her register fear. She ventured onto the walkway and—*woop*—all eighty pounds fell backward as her feet moved forward. I pulled sharply on her arms, bringing her center of gravity back to square. She broke into a grin, like a child dropped in play by its father and then magically swooped and caught just before hitting the floor.

Whew, okay, I thought, then looked down at her feet. Only the rear two inches of her heels remained on the moving stair while the rest of her feet pointed out into space. I bent over to adjust her stance, but she began stepping downward.

"Okay, walk," she said. Now she was telling *me* to walk. "Why are we just standing here? Let's go."

"We don't have to go, the stairs will take us," I said.

"Sure, but let's start walking, or we'll never get there."

I pointed to the approaching lower landing where people with carts milled about languidly, waiting to claim baggage. I shared her perception that the lower floor was rising toward us.

The baggage claim landing threw her forward. I caught her again.

"My feet just shifted forward in my shoes, and my toes are pinched up inside the front of them," she said, looking up at me like a young girl. Along with the gradual shriveling of her diminutive frame, her feet may have shrunk since the last time she had worn her tattered Indian cloth sneakers, or her feet may have shortened as they broadened from scrambling across boulders and climbing trees, barefoot. A half-inch gap showed behind her heel, and the sneakers flapped softly as we walked away from the escalator.

In our room at the Airport Hotel, I stayed awake only long enough to drink a glass of water and note where the light switches were located. Later, at a timeless international hour, I awoke. Aama was not in the room. Only a faint rumpling of the cover on the other bed indicated where she had curled up. I lay quietly, waiting to hear a sound from the bathroom. Slowly the door opened.

Her eyes were bulging. "There's another old Gurung lady in there," she said discreetly, as if we shouldn't disturb the woman. She guided me to the door, looked back to see that I was still with her, then peeked in and slowly entered. A brightly illuminated mirror spanned the full length of the bathroom counter. Staring intently, she confronted herself again, exhibiting more confidence this time than in her first viewing. The more the woman in the mirror smiled, the more Aama smiled, in a snowballing reaction that I thought might cause her grin to burst. She clearly recognized the reflection as her own image, but to behold it unveiled in its fluorescent-limned entirety and in the context of the mostly light-skinned, strangely dressed foreigners we had seen over the past day was plainly shocking. This was a reality check I was familiar with. Catching sight of myself in a mirror after months in a Nepalese village, I would be startled at how unnaturally white and tall and ungainly I appeared. My blue eyes seemed albino clear and shallow, too easy to read.

I thought of Didi's eyes, which were bluer than mine; they glimmered with a baby's soft iridescence. A long time had passed since we had left Kathmandu, it seemed, and I looked forward to seeing her. Then my mind stirred with visions of the other women I might see again in the U.S.

Aama snoozed on our seats while I deplaned at Tokyo to look for Didi in the transit lounge. As I walked into the pod-shaped transit area, an American woman stepped up to me. I had watched her do stretching exercises in the aisle on our flight from Bangkok.

"Excuse me, but why is the older woman going to the U.S.?" she asked.

"Well, she has some business there that just couldn't be done by fax," I tried to remark in the voice of a road manager, but my jet-lagged words sounded as if they had originated elsewhere and were broadcast through a toilet paper tube. The woman laughed anyway, and I related Aama's story, or part of it, as I casually looked beyond her for Didi. The woman smiled and with genuine sincerity wished us luck, an American kind of blessing. But for some reason I felt nervous.

Didi was sitting in a group of mostly Japanese, leisurely swinging a crossed leg. Her hair was gathered into a dusty blond topknot, and she wore an attractive white dress. We kissed lightly, and I sat down next to her. With a sisterly, or perhaps motherly, expression, she said that I looked as if I could use some help. I smiled and shrugged, but the expression she shared with me was only partly sympathetic. Her face was relaxed, yet pensive—tentative, as if she were withholding an enthusiasm for our adventure.

"How's your sister?" I asked, trying to lead off in an open, personal tone.

"Teddi's okay. Business is going well for her. Her thirty-eighth birthday is coming up in a few days, and she said that she'd like to get married and have children, but she doesn't have a boyfriend at the moment." I was taken aback by Didi's clipped delivery. She said she had urged her sister to fax a high Tibetan Buddhist lama in Nepal, to request a *mo,* a divination, in order to determine the future and her prospects for a lasting relationship. But Teddi was already consulting a popular psychic, a British woman who worked out of an apartment in Kowloon. During their last session, Teddi set up an appointment for Didi. Yesterday Didi consulted the psychic. I didn't ask her what the psychic said, but I could sense in Didi a new volition, an empowerment likely fueled as much by her sister's widening search for a suitable partner as by the psychic's words.

I groped for comic relief to deflect the tension. I suggested that she could have saved money by consulting the Perfectly Scientific Electronic Fortune Teller in Kathmandu, a vendor who pushes around an aluminum cart displaying an antique television set. I described to her how I paid a rupee and placed my hand on top of the machine. Colored lights flashed, an alarm bell rang, voltmeter needles twitched, then the machine emitted sounds from distant space as a tape-recorded voice spoke to me through a set of well-used headphones: "You are lucky man and will have many children, but only after much hardship and penance. . . ." A hand-printed warning on the side of the machine read "No matter how many times you listen, the machine will tell the truth about you." If it kept repeating the bit about the many children, I thought, once was enough times for me, though I didn't express this to Didi.

She blew air from her nostrils. She had been looking at something on the floor, waiting for me to finish. "Anyway, the psychic confirmed what the Tibetan lama told me in Nepal," she said without looking up. I took a moment to muster an air of casualness and control.

"I didn't know you consulted a lama."

"I didn't consult a lama; I attended one of the lama's morning teachings on Buddhist philosophy and afterward took a blessing from him. He looked into my eyes and spoke a few words that were consistent with something I've been reflecting on for some time."

We sat in silence, listening to a woman's tape-recorded voice on the public address system repeat monotonous, singsong advisories in Japanese.

"Teddi also said that there might be business opportunities for me in Hong Kong if I want to pursue them, and she offered to share her apartment with me for a while." Didi was only a year younger than Teddi.

Uneasily I stood up to go to the rest room. I hadn't expected this change in Didi's disposition, this new, detached manner. It was typical that she would mess things up just when they were going smoothly, I thought. Hell, I have other opportunities, too, I reassured myself as I gathered my pride along with my shirt tails in the men's room. I could be as unsure about her as she was about me, if necessary. Didi might not adjust well to America; she might withdraw or become anxious or different, or weird. We would be regrouping with friends who had forged their careers, while we had foraged as expatriates in what sometimes felt like a state of suspended animation. Or avoidance.

A trial run for the two of us sounded fine with me, better than marriage. Too many adventures remained to be tasted and too much work to be done, I figured, to waste time trying to fine-tune an intangible such as a relationship. I sometimes wondered if Didi and I were together for reasons of habit and a shared distance from our country of birth.

Didi was justifiably cautious about me, and frustrated. I would have been willing to work harder on developing our intimacy, but first wanted her to share the affection that I felt for Aama. She had been helpful and cordial toward Aama, but not overly warm.

In the inadvertent way of the elderly, Aama could be obstinate and demanding, characteristics that Didi had little patience for. Traditionally, the daughter-in-law must treat her mother-in-law with respect and deference. Similarly, it is customary for the mother-in-law to scold, regardless of how carefully a wife completes a chore. Didi could appreciate this societal casting in its context—while sitting in a village in Nepal—and could abide by it as a social grace. But now protocol prescribed that the daughter-in-law, the favored son's wife, bear the responsibility for caring for Aama on a visit to the U.S., an uneasy role for a California girl who was not a wife and didn't feel like one.

But there was more. In Kathmandu, Aama and Didi had exchanged another kind of tension, a subtle competitiveness expressed through body language, tone of voice, or other channels that I was unable to tune to or didn't want to receive. Neither was convinced that the other woman was what I needed.

When Didi and I found our three adjoining seats on the plane, Aama was awake but sleepy. She looked up at Didi and smiled in wonder.

"Why have you been hiding on the plane all this time?"

"We're in Japan, Aama," Didi said gently.

"You mean the plane is on the ground?"

Didi remained standing to observe Aama, which she did with a fondness and warmth that surprised me. She asked me if I realized that we were bringing into a new world the equivalent of a welcome but unexpected and totally dependent child. Didi knew; she had been raised by the elder half of thirteen brothers and sisters, and in turn had helped raise the younger half. Catholics. "Though you may not get along with all of them," she had told me, "you love them unconditionally." She was including Aama in that spacious family, and an affectionate spirit of trust appeared to flow serenely between them.

For an odd moment it struck me that Didi might simply be forming an alliance with her, seeking from Aama the support that I wasn't prepared to give her fully, conspiring to work with Aama to get what she wanted. But this cynical notion evaporated as Didi continued to direct her blue eyes on Aama, gently assigning to her a love and faith that she had kept in reserve for me, or some man, a husband, somewhere. I had never seen her display it. There it was. Aama looked up at Didi and wrapped this tenderness around her, a welcome substitute at this point in her life for livestock, farm, and family.

Two cabin attendants pushed a cart stacked with trays of food past our row, and dinners soon appeared before each of us. Aama held her hands apart, palms and fingers loosely cupped in an open supplication to the scene in front of her. "This meal, these different colors of food, all wrapped up. . . . Here I am, the mother of a British Army officer, walking through a dream."

Didi helped her remove the foil and plastic, and Aama sampled each item to select the one she'd like to work on first. Once the silverware was abandoned, she ate everything. Didi could see Aama observing the dessert cake on her tray, and she handed it to her. Aama ate it in large but polite mouthfuls, then peered over at my tray, then up at me.

"You already ate your cake," she said with no particular inflection.

"Of course I did, because I figured you might try to swipe it from me. Didn't you get enough? Look at your stomach."

"Hunnh," she moaned, and gazed down at her sash, the three-yard-long *petuka* that hill women wear for strengthening their backs when they work and carry loads. It appeared to conceal a rugby ball. "My stomach hurts if it swells up too large, because I haven't figured out how to loosen the string to my new petticoat. But if I don't keep the string tight, my petticoat slips down. I may eat a lot, but it's hard for old people like me to keep meat on our bones, and our clothes tend to fall off." She held up a miniature tub of butter, examined it and shyly tucked it into her sash, then smirked at Didi and me. "You think it's funny that we don't have this sort of thing in our village." Didi gave her a mother's look, wondering where that small item would end up, and in what condition.

A ripe peach remained, and Aama gummed through it slowly. She circled her tongue inside her mouth, then absentmindedly backhanded the pit toward the window of the 747, forty thousand feet up. It hit the clear plastic and deflected into her lap. She looked down at it, then turned to Didi. "Can you open the window and throw this out?"

In the middle of the night high over the Pacific, the jet hit heavy turbulence. It shuddered, plunged, and rolled in a jarring, gut-level reminder that we were sitting in a fuselage full of people hurtling through space and darkness. Anxiety filled the cabin as passengers placed drinks on the floor, fastened their seat belts, and stowed their tray tables. I looked toward the attendants for some reassurance. They looked worried.

Aama was reenacting a conversation with her relatives about the buffalo shed that blew down one night, thirty-five years ago.

"Did I tell you about that?" she said, making sure she recalled the details in precise order. "On its way down, the falling shed damaged the corner of my house, and then somebody ran over and said . . . let's see, what did they say. . . ."

"Do you feel the plane tossing around?" I interjected, wondering whether the heaving and shaking affected her at all. If one hadn't been told of the danger of flying, perhaps it didn't exist, or something. I was sinking into an intense, toxic fear of death, not helped by Didi's rigid clutch on my hand, nor by the Buddhist teachings that were meant to prepare one for death.

"Planes do that, the Gurkha boys told me," Aama said. "Like buses. It bothers some people. It makes them feel sick and many vomit, but it doesn't bother me. I'm not afraid of heights, and I'm not afraid of flying in airplanes. I'm only afraid of falling over when I walk."

Didi's eyes met mine, and we logged a silent note. We've got to hang onto her. Or, if we fell from the sky together we would avert the troubling likelihood of Aama slipping on a sidewalk somewhere.

". . . And so I decided not to rebuild the shed on that site, but instead repaired the house, the one that has since been torn down to build the present house, for which we used the original stones. Anyway, my brother told me . . ."

The storm passed. Didi pointed to the eastern horizon, where a narrow vein of orange light refracted through rainbows of stratospheric ice crystals. The 747 began descending into the sunrise and crossed into the U.S. at the northwest corner of Washington state. Tubes of warm sunlight traversed the cabin walls as the plane banked south, and when we leveled out Aama scanned the sunny brilliance of the Cascade range.

"Those are our Himalayas, our Abode of the Snows," I told her.

"They look like the stacks of hay we pile up near our houses." She leaned into the window bay to take in the breadth of the scene, alone with the plane and the sky and earth. She spoke quietly to herself. "What was it in the planets on the day I was born such that I am here now? What was different about that day? What will it be like and where will my thoughts be at the moment I die?"

By departing Asia for America, Didi and I were leaving the exotic, while Aama was going to it. For Didi and me, America evoked familiarity and comfort, tinged with hesitation. Could we blend into America's fast pace and professionalism, and its literal-mindedness? Was a critical attitude toward our country mostly a symptom of our fear of dealing with what we had avoided by living abroad?

I took refuge in thoughts of what Asia had tried to teach us: that happiness and inner peace, unattainable as they are, are not strictly a product of external events or one's upbringing. Ultimately, who we are as humans shouldn't be affected by where we are.

In America, there would be fewer curious paradoxes. Didi turned to me and grimaced. "I *like* all the chaos and craziness in Asia." As we approached the Seattle-Tacoma airport, I recalled the time I flew to the western Nepal town of Pokhara, en route to visiting Aama, and talked with a young Sherpa pilot as we stood on the grass airstrip waiting for the ground crew to unload the baggage. Instead, loaders were guiding carts filled with luggage to the tail of the plane, for the return to Kathmandu.

"Why don't they offload the luggage that came with us from Kathmandu before they load the return luggage?" I asked the pilot.

"Pokhara doesn't have enough carts. We have to load the plane first, in order to have empty carts."

America's punctuality and predictability would simplify planning for our trip to California, if we were to make it that far. Phone calls would go through. Water and electricity of good quality would be provided consistently throughout the day. People observed and respected the schedules of a culture based on efficiency. Capitalism worked. I wondered if Aama might figure out what was or wasn't behind it all. She was well situated to deliver an unbiased account of the country's health; her view was undistorted by an urgency to find a job or carve out a career, live a life, prosper and procreate, as growing numbers of immigrants were doing there now. She had no agenda.

Aama placed her arms on the immigration agent's counter and explored the features of the small kiosk, her eyes moving about like fingers reading Braille. The agent flipped through our passports without asking questions of us; Aama inquired about his race and if he had any children.

I was disappointed that my father and stepmother were out of the country and unable to meet us. But when we strolled out of customs, our friends Mrs. Withington and her daughter, Tori, welcomed us from across the arrival lounge. They waved small U.S. flags back and forth.

In Kathmandu, the American flag stood resolutely within the bomb-resistant confines of the U.S. Embassy—attached to a varnished pole crowned with an eagle—and it symbolized our heritage of power and high technology. Now, beside Aama and Mrs. Withington, the flag connoted something else: It was a symbol of home. Mrs. Withington opened her shoulder bag to show Aama a clear plastic container holding several chocolate chip cookies, identical to the ones Tori passed around on weekend outings twenty years earlier. The favorites. Aama pushed her lips outward and glanced up at Mrs. Withington with a look of hunger and approval.

Outside the terminal, the smell of Douglas fir needles, pulp mills, and marine life saturated the temperate air. Aama breathed in the freshness of a young world. She seemed at home, too. And young.

"All my relatives and friends have died ahead of me. I wasn't able to die when I should have, when I became an old lady. It was the gods and fate that willed me to live, so that I could be brought to Amrita and stand here now with my dharma son and daughter-in-law."

Chapter 4

"Where have I come to, now? An old woman who for months hasn't been down to the spring at the edge of her village is now traveling all over America!"

Head reclined, jet-lagged by centuries, Aama surveyed the blurred surroundings from the car hustling us into the center of Seattle. The incline and tilt of the freeway viaduct gave us a sweeping, futuristic view of the city.

"Haré, Haré," she mouthed in wonder and reverence, invoking Vishnu. Didi, Tori, and Mrs. Withington sat in front, blending news with old stories as they glanced back occasionally at Aama. I sat next to her,

my feet cramped by piles of baggage. Tori changed lanes, caught the exit ramp onto Third Avenue, and we coasted quietly to a stoplight.

Aama peered out the window. "They are just building this city," she proposed casually, as if critiquing a modern painting. "This is a new settlement. People haven't moved here yet."

Hmm. "Why do you say that?" I asked.

"Where are all the people? I see only cars and cement and tall buildings. If people had moved here, they would be out walking around; stalls would be set up on the street; there would be more of a crowd." Of course. By comparison, even a small market town in the hill valleys of Nepal would be thronged.

Tori found a parking place and armed the car's security device. Didi and I grappled with some of the bags as Tori and Mrs. Withington led Aama to Tori's downtown loft.

Quietness replaced the remnant whine of the jet and airport and freeway. Aama stretched out on the studio loft's luxurious decorator couch and observed a swatch of Northwest sky through the skylight. The green canopy formed by two potted tropical hardwoods evoked a forest as much as an apartment.

"This looks like a good fodder tree. Do they lop its branches?" Aama asked. Her eyelids drooped from the jet lag.

"No, only if it grows too big for the room."

"So your friends don't have livestock?"

Tori carried in a tray of Nepalese-style tea, heavy on the milk and sugar, a source of nutrition, and muddy with caffeine. Didi unpacked a trunk while I thumbed through my address book. Tori's husband, Bill, had been talking on the phone from within another nook of the loft, negotiating a deal, by the sound of it. Two other guests, working with Bill on a photography project, fiddled with equipment and papers. As she sipped tea, Aama glanced back and forth between each of us, curious how our activities interrelated. Already I felt captive to a culture where the grains of sand in an hourglass are bought and sold and bartered. And we had only just arrived.

Like a careful archaeologist, Aama explored the loft, probing cautiously with her senses, tentacles of discovery. Tori showed her the electric stove, and Aama ran her hand slowly along its metallic surface, needing to connect a tactile sensation to its unfamiliar look. I wondered if the effortless operation of a modern range might aggravate her, inflaming memories of the years of gathering burled, damp firewood, splitting it, and coaxing it to burn.

"The stove must be large like this in order to store all the fuel it consumes," Aama said. "When you are done cooking do you have to extinguish it, or does it burn out by itself?"

Tori turned a knob and demonstrated expertly, like the televised user of an improved new appliance. Aama studied the luminous red coil on the range top. Wonderful, but too easy, her face seemed to say. Tori turned on the water and reached for a saucepan. Aama moved closer to watch the water splash into the sink.

"Is there a spring uphill from here, or do you carry water to a cistern on the roof?"

"Underground water pipes are laid through the city, and it flows into the apartment on its own," I responded for Tori. "They have to pay for it."

Aama looked to Tori for confirmation. "Then do all the people of the city come here to fill their water jugs?" she asked. I was about to answer, but her eyelids sagged in a prolonged blink. "If it is night in Nepal now, then no wonder I want to sleep during the daytime," she said drowsily.

In the guests' corner of the loft, Didi made up a thick foam mattress with contoured pastel sheets for Aama. She turned down the covers, then showed her the bathroom on the far side of the studio space. From experience with the airplane head, we figured she could understand the function of a household toilet. Didi cranked the lever while Aama watched the water in the bowl corkscrew down and disappear —perfectly good water used for disposing of excrement. And the bathroom door, Didi demonstrated, opens and closes this way. She left it open with the light on.

The bathroom tour was a cue for Aama to talk about her regularity, a universal concern of old age, we were finding.

"Leafy vegetables help my bowel movements come on time, at uniform intervals, but I usually end up eating whatever my stomach is hungry for or whatever is placed in front of me, even foods that require teeth. It all goes in, and some of it gets ground up in there and some of it doesn't."

Aama followed Didi to bed. Didi and I retired, exhausted, on a nearby mattress.

At two in the morning, we awoke to a rummaging sound. Aama wasn't in bed. Footsteps and mumbled whispering echoed softly like small animal noises across the studio space. She had shuffled past the bathroom and into the living room, where Bill's associates were asleep on the floor. One of them had switched off her beacon, the bathroom light.

"Where is that machine, the vessel made of bone that people urinate and defecate into inside the house? Wait. . . . What's this? Why would someone leave piles of blankets on the floor, not folded up? Here, I'll fold. . . . Ah! There are people under them! Are they alive? They must be sleeping, and they are men, probably Tori's husbands. Why would she make *both* of her husbands sleep on the floor? Oo, one of them is stirring. He wouldn't understand me, probably. Now I'm lost and I have to pee, maybe I can find a corner where no one will notice. I might fall."

Didi guided her to the bathroom and turned on the light. Aama shut the door, and the bathroom wall echoed Aama's voice as she spoke to herself. "Where have I come to? Can anyone in the village imagine that I am here right now?" She opened the door softly, and Didi returned with her to bed.

For some time, Aama and the city beneath the loft windows were quiet. Then, alarming us at first, she began to sing a *nirgurn*, a dirge-like devotional song, in a guttural yet flowing voice. The silences between each passage rang with an empty tranquility. I found it soothing, and soon lapsed into what felt like a dream state devoid of either tension or pleasure. Literally, this feeling itself was *nirgurn,* a state of no *gurn* or characteristic, containing neither form nor attribute.

Singing mournfully, Aama's words described the emptiness that characterizes the nature of our minds. Despite our ability to accumulate knowledge about that which we experience, ultimately we are unable to say why it all exists or what will happen, except that it will end. Our thoughts, our bodies, and the life that vitalizes them, are no more than a bead of water on the petal of a lotus: The droplet sits in perfect roundness and beauty, reflecting the entire spectrum of radiant light. But a mere breath of wind blows, and it falls from the petal and merges its form with the water below. The drop becomes indistinguishable from that water and leaves nothing behind. No moisture remains on the lotus petal.

My battered two-tone '68 Ford LTD sedan, nicknamed the Street Sweeper, had been parked for the past several months in a friend's driveway. Praying that it had recovered by now from the exhaustion I had driven it to, I reconnected the battery terminals. It started up, hacking and expectorating, yearning to breathe after its hibernation in the Northwest rain. Comfortable and respectable though the car had been in its day, it was unlikely to impress Didi, who dressed well and enjoyed living in style, which I considered largely a waste of time. I duct-taped the torn upholstery and threw a Tibetan blanket over it as a poor man's custom seat cover.

"Aama is going to need better sneakers," Didi said to me abruptly when I returned to the loft. She was anxious to set out into the city to acquire items we had been unable to find in Asia. She looked down from the fifth-story window at the LTD parked on the street below, and I waited hopefully as she appraised its looks. She groaned. No, I admitted, turquoise and ivory were never great car colors.

We helped Aama into the front seat and drove across downtown to Nordstrom's department store. In the shoe department, Aama tried on five different pairs of sleek competition sports gear designed for the youthful, narrow, arched jogging foot bound in shoes since infancy. Nearby, the dress shoes sat lined up stiffly. She picked up a high heel, examined it inside and out, held the toe in her hand, then pivoted and jerked the heel in a pecking motion.

"These look like the beaks of egrets, the birds that wade around in our rice paddies looking for fish and insects. These pointed parts would probably break off if you tried to wear them in our hills—what kind of work do you do in them?"

Her feet were the color and texture of elephant hide, and their hard calluses scratched my hands. From the straps of a plastic sandal, an independent-minded toe stuck out at a 45-degree angle, nearly opposable like a thumb, as if it had evolved for grasping rocks.

No shoe would fit. Before we left, Didi checked the children's department and selected a pair of boy's wide sneakers with Velcro closures and a neutral blue appearance.

We stepped into the department store's free shuttle bus for the four-block ride to the Pike Place farmer's market. Aama was still puzzled by the city.

"What goes on here? There's a low noise, everywhere we go, all the time, *ngyung-ngyung-ngyung,* like a flour quern constantly turning, milling away. Do the buildings make that noise, or is it the wind blowing through them?" She twisted and leaned across Didi to peer upward at the skyscrapers, like a farmer checking the underbelly of her farm equipment.

"These buildings are not short, either. How do people agree to go up in them, I wonder. They must get dizzy, but force themselves to for their work. All those stairs to climb. And how do they fit all the pieces of wood together to make such tall buildings, anyway?"

"They're made of metal and cement," Didi said.

"Good, that lasts longer than wood."

Four blocks later, we climbed out at the Pike Place Farmer's Market. Immersed in people and motion, we strolled past fruit stands and potted flowers and shellfish on ice. Aama dug a few coins from her sash for a street guitarist, prompted by the sight of his hat on the pavement.

"Are there many beggars here?" she asked.

"There are some, especially in the cities. But poor people don't beg door-to-door. Usually, rich people collect money and then distribute it to the poor people, or it's done through taxes."

A flower stand captured her attention. A woman holding a bouquet leaned across the table and handed money to the flower vendor. "And they sell flowers, too?" Her question curled into an answer. I recalled trying to stop the neighbor girls from picking, for offerings, the last few marigolds that grew along the margins of Aama's small courtyard. Aama had scolded me for scolding them. People preparing to perform a ritual or make an offering should never be denied flowers; they should be encouraged to pick them wherever they wished.

Aama's upper torso rotated to follow her head, which was turning to observe the tide of people walking by. "People in Amrita are fat and tall. There must be some reason for it. Maybe it's the food, which tastes good, but I didn't detect anything strange in it that would cause this. I imagine that eating fruit and meat is what makes your bodies long and your skin white."

Shoppers halted in midstride and broke into relaxed smiles, disarmed by Aama's childlike openness and her print sarong and velvet blouse, all of which naturally complemented the fruit and flowers. We sat on a bench, and Didi released her hair. Aama extended her hands and carefully ran them through Didi's hair, and then retied it for her. Two women sitting near me asked, with some trepidation, "Is she putting a spell on that girl?"

"See that red-faced man?" Aama said quietly. "Why do some people leave hair on the sides and back of their heads and then shave the front and the top?" I thought for a moment, and couldn't recall having seen a bald person in Nepal. No gene for it.

As Didi led Aama to another booth, a woman stopped to look at Aama, then stepped up to Didi and said, "God bless you." Didi was about to respond when the woman motioned to her that nothing need be said; she turned to hide a tear forming.

Didi and Aama bought fish and vegetables while I retrieved the car. As we idled back to Bill and Tori's loft, Didi observed the dust that filtered up through the floorboards. "You're going to have to get a new car before we leave town," she said. "Aama and I aren't driving to California in this enormous, stinky, funky thing."

"Well, I'll think about it," I said, aware that the Street Sweeper was near the end of its lifespan. I mildly resented Didi's claim to speak for Aama. It was unlikely that Aama would notice the difference between the LTD and a newer car, and she would prefer a larger vehicle to a smaller one, I figured.

From the loft window, Bill spotted us pulling into a parking place and he shouted down that there was a phone call for me. We stepped into the entryway of the loft's bottom landing, and I looked up at the four flights of stairs. I took a breath, dipped to one knee with my back to Aama, then told her to climb on. Without a word, she interlocked her fingers—making a tumpline of both hands—and cupped them around my forehead. With one hand on her ankle and the other on the banister, I portered her up the stairs. Aama's voice droned behind me as if it were coming from headphones, pleading with the deities to tell her how it was that a dharma son like this had befallen her, one who fed her and clothed her and now carried her on his back. Thankfully, her pride kept her from allowing me to carry her again. And I could do without the load, and the admiration.

"Family wagon, PS, PB, AT, AC, exc. cond., $1,600" read the classified ad in the Seattle paper. I called the number, then Didi and I drove to a suburb on the east side of Lake Washington, trying to discern how the main arterial correlated to North 136th Street and West 204th Avenue. Seattle's suburbs had outgrown the city itself, a regrettable modern tale of the offspring devouring the parent.

Feeling for a switch in the dark, the woman flicked on the garage light and opened the electric garage door. Didi and I climbed into a maroon, imitation wood–paneled Ford Country Squire wagon, late seventies. No need to ask why they were selling. Alongside it was parked a fat but sleek snub-nosed family van, a logical trade up. We backed the wagon into the suburban cheerfulness and worked our way toward the arterial for an Italian test drive: Didi played with the knobs and ran the electric seats and windows while I stomped on the gas, hit the brakes, and cornered at high speeds around neatly trimmed hedges, listening. The car maintained a solemn, quiet rumble, reacting to my foot by shrugging at first and then yawning into a muted roar. Sounded good. And the front seat was fitted with three seat belts. The woman accepted a check. Son of Street Sweeper.

The next morning, we awoke to Aama's description of what she had seen and heard during the night. Shamans and relatives from her village had wandered through her fields, all with something to say to her, and it was all good. But she feared they were hiding something. She reached her arms out to them, and they walked away before she could find out more. Her livestock ran from her, too. She reminded me that bad images are good omens in Gurung dream interpretation. To see a dead body is auspicious, to see a wedding is not. It is especially favorable to see water in a copper urn.

I had slept fitfully through a similar angst-driven dream. My carry-on luggage was lost in an airport; I was certain where it was but couldn't quite reach it, just couldn't connect with it.

Within a few days we would begin to sleep through the night. Lying in bed, I worked on convincing Didi about a study that confirmed that sex was the best known cure for jet lag. The process wasn't well known; neither was the location of the clipping where I had seen it mentioned.

"I want to wait until we have more privacy," Didi said predictably. "And I haven't been in the mood, anyway, because I'm tired from looking after Aama."

More likely, I told her, the tiredness was from the jet lag. "I'll help out more when we're on the road," I offered.

After breakfast, we packed up and took Aama to the curb. "This is the new car, and we're taking it to visit our relatives," I said, pleased with its boxy, solid lines.

"We can't walk?" she asked.

"No, because first we have to pick up my clothing and things at the house where I have them stored. Then we'll see one of Didi's sisters, and her daughters, then visit my maternal aunt and uncle—the ones who are farmers on the other side of the mountain range that we saw from the airplane. From there, we'll drive several days to Didi's mother's home, a long way south of here." I placed more emphasis on the long way than I had intended to.

Didi told Aama to hold still while she fastened her seat belt. We waved chaotic good-byes to Tori and Bill, and the wagon power-steered easily out of its parking slot. "We'll be back in a month . . . or so," I yelled from the opened door as I struggled to find which of the brushed-chrome toggles operated the driver's window. My camping gear was stored at the home of friends, Ann and Greg, who lived at the edge of a cow pasture overlooking Puget Sound.

"Oh, no!" Aama blurted. I shuddered each time she said that. She was looking at her waist as if noticing her seat belt for the first time. "I've taken that big belt that I was wearing in the other car into this car with us."

I made sure that Didi was listening, then asked Aama if she liked the new car better than the older car.

"Both cars are good. They're all the same to someone who never dreamed they would ride in one, although this one is bigger. When I return to Nepal, you keep the old car and I'll drive this one along the ridge trail up to the village—I can transport more grass and firewood in this."

Weekend vacationers heading to the Olympic peninsula crowded the ferry loading zone at Mukilteo. We pulled into a holding lane, and Didi headed for the rest room of an oyster bar adjacent to the loading dock. She returned with three soft ice cream cones, and presented one to Aama.

Welcome to America, I thought. The sun shone radiant in a patriotic blue sky adorned with nautical flags and sea gulls in unhurried flight. On the pier, tourists in shorts and sandals tried to keep food from falling from its packaging as they ate. Aama watched Didi bite off the slumping top of her cone, then bit into her own. "Some of the ice cream melts off onto the tongue with each lap," Didi demonstrated.

Aama took a big lick, draping her tongue out to the tip of her chin, and power-licked like a leopard lapping milk. Her eyes peered up at Didi with smiling approval as she licked sideways, no time to talk. Good food for the toothless. Gradually one side of the cone disappeared, and the other began to lose balance.

"You have to rotate the cone as you eat it," Didi showed her. Aama stopped for breath. I crunched into my sugared cone and swallowed it in two bites.

"What? You just ate the holder!" Aama said, astounded. She announced that she was full and turned to Didi. "Here, put this in your handbag and I'll have the rest of it tomorrow."

Didi expelled a single snort of motherly exasperation and handed me the cone. An attendant in a reflective vest waved our line of cars toward the ferry, and we pulled onto the car deck. Aama sat up and gazed across the hood at the water. Several boats passed silently in the distance, while others moved in phantom double exposure across the glass of the passenger window.

"That's another boat, not this boat, right?" she said, not sure where to point.

"Yes, we are in a car that is now on a boat that is distinct from the boats you see over there, or over here," I summarized.

"Ahhn." She sighed, acknowledging in one syllable the complexity that her life had assumed. We stepped onto the car deck.

The ferry's elevator doors glided open, and three people entered. Didi returned to the car to get her sweater. Aama watched the doors close.

"We'll go in there in a minute," I said, "but let's wait for Didi."

Again the elevator doors opened. Aama braced her arms between the metal jambs and leaned inside. She looked concerned.

"Where are the people who just went in here?"

"The room went up, and they got out one floor above here, at the place where people sit while the boat crosses the water." We stepped in and the elevator shuttled and moved upward.

"This must be where we are weighed, to determine how much we pay for the boat ride. We *are* on the boat now, I think. No, we just got out of the car, near the water. Is the car going to the same place we are? If it is a big boat it shouldn't flip over, which would be good because I don't know how to swim. . . ."

As the ferry slipped fluidly from the landing, we followed the stairs to the top deck. The trees and houses of Whidbey Island were plainly visible across the strait. "That must be Malaysia," Aama pronounced. "We're heading west, and I've always been told that Malaysia is to the west of Hong Kong and of Amrita. Will we meet some of the Gurkha recruits who are enlisted there?"

"Malaysia is much farther to the west, Aama. We won't get there this trip," I said, as disappointed as she that there were none of the British Army's prestigious Tenth Gurkha Rifles regiments within the U.S.

The Son of Street Sweeper bumped off the rural island road onto Ann and Greg's narrow driveway, and tobogganed crudely down ruts established by smaller cars. Ann and Greg met us in their parking area.

"So this is one of your houses, and these are your caretakers when you are in Nepal," Aama said to me, in Nepali, fortunately. Andrew and Adrienne, ages four and six, were uncommonly quiet, but only long enough to study their parents' reaction to Aama, which was lively and gracious.

The kids led Aama to the bluff overlooking Admiralty Inlet, Puget Sound's main shipping channel. The Olympic Mountains stood elegantly across it to the west, about as distant as the Himalayas are from Aama's village. Aama scanned the forested foothills of Olympic National Park. "So then *that's* Malaysia," she voiced with finality. "And it looks fairly close."

She inspected Ann and Greg's cedar-shingled home, then turned to me. "Nani this house is all wood. When you get enough money, you can have them cover it with tin for you." Corrugated sheet-metal roofing had become popular in her village, I was painfully aware. It reflected sunlight harshly and made a racket during hailstorms. Most of the young men in the village had no interest in learning how to thatch a roof properly, and Aama said she wouldn't trust them to do it right, anyway.

The kids grabbed cookpans and ran bouncing and stumbling to the garden, to pick peas and beans. They waved at Aama to follow them, which she did without glancing back. Squatting in a line in the midst of the vines, they duck-walked ahead after each section had been carefully picked.

One of the children pointed to a slug.

Aama said, "Save that. We can fry it up and eat it. They are good medicine, too, for sprains and bruises. You dry them, grind them, and mix them with nettles and corn flour before you eat them. But for tuberculosis, it's best to eat them raw, or while they're still alive." I translated Aama's advice for the kids.

"Yuck," Andrew said. They made faces.

"Some people like the taste," Aama continued, "and they hunt for them. Others are disgusted by them, and you have to feed slugs to them without their knowing what it is." She picked up the slug and wedged it between two large rocks.

Like a Christmas ornament in summer, the sun hung well above the Olympics though it was past nine in the evening. Ann and Didi set the table, and we sat down to dinner, our third night in America. Didi called Aama to the table.

"I'm not hungry," she said from the couch in the living room.

"You go ahead and eat, I'll just sit over here. If I sit at the table with you, the smell of the food and the sound of eating will make saliva come to my mouth, and I'll want to join you, even though I'm not hungry."

Maybe she was sick, or just being polite. "Come join us anyway," I said, knowing that for Nepalese, despite their lives of socialities, the act of eating was not a social occasion. Aama may have felt awkward sitting down to eat with men, who are usually served before the women begin. In her village kitchen, Aama would first place a small amount of rice on a plate by the fire, for her ancestors, then a bit into the fire pit for Agni, the god of fire, before dishing out the first large portions to any male guests.

"What we don't eat might be thrown away," I said, conscious of the extravagance of doing so. Didi and Ann guided Aama to the table. She picked up a spoon, haltingly but delicately, and her appetite slowly gained momentum. She ate a large plateful, partially filled her plate again, ate that, and belched. Ann brought over some more food for her.

"No, I've had enough now," Aama responded. "I didn't think I was hungry until I started in." She smiled demurely. " 'When those who never have, then find, they eat it right along with the rind.'

"You young people grow bigger the more you eat, while I just grow smaller. What did Ann put in the food that makes it taste so good? There was enough salt this time, I guess."

"Here, have some more," I persisted. In the village, forcing food upon guests was polite, expected behavior, just as declining it was. To ask for something or say what you were thinking, on the other hand, would be impolite. "You know those slugs you found, Aama? We're frying them up in butter for dessert, so be sure to save room for them."

"I thought the kids threw those away. I couldn't find them," Aama said seriously, then loaded up a serving spoon with potatoes and carrots from the serving bowl. She steadied the spoon with both hands and guided it to my plate, then delivered spoonfuls to Didi's and Greg's plates. Others always come first.

Greg and Ann talked about life on the island, thankful for the seclusion one moment and longing for company the next. Ann contended that they were more isolated than Didi and I had been in Nepal. While we spoke among ourselves, Aama observed our motions and mannerisms. Her stomach jiggled, amused that our words, composed of sounds made entirely in the mouth rather than the chest and stomach, could convey useful information. At one point, she chortled during a lull in the conversation.

"What's so funny?" I asked.

"I—" She faltered, laughed uneasily, then gave me her look of confidentiality; I leaned toward her and she began again, privately. "I can tell when you are talking about me when I hear my name, mixed in with all that gibberish you speak. You know, I can't be certain that you're not talking about cutting me up and eating me."

When I first moved into her village, I was seized by the same fleeting uneasiness. The villagers must be scheming to rob me or—even more damaging—ridicule me. "You're right," I said brightly. "But Ann and Greg agree that we wouldn't get much meat off those bones of yours, thin as you are. That's why we're feeding you all this rich food—to fatten you up." Aama's villagers retorted with a similar line when I had interrupted their discussions to ask what they were talking about.

Aama laughed, then looked down at her tiny, distended stomach. She scanned around the table at each of us, her eyes twinkling.

Ann took the children to bed.

"Mom, do you have any earrings like Aama's?" Adrienne questioned as her mother tucked her in. Before Ann could answer, she asked, "What's it like to die, Mom?"

"I don't know, dear."

"Has Aama ever died before?"

"Do you think she has?"

"I think she has, because she's so ancient." Ann later told me that she had never heard Adrienne use the word *ancient,* but Adrienne had been searching for someone who has died and returned, perhaps because it would be reassuring if they had. I said to Ann that Aama and the Gurung believe that all of us have died and come back, and that we can expect to again.

Chapter 5

Her lips moved in bewilderment, attempting to identify and account for this mockery of her subsistence existence. Agriculture shock.

A box boy nonchalantly hickey-bobbed the back of a train of shopping carts as they accelerated downhill toward the entrance of a Safeway outside of Buckley, Washington. Aama, Didi, and I had stopped to buy food en route to a campground in Mt. Rainier National Park, where we would rendezvous with another of Didi's sisters, Stephanie, and Stephanie's two daughters.

"Listen to them, those carts go *garararar-gyat-gyat-*

gyat as that boy pushes them. What a marvelous noise," Aama said. The young man lined up the carts outside the store and nodded to us smartly.

I was about to show Aama the stacked-up Presto-logs, our American type of firewood, but the hydraulic glass doors had magically opened and were humming at us to enter. Aama was already mesmerized by the colors and bustling sounds and curious mix of smells streaming over us. Didi introduced her to one of the carts, and Aama instinctively placed both hands on the handle and strained at it. The Human Shopping Reflex.

We embarked into the aisles, Aama taking to the cart like a teenager to a hot rod, no instruction wanted, really, just a second or two to get the feel. She headed straight for the meat and dairy coolers.

"Now, *turn* it," Didi said loudly from behind her. Shoppers' heads rotated. Aama leaned on a corner of the cart, confusing the motion of turning with tipping. It rose onto two wheels and nearly crashed into a display as I lunged to catch it. She took off again, banging into the food racks like a windup toy hitting a wall, then whirling about in search of a new wall to head for.

"Méro baajay"—my old man—"look at this bazaar, I can't believe it—all this food lined up, one kind of meat in this line, another kind in that line, fish set out over there. You would think it would all spoil before people had a chance to eat it." Her eyes seemed to absorb energy directly from the flickering lights and buoyant shopping music, as caffeine and refined sugar pulsed from the shelves into our veins through osmosis. We were on an inspection tour of a dream factory.

"This garlic is so big. . . . And there are eggs everywhere, stacks of them, but I don't see any chickens." Her view shifted to the produce. "I look at these green vegetables and want to cook them and eat them, if only I had teeth. The fruit looks ripe and is probably sweet. The kids in our village always steal fruit from the trees before it ripens."

Didi bagged some bananas, pears, plums, and strawberries.

Aama peered around her, then turned to me. "Do the people who own these items leave them all in this bazaar at night, or do they take them home and set them up the next day? And where are all the people who will buy this? They must not have heard that a bazaar has been located here; when they find out, this place will be packed."

Each aisle offered up an associated memory. "Don't let that scoundrel son-in-law of mine in here," she said, laughing her way through the wine section. I could see her picturing his stupid stagger, choreographed to dog-eared philosophical musings. He used to be only an embarrassment but was now the village joke.

Didi threw a plastic bottle of mouthwash into the cart, and said to me that she hoped it would do something for Aama's breath. Aama's teeth were rotting, the two or three that remained.

Aama placed her hand on Didi's forearm and spoke quietly. "My teenage granddaughters are now wearing what they call *feshion,* and they asked me to bring them the cloth that their friends use nowadays to cover their breasts. Can we get that here?" Didi added bras to our shopping list. "And I'm supposed to bring wristwatches back for the villagers, but what need of watches do village people have? Watches are expensive, and they break. I'll say that we weren't able to find any good ones in America, if you'll agree to say that, too, okay? Ha!"

A woman stood alone at the head of an aisle, passing out free food samples. When we rolled the cart past her, she cheerily offered us small chunks of a new brand name of chicken that had been specially prepared for microwave cooking. Aama placed a piece on her tongue and mouthed it slowly but hungrily.

"Tastes good. It's soft, too—I can swallow it without chewing."

The woman noticed Aama eyeing the lined-up morsels and offered her another. Aama took one and again savored it.

"Tastes good," she reiterated. "How much do we pay her?"

"Nothing. She gave it to us to try."

"Then you should go and buy something here to give to this woman."

"I'm not sure we really—"

Aama dispatched Didi and me into the aisles with a wave of her hand. Reciprocity was woven into the fabric of Gurung tradition. She was content to wait for us, and turned to accept a third sample offered by the hostess.

"Aama, I don't think we need to . . ."

"Why would she stand here and just give this away for free?"

"She's trying to tempt us into buying this new kind of food."

"What do you mean, *new kind of food?* Since when is chicken a new kind of food?"

We rolled the cart up to the checkout counter, and Didi and I placed the groceries on the conveyor belt.

"Hunh. You don't bargain with them," she deduced from the movements and expression of the cashier. "How does the woman remember the price of each item? I didn't see her look at the boxes, where you said the prices are written."

"There's a machine connected to that red light," I said. "And the light is like a mechanical eye that reads the price on the box and tallies it inside another machine."

She sighed. "I figured it must be done by machine, since everything else is. It's all so easy. But I bet this stuff isn't cheap."

Didi rolled the groceries outside. "Do we get to take this cart with us?" Aama asked. When I didn't respond, she looked up at me. "They seem useful and durable, and we could use one to store all those bags and bottles we've collected," she amplified, as if the cart's mere practicality warranted owning one. Didi and I glanced at each other and collided with Aama's deduction. If we lost her in the city or suburbs, we knew the profile to begin a search with. She had already cached several paper and plastic bags beneath the car seat, the ones she had caught us trying to dispose of, the smaller ones carefully stored within the larger. Bottles and cans lay next to them, exhibits from a harmless collection that we hadn't taken much notice of.

As we swept back onto the highway, Aama noted the oncoming traffic.

"Look at all these cars. They must have heard about that spontaneous bazaar and are heading for it now."

At the White River campground in Mt. Rainier National Park, we abandoned the cruise wagon and joined Stephanie and her daughters in their camper. The van climbed toward the parking lot where the road would end in a pasture called Sunrise, near the tree line.

Halfway up the switchbacks, Stephanie slowed for a small white-tailed deer nosing about for crumbs at the edge of a gravel turnout. Didi slowly opened the door as Stephanie pulled over. Aama asked for some food, then crawled out and approached to within a few feet of the doe. The doe looked up at her but was curiously unafraid.

Aama squatted, avoiding eye contact, her head lower than the doe's. "Ahh, ahh, ahh . . ." she repeated in a rasping but gentle voice, the call she uses for her chickens and livestock. She held out her hand, and the doe took the piece of bread.

"It's hard to approach wild animals," she said when she returned to the car. "You don't know what they're going to do and they don't know what you will do. As tame as they are here, there must be no tigers or hunters."

The pungent aroma of alpine wildflowers awakened and cleansed our nostrils. Aama and Didi ambled on a graveled tourist path across an alpine meadow that merged seamlessly into the backdrop of Mt. Rainier. The Mountain, as northwesterners refer to it, looked massive and desolate, but in the congenial two dimensions of a painting. When I glanced away and again turned to look, its icy outline vibrated against the dark-blue sky, emitting a profound and frightful air of volcanism.

Presiding monumentally over the surrounding forest, Rainier evoked Mt. Kailash, the solitary, sacred peak in the far corner of western Tibet, the source of the Ganges and the blissful realm of Shiva, the Destroyer. The Hindus say that Kailash is the heaven where the Aghori Babas, those saddhus who have fully taken Shiva's form, will go to reside. It has never been climbed. To do so would defile it, for Kailash is a state of mind as much as a location, and it embodies liberation from the material, physical realm.

"Just as pilgrims trek to Kailash, Americans come from a wide area to see this mountain," I said to Aama, "except that people here don't generally walk to it, nor do they worship it, really."

"But they do come to see it, and simply by seeing it they will gain merit," Aama affirmed.

A woman walked up to me, trailed by her husband and two children.

"You know," she said, as if holding a discussion, "on the way up here, we were trying to take a picture of this woman as she fed the deer, but we couldn't get our camera to work." When I realized she wasn't going to report us for feeding a park animal, I expected her to ask, as most had, where Aama had come from. "But somehow," she continued intently, "it didn't matter, because all of a sudden it was like we became focused, like we slowed down, we stopped, right there, as if this woman's aura was the only thing visible. We could feel it."

Her husband nodded in agreement, and the children stood riveted by Aama's jewelry and wrinkled face. I could think of nothing to say to the woman except that I had seen it, too, and that Aama emanates a comforting animal energy while working with livestock and walking through her mountain forest.

Another middle-aged woman intercepted me on the trail and canted her head sideways with amiable curiosity. "Excuse me, is this woman an American Indian?" she asked. Behind her, a loosely formed line of people had gathered to see Aama up close, as if she might be an original source of the native American legends of the mountain, a holder of the key to their grandeur. The mere presence of a crowd had generated around her an air of authority and mysticism. Captivated by their intent looks, Aama was getting a contact high from their contact high.

"No, she's from Nepal," I said. "But she's of the same race as the American Indian. Their common ancestors came over the Bering Strait land bridge from Asia many years ago and settled in North America."

"Well, we came over from Brooklyn two weeks ago." The woman placed her hand on my forearm and spoke to me directly. "Tell her that I think her clothing is *very special.*" I conveyed the woman's impression to Aama.

"Would she like to have my clothes?" Aama honestly offered. "She can have them if she wants them."

"How does she like America?"

I relayed the woman's question.

"I'm thinking of living here," Aama quipped, "so that everyone can stop and look at me and take my picture."

"She likes it," I said.

"Well, we'd love to see you again some day," the woman said.

"If I'm not dead. I could die today, but it might be tomorrow," Aama retorted. Majestic and spiritual places, such as the Himalayan shrine of Muktinath, the Realm of Liberation, enlivened her with a playful mischievousness and sometimes philosophical advice. By not knowing English, she could speak as she pleased, leaving me to modulate her words to fit the context of a social conversation, to turn the literal into the figurative.

"Now you know how I feel when I hike around your hills," I said to Aama. "Everyone there looks at *me* just as people here look at you."

"Well, sometimes I feel like a lamb in the middle of a pack of jackals." Aama caught my glance. "Nani, I may speak to you in Gurung sometimes, so that people won't overhear me when I have private words to tell you," she said, as if there might always be bystanders who understood Nepali. Didi didn't understand Gurung, and I wondered if Aama might at times want to exclude her.

"I can tell that people are wondering about me, and I sometimes see you writing in your notebook. Now, if anyone asks who the old lady with you is, or if you write anything about me, I'll tell you what to say: 'She's a farmer. She's not a rich person, neither is she poor. She's right in the middle, an ordinary woman, the daughter of regular people, in between. She's not overly happy nor overly sad. In between.' That's what you should tell them." Didi looked at me, questioning how ordinary Aama was, really.

"Poverty is relative," I said to Didi, endorsing Aama's self-ranking. "Even though she'll pick up cow dung she finds on the trail—manure trouvé—she could build a decent stone house with her jewelry and, as you've seen, always goes out of her way to give money to beggars and homeless people."

". . . And I bet they're asking how old I am," Aama continued. "Tell them that I'm eighty-four, and that I've been alive this long precisely because my scoundrel son-in-law wants me to die, and I don't want to give him that pleasure—that's what keeps me going!" Stephanie's camper quietly descended to the campground while Aama continued to roast her son-in-law. "That ingrate asked me if I would divide up and distribute my land before I die, and I told him no. He's probably sitting in that house of his down there below mine right now, privately hoping that I'll become a corpse while I'm away. . . ."

At our riverside campsite, we unloaded grocery bags while Stephanie's daughters, Genna, ten, and Nicole, seven, led Aama to the picnic table. Delicately Aama ran her hands through Nicole's hair and turned her head from side to side, pausing at each feature and curve like a phrenologist uncovering her fate.

The girls carefully examined Aama's hands and face and wrinkles as if she were an imaginary character who had stepped out of a children's television program and into their private forest. In the car, Nicole had introduced Aama to some of her stuffed animals.

"You have two girls," Didi said to her sister as they pulled beers from a cooler. "And now I have one." Didi's smile was ironic, with a hint of pride.

"Didi," Aama called from the table, "your sister's daughters should have their ears pierced. Your people must not know that you can go deaf from leaving your ears naked. Ours are pierced when we are three days old." The girls looked at me, and I translated.

"Yeah, Mom, can I have my ears pierced?" Nicole asked her mother as she must have repeatedly, awaiting the inevitable, but now unlikely, yes answer.

"You can, Nicole, when you're older. You're too young now to be wearing jewelry around everywhere, and the holes would only close up if you didn't." Moms always had good reasons. Aama had one, too.

"When I was young, we heard that children with unpierced ears attract the 'jungle shaman,' a man-demon about three feet tall, with long, ratted hair. His feet are on backward, and he lives in a cave lined with gold, like a king's palace. The jungle shamans eat food not from their fingers or palms as we do, but from the backs of their hands. If you're infected by a hex from one, you have to eat food that way in order to expel it. They chant *kururururuu* as they go out to capture children. They eat the girls and teach the boys to be jungle shamans like them, then release them to capture other boys and girls with unpierced ears. But a simple net will stop them. When we were children we used to carry a small net with us whenever we went into the jungle."

I caught myself looking briefly into the forest, which was being overtaken by dusk. I gave an edited summary of Aama's story to the girls, not wanting to scare them or antagonize Stephanie. I was tired of translating everything, anyway.

"You see these large earrings of mine?" Aama said, as if we hadn't noticed her medallion-size gold earpieces. She turned her head each way.

"They used to be much bigger, but I had them resmithed into

smaller ones so they'd be less of a load to carry around and wouldn't burn my cheek when I sat in the sun and turned my head to talk to someone. Also, I was afraid they'd get stolen. Large jewelry is not appropriate for older women, anyway, and I needed the money."

Nicole gently lifted them, then inspected the numerous empty holes ringing the perimeter of Aama's ears. The mystery holes. Each open slit and stretched loop of ear tissue was like a notch denoting time, a medal of experience telling a story of happiness, grief, or adventure, financial gain or loss. She studied them as if trying to decipher their history, to read back into a time long before her birth.

"My original earrings were pure," Aama continued, "but the goldsmiths adulterated them with inferior gold when they made these. Every time you melt and rework gold, its quality drops a level, from what we call 'eldest son' down to 'third eldest.' 'Youngest son' is the number-four quality, and is lighter colored, like brass."

I had seen Aama rub corn kernel-size chunks of gold on a smooth black rock, then scan for a yellowish color. To villagers, the qualities of gold are general knowledge. They don't trust paper money, and convert any that comes their way into gold or silver. Wearing it as jewelry is more secure than storing it in houses that are difficult to lock.

"You know the coral she has strung on either side of the gold pieces?" Didi interjected. "It isn't real. I don't know where the Gurung get them, but those large coral beads are imitations."

"What do you mean?" I said indignantly. "Of course they're real —do you think Aama would knowingly wear fake jewelry?" Maybe Didi was jealous, or simply wanted someone to pay attention to her appearance, as well. I couldn't give my full attention to both of them at the same time, and right now was Aama's turn. But Didi did know jewelry.

"Maybe she doesn't know the coral are fake," I allowed, "but the rest of it is genuine."

Amused at first, Aama watched as we argued, then became impatient.

"Oh, I forgot," she said, raising her arm to distract us. "Did you know that my nostrils have been pierced here in the middle?" She pinched her septum and held her thumb and forefinger in a circle. "This hole will never close up on its own, but the other ones will. I had a thick gold ring in it, a *bulaanki*, fitted with tiny gold chains and decorations that hung down in front of my mouth and swung back and forth whenever I nodded my head. When I ate, I had to hold it up with my free hand." From the ground beside the table she picked up a small stick, then passed it through her septum. It held her nostrils in a flared position and created a temporary speech impediment; she looked like a cartoon cannibal. The girls broke out in noisy laughter, and Aama moved her head back and forth comically so that everyone could see. Didi and Stephanie laughed as loudly as the girls did.

"To pierce our noses, we take a long thorn from a high altitude bush," I interpreted for Aama, "dip it in melted gold, let it cool, and then punch a hole." The girls squirmed. "You have to keep the hole open by gradually widening it further with a twig, which must come from a certain tree; otherwise, it could get infected."

Didi and Stephanie set out cold chicken, fresh corn on the cob, and salads in plastic tubs. We ate heartily, enjoying the change from Nepali food, which tended to be healthy but monotonous, except for the chilies.

"I love to cook for people like Aama," Stephanie said, "someone who simply appreciates every detail of food, even the act of eating. She feels like our mother, too." Stephanie had Didi's soft family features, and shared the warmth that Didi radiated when she first saw Aama on the airplane. "When Aama was in our house, I felt—" Stephanie paused, somewhat embarrassed "—a kind of purity, or safeness, a goodness, like having an older grandperson in our presence."

Sitting uncomfortably on the bench, I lifted a cheek and carefully released some pressure, controlling it so as to be barely audible. A

moment later, I had to do it again. Aama waited until she had swallowed her mouthful, then spoke without looking up from her plate.

"So that's how you eat—you chew one bite and fart, chew another bite and fart—ha!" Her hearing must have been better than I
thought. She was the only one to catch me, and reacted with the tone
of voice and expression that my own mother would have: disappointed, but not resentful. I stared at her a moment to freeze her
image, to hang onto the déjà vu that swept by me.

"But you just said yourself that you don't hear most things anymore," I responded.

"My ears seem to hear bad things just fine. They don't hear good
things very well, or very often."

"What is Aama talking about?" Genna questioned.

"Uh, she's commenting on my table manners. You know how
mothers are." Aama cleaned her plate, then ran her tongue along the
outline of her blank gums. She leaned back, said that she was full,
picked up the paper plate by its edge, and held it between her thumb
and index finger, then in a spontaneous motion flung it toward the
trees where the tent was pitched.

"Hey!" three of us exclaimed at once, the words leaping out as if
to capture the plate in midflight. We looked at each other and
laughed at our conditioned response.

"We don't do that here," I said to Aama, mildly shocked, trying
not to laugh.

"What, you want to reuse a defiled plate?" Indeed, for remote
villagers, litter from packaging was a minor status symbol, a rare
item to be casually garnished around the front of the house to show
passersby that they have consumed an expensive modern product.
She viewed litter also as a minor act of generosity toward the low-
caste paper collector who would come by to gather it for recycling. I
devised a short version of a lengthy explanation of litter, comparing
our national parks to the queen's forests that surround Gurung villages, but lost her early in the telling.

In the cool morning along the stream bottom, Stephanie and the girls gave long hugs to Aama and we departed for the frying pan of eastern Washington. At the park's entrance station, Didi pulled the wagon into the adjoining rest area. I jumped out to go to call my aunt and uncle to let them know we were on our way. When I returned, Aama pointed her lips through the windshield at the phone booth in front of the car.

"How did you know that you would receive a call at that phone there, right at this time?"

A gas station outside of Yakima was our first stop after dropping onto the orchard and desert country east of the Cascades. I was reticent to fully crank the air conditioner; a heavily weighted older car would have trouble handling the additional load, especially in hot weather. I asked Aama if she wanted anything from the convenience store.

"Feed the car first. It's been doing all the work, while we merely sit. Don't worry about me, I haven't done anything."

As I pumped gas, Aama observed a sedan parked beside the water and air stand on the side of the service station. A man got out. With a paper towel in one hand and a bottle in the other, he sprayed his windshield, then leaned over to wipe it, careful not to let his clothing touch the film of dust that covered his car.

"Why is that man washing his own windows?" Aama asked when I got back in the car. "Aren't there people who do that sort of thing for you?"

"Not anymore. Servants and laborers are too expensive now for most people to afford. We try to do everything ourselves."

"I'm having enough trouble telling men apart from women. When everyone looks the same, how can you tell what caste or tribe they are? Doesn't one caste farm, while others do another kind of work?"

"We have laws here, Aama, that we can't hire people of one color or tribe or sex in preference to another. So we don't really have castes."

"I bet that your people had castes years ago, and you corrupted them and forgot them such that they are all mixed together, *luttar-puttar*. I heard in the village that Amrita is a country of only one caste of people, as you say, but we've seen black people here. When I was younger, the villagers said that black people ate human flesh. That always sounded strange to me, and the ones we saw in the city and near the mountain didn't look as if they would. Do they speak your language?"

"Yes. A hundred years ago, black people were slaves to the white people, but no longer. In many ways they've become like the white people. One ran for President of America. But still, the black and white races don't get along with each other as well as the Brahmins and untouchables do."

"I've seen white and black people, but not many like me. It's nice that some people bend over and speak to me, although others, I noticed, pretend I'm not here. Maybe they're embarrassed to see someone who is not like them."

The loess soil of the Palouse, dark with organic matter and volcanic ash, was covered with a gilded fabric of wheat. In Dayton, near Walla Walla, my Uncle Chad and Aunt Darlene shared a life of land, crops, and community. Darlene was close to the church and had spent years working on restoration of the town's railroad depot as a museum. Chad had taken over the farm from his father, and when he wasn't in his office he drove about in a pickup truck, testing soil and chasing cattle.

A layer of grain dust coated the seats of Chad's pickup, and well-used tools and an issue of the *Wall Street Journal* sat in a brown clutter on the floor like memorabilia of the contemporary West. We squeezed into the front, and Chad drove us through dried-up gullies shaded by occasional oases of honey locust trees. In their impatience for harvest, swells of bronzed wheat rippled and waved to the summer breezes, reflecting warm light onto our faces and the ceiling of the cab.

Columns of dust rose from beyond a distant rise like smoke signals, the first sign of harvest. Chad pulled off the gravel road and into a field of stubble, and we drove to the top of a knoll. In the valley below us, three high-speed combines with headers twenty feet wide moved in formation like ravenous Cretaceous herbivores. Reaching our hill, they swung U-turns in sequence, spinning about at full speed as if trying to escape the dust and chaff that swirled about them like insects. The combines slowed only for the trucks that sidled up to them and docked like pilot fish, taking dumps of three tons of grain at a time.

We stepped out of the cab. Aama grasped Didi's hand and stood motionless, calculating the scale and speed of machines that in two minutes harvest what their entire village reaps in a year. Her lips moved in bewilderment, attempting to identify and account for this mockery of her subsistence existence. Agriculture shock. The grain and the hay and the land, the largess of the gods, were being upstaged by machines parading about as arrogant, impostor deities. And where were the people? There was no singing or teasing banter in the fields, no popped corn and sweet foods wrapped in leaves and carried out in baskets, no socializing, no communion of hand with soil.

After a moment, she seemed to suppress her alienation, and the scene began to register. She saw how it worked. "I wonder if the wheat was planted at the right time," she said finally, as if wanting to contribute, to help with the harvest. "Did someone look first at the alignment of the planets? We do this before each planting season to insure a good crop and protect it from hail. And if the wheat doesn't ripen long enough on the stalk, it might rot during storage." She watched closely as Chad husked a head of wheat between the palms of his hands and poured the grains into Aama's. "These are large, full grains," she confirmed, "and it appears sufficiently dry." She looked back to the combines.

"But what happens to the wheat stalks after the machines take the wheat?" she asked, as if such giant eating machines would certainly leave behind bones and gristle or some other by-product.

"When the harvesting machine threshes the grain, it chops up the hay and scatters the residue over the field, which then acts as mulch and fertilizer," I said.

"Then where is the grain taken?"

"We'll go and see."

The terminus of the county's rail line was at the edge of town. Aama craned up at the cluster of cooperative grain elevators beside the tracks. "You Americans are all so wealthy, you own so many things, so much grain and land. And you don't even grow rice!"

"It's too cold here, and there's not enough water for rice."

"Yes, it looks as if the only water you get falls from the sky, unless you lead irrigation water from those large rivers. But why do you even bother to grow grains when you eat mostly meat? When the new generation comes, will they grow crops with machines—I imagine so—or will they scratch the earth with their hands as we do? Here young people study while the machines do the work."

Darlene prepared a summer farm breakfast of omelettes, cantaloupe, and coffee, and set out the morning newspaper for Chad, who scanned the commodity prices through the bottom half of his bifocals. We sat looking out at the cherry tree and the foothills of the Blue Mountains, and spoke of changes in our lives. I recalled my college summers on the farm driving a wheat truck, and we agreed that we missed my mother—Chad's youngest sister—and their father, Gramps. Darlene told me privately that Didi was a gem.

After breakfast, I made some phone calls and changed camera film. When I came into the foyer, Darlene and Aama were sitting together on the small couch near the door with a photo album spread open between them. Didi interpreted as Darlene named the relatives in each photo.

Aama told Darlene that she envied and admired her good fortune to have healthy children, and lamented that our lives are short and frustrating, because just as we fall in love with something, we must leave it. She summoned images of her only daughter and her deceased kin, and a tear dropped onto her blouse. Darlene looked away, but she, too, had begun crying. They were crying in unison.

"Even though life in our hills is difficult, as it must be in yours," Aama said, "I can't help but think of where I was born and raised. How can people forget such a place? Their soul never leaves it. My mother died when I was nine years old and younger sister was seven. Younger sister foresaw better than I that children of the next generation would lead a difficult life, so she never married. Here, when I eat good food and see beautiful things as I have this morning, I think of Sun Maya, suffering the pain of both my life and hers."

Darlene remembered her own relatives, the departed ones and distant ones, and her children, grown up and moved away. "It's sad that only one son is farming, but is perhaps just as well. Farming yields little reward for our constant attention and effort." Aama had said the same thing herself. She appeared to understand Darlene's words before Didi could translate.

"Yes, but if good things are meant to happen to you, they will. We don't know how we got here exactly; we just know that we have been stationed on earth by Bhagwan to do some work. And if we work and play honestly, we will stay healthy and thrive. Yet, as if swimming across a wide river, we may swim and swim, but regardless of where we reach, our time runs out before we can touch the other side."

I looked at my aunt. The glint of an embarrassed but hopeful smile sneaked through the tears that ran down her cheeks.

Chapter 6

Aama was withdrawing. "What kind of people are these, what kind of country is this where we have to pay money to spend the night outside in a forest?"

The station wagon's chrome bumper scraped the concrete incline as we swerved into a gas station on the outskirts of Walla Walla. Squinting at the midday brightness of the pavement, I pumped gas and added water to the radiator while Didi took Aama to the rest room. I closed the hood and turned the flat, luxury car hood ornament sideways, hoping to reduce the wind resistance some and save gasoline. Especially when accelerating, an expensive diarrhealike funneling sound issued from the carburetor. The wagon was doing no better than its previous large-car incarnation, the LTD. Earlier, Didi had reminded me that our gas mileage might improve if I released the parking brake while driving.

Lounging behind the wheel, one foot on the dash, I checked the road map. Didi opened the passenger door. Aama looked in, gripped both sides of the door frame, and pulled herself onto the front seat, standing. Her diminutive figure bent at the waist, she took two wavering steps toward me and grasped the rearview mirror for support, twisting it, as usual. She then made a standing 360-degree turn and installed herself on her perch—the bottom section of a large child's booster seat—as if climbing into an early-model space capsule. Nepal's pioneer into the inner space of America.

Didi fastened Aama's seat belt.

"Do we have to attach this strap each time we get in, the way we did on the airplane?" Aama asked. "It keeps us from falling out? I know—you're doing this because you're afraid I'm going to run away!"

"It's illegal to ride in the car without it fastened," I said as partial explanation. "The police could arrest us."

"Arrest the two of you, maybe, for tying down an old lady."

Wind lightly buffeted the car as we cruise-controlled the freeway that parallels the south bank of the Columbia River, heading toward Portland. To our starboard, the river's whitecaps nearly lapped at the road, reflecting starbursts of sunlight. Baked brown columnar basalt pillars loomed above us on the left, accenting a cobalt sky. The highway was smooth and clean, perfectly engineered for relaxing modern driving. "What are those patches in the middle of the road?" Aama asked, waving her hand at the intermittent white line. "It looks like stitching. Does it hold the road together?"

She selected road signs and items of contrast, and watched them approach and pass. A yellow CURVES AHEAD wavy arrow sign went by. "That looks like a centipede," she noted. "Maybe lightning will strike. Just before a storm, centipedes come out from under rocks, turn onto their backs, and wave their legs in the air, and we say that they are teasing the sky. Then lightning strikes in revenge. It looks like rain, doesn't it? I can't tell."

The tinted upper margin of the windshield had earlier led her to presume that the sky was cloudy. She hadn't mentioned eye problems, but I wondered if her vision was worse than we had suspected. I held up two fingers and asked her to count them.

"Of course I know how to count. That's three fingers. Or do they count differently in Amrita? Are you trying to trick me?"

"I think we should get glasses for you, Aama," Didi said.

"My eyesight *is* getting a bit funny, and dim. One candle looks like two or three candles, and the full moon looks like a white rose with its petals about to drop off. Would glasses help?"

"Maybe. If you don't have cataracts." Didi shifted to the edge of the seat, turned sideways, and told her to open her eyes wide. She peered in and saw deep brown darkness.

Aama chuckled. "I don't know why you would go to the trouble to get glasses for someone like me who is about to die, but if you do, be sure to get the power kind. Actually, I need teeth more than glasses, now that my mouth mill is worn smooth. I see people eating food that must be chewed, and it makes me envious. The villagers say that teeth doctors can make artificial teeth out of bone or something." She twisted the rearview mirror again to see herself, opened her mouth and looked in. Empty. No different than it had been for a long time, her look of surrender said. "Now, if you go to a doctor to get me glasses or teeth, make sure he checks Didi to find out why she isn't having any children."

Didi and I exchanged glances, surprised by this tangent. Aama gazed straight ahead at the pavement, locking into the steady beat of the broken white line. Her statement required a response, from me, I assumed, but I wanted more time to draft one. Didi observed me, curious to hear what I would say.

"We use family planning here in America," I told Aama. "It's expensive to raise children, so we have to plan them carefully."

"How can you plan something like that?" She contorted her soft, alligator-skin hands and callused fingers into question marks, as if she had expected my excuse. "Children come whether you want them or not. In any event, you need them to support you in your old age. Whatever the degree of your suffering, it eases your mind to have children. If your karma is good, you will have them."

Her lips moved, attempting to form additional words; with a small sigh, she gave up, then looked at me as if confidentially. "I haven't told you this, but I've been thinking that by my coming to Amrita, there might be some way I can help you two to have children." I could feel Didi's gaze. For the moment, I avoided them both by glancing back to check for traffic, then changed lanes. I told Didi that it was true; without children we were not much of an extended family. But by bringing Aama with us to America at least we had begun to expand it.

"You can't just hoard money and not have children," Aama expounded. " 'Her calf, the mother cow finds inside a large mass. What can a barren cow find, except grass?' "

She rested her head at an angle and looked at me. "You know, if a wife is infertile, we call a priest, who sometimes attributes the barrenness to a planetary misalignment. If so, he usually recommends that the husband take a second wife." Her tone clearly implied a younger wife. At thirty-seven, Didi was considered old by Nepal's marriage and motherhood standards. Aama again turned to watch the oncoming road.

She was playing both mother and mother-in-law. It was simple. Two daughters-in-law would be better than one. The reserve one could return to the village with her to help with the perpetual chores. In an attempt to lighten up the discussion, I feigned an exaggerated, portentous look to Didi. With a genuine furrowed brow, she promptly stared me down.

"Hey," I said to Didi, upbeat, "I heard—I think—that only the second wife is obliged to commit suttee and throw herself on her husband's funeral pyre, so you don't need to wor—"

"Well, I'm not even your first wife yet," Didi interjected, betraying a slight smile.

I asked Aama. "If I were to die, should Didi commit suttee?" Didi held her remarks and waited with me for Aama's reply.

"We Gurung don't do it, but they say that suttee is good for the karma of both the man and the wife." Aama resumed sitting, expressionless, preparing for a reaction from Didi. Didi formulated.

"Aama, taking two wives doesn't work for us here," she began, easing into the issue. "For one thing, the wives would have a hard time getting along with each other."

Aama nodded. "It's true that there can be trouble between the first wife and the second when they live in the same household. But a first wife should be pleased when a second wife has a child by their husband." Aama could tell that Didi was in no mood to endorse her proposal. "Okay, then—have no children, keep only one wife and hoard money, along with all that clothing you are already hoarding in those big bags you carry around. We Gurung don't have enough cloth to cushion and cover guests when they come to stay in our village, and here in Amrita you have so much clothing that you need little rooms in your houses just to hang it all up in. And you walk on top of thick wool carpets, wearing shoes, which makes us feel funny because we can't afford carpets even for use as mattresses."

A spasm of guilt wedged itself onto the seat between Aama and me—the guilt of affluent Americans who send charity to poor Asians, but with an extra dose of it considering here was a poor Asian sitting right next to us, voicing what we hear normally only from magazine appeals, or our consciences.

"Here," I clumsily tried to explain, "money, for better or for worse, much of the time, is how we relate to each other. Most people don't own land. They have to work constantly in order to earn enough money to save some to support themselves in their old age."

"Don't the children take care of their elderly parents?"

"Sometimes. But the government pays money to old people, too."

"Why? What do old people do for the government?"

"It's like a pension, for those who have put in years of work for the government or their company."

"How easy," Aama said matter-of-factly. "Maybe I should live here."

Aama could live here, and Didi and I could take care of her. Mostly Didi, Didi harumphed. ". . . Bathe her, help her in the bathroom, puree her food, and hold her hand. Everything." Already our lives were being altered, like having children of our own. Here was one large one, impulsively adopted out of wedlock. I recalled warnings from friends with kids that it was easy to both spoil and be manipulated by demanding children.

We drove in silence, then I asked Didi whether she thought Portland or San Francisco might be the better place to get Aama glasses, and possibly new teeth.

There were no free campsites along the Columbia River Gorge, and in the height of summer we might not find free camping anywhere near a highway. Tired from a long afternoon in a warm car, we swung into a state park campground near Multnomah Falls and secured one of the last slots. The Country Squire appeared a lean Third World size between two deluxe aluminum recreational vehicles that were nurtured by electricity and water from umbilical cord hookups. At least the hookups relieved us from having to endure the RVs' fuming and noisy generators. Aama studied the curious metal monoliths. Their awnings scowled like primordial eyebrows.

"Aama, these are houses on wheels," Didi explained. "In addition to their country house or city house, some people have a house that they drive around."

"So why would they need the other houses if they have smart-looking ones like these, made out of metal and on wheels, no less?"

"They probably have the money to afford two houses—or they borrow the money—and they need to work in one place but like to travel, just as you do. So why shouldn't they?" Didi added. Her voice sounded a bit indignant. She was still irritated by Aama's clear counsel that I find a younger, second wife. Since our return to America I had sensed that Didi also was thinking of settling here, and looking for a home, with or without wheels, which may have been part of her motive for joining us. It was Aama who had joined Didi and me, rather.

The campground attendant walked into our parking space to collect the fee. He wrote the slot number on a clipboard, recorded our license plate number, then eyed with suspicion our Tibetan carpet and Gurung blankets laid out on the small patch of grass. As I spoke with him he continued to write something—perhaps a note designating us as problem campers. I handed him a ten-dollar bill and pocketed a scribbled receipt. Didi began to unpack the car.

Aama pulled on my sleeve. She wanted to know how much the ticket he handed me cost, and what it would allow us to do and have.

"About 250 rupees, and we can stay in the campground one night."

"Hunhh?" She looked up at me, taking a moment to register. "That's expensive. Like everything here, I guess. Well, when do they bring the food?"

"Food?" I nearly choked on the word. "They don't bring any food. We have to buy our own food and then cook it—that's why we brought all these pots and pans and a kerosene stove, the stuff there that Didi is taking out of the car." Didi had thrown a red checked vinyl-ply tablecloth over the picnic table and was setting out boxes containing groceries, aluminum pots, and plastic kitchenware.

"You have to pay for a place to stay, outdoors, and they don't even bring you food?" Aama stood suspended in thought, staring blankly at Didi and the boxes. "No food. . . . We pay to sleep. . . . Two hundred fifty rupees. . . . Hunh." I stopped puttering.

Aama was beginning to withdraw. She spoke quietly. "What kind of people are these, what kind of country is this where we have to pay money to spend the night outside in a forest?"

I couldn't find an adequate response. "Well, this place is run by the government, so it's cheaper than the privately owned places."

"If it is run by the government, they shouldn't charge money, should they? Isn't anything in this country done for dharma, for religion, for passing travelers? It's our religious duty—and we gain merit—by offering food and shelter to overnight guests, whatever time they arrive. 'An evening guest brings luck,' we say, and we never ask a visitor for money. My house is directly below the trail, so I often get travelers dropping in, many of whom I don't even know." She paused to qualify her thought. "Morning guests are not as important."

Gradually Aama became agitated, jerking her hand to solidify each point, gnarled fingers trying to gain purchase on the familiar. She first addressed us, and then turned to the trees, then the tops of the trees, beseeching them, hoping that a wider audience, the people who need to know, somewhere, would hear and comprehend and clarify this for her. My gaze followed hers into the forest, hoping to be there with her to respond and react.

"And you would expect to see at least some sign of your people's offerings to the deities, deities who are certainly here, everywhere, within all that surrounds us in this wonderful, beautiful and natural land. Bhagwan, the god of gods, the spirit of dharma, is here; I can feel that, but your people don't seem to know it."

She squatted next to the picnic table and her eyes searched for an object she could identify. I settled next to her on the table's wooden seat and methodically ran a thumbnail back and forth across its layers of chipped paint, digging for an example or metaphor she might relate to. I found nothing. The close-up radiance of the Cascades had delighted her, as had the endless wheat fields and the elegance and thrill of technology. But I sensed on the road that she was looking for something more, searching for an affirmation of

American peoples' respect for the spirit that most certainly guides and enables our lives. Such an orientation to sacredness might not be found readily or nearby, I feared, and possibly not within America.

"Most Americans don't know how good and beautiful and abundant our life here is, Aama," I said tentatively, "because they haven't seen anything else. They have never been to a place like your village, and most have never been to a foreign country. I feel embarrassed to show you my homeland because of our lack of religious devotion."

The evening bird calls and background murmur of camp life took on an intense vividness. A camper coasted by slowly, silent but for an almost imperceptible rattle and dull *whoosh* of tires on asphalt.

"Well, I look around and I wonder what these people do—isn't anyone here religious?" she challenged. Her look was piercing, severe. Discomfort and aloneness radiated from her face and the tips of her trembling fingers. Visibly, she grew self-conscious of her small stature, her dress, her isolation, her powerlessness. I felt helpless to transform her disenchantment. To apologize for our country would be cavalier, and futile.

"We may meet some people who are religious," I ventured, attempting to defuse her mood. "There are gods here; Bhagwan is here. Just take a look, as you said. Religion and spirituality are not everywhere, but there are people here who worship." A hopeful but not unrealistic prospect, I reasoned.

She wouldn't expect Americans to act like Hindus, but she hoped that they would share her spiritual foundation of strong, implicit values, including devotion and service. The Buddhists and Muslims she had encountered in Nepal behaved as she did, and she considered them as spun from the same spiritual fiber. Only their icons, visualizations, and explanations were unlike hers. Where were ours? Somewhere inside the televisions in the RVs next door, I guessed.

Didi sensed that Aama was hungry, a common trigger of her aggravation, and she prepared the food hastily. Pouting, Aama moved toward the picnic table. In silence we ate a meal of Didi's outdoor cooking. Like parents awaiting the latest statement from a rebellious adolescent, Didi and I sat tensely, then gave up. Didi took some melting ice cream from the cooler and scooped out a dish for Aama. Aama recognized it from our wait in the ferry line, and her eyes followed its path to the table. Observing its slumping form, she slowly consumed it, soothed by the easy, toothless enjoyment of massaging ice cream in her mouth and then swallowing it. She roused the image of her relatives reacting to the implausible news that she had paid to sleep outside. Together, we laughed for them in advance.

In what came forth as a pessimistic tone, I told Aama that I shared her uncertainty about the spiritual character of our continent —a community of persons without a persona. How could so many of us drift so far from simple principles and pleasures? Undeniably, America was inhabited by neighborly, even friendly, people devoted to their work and families and recreations, but it lacked the kind of universal, binding belief system that held together a Gurung village. Money was a universal feature of America, but perhaps it bound people more to debt and obligation than to kin and community.

Aama knew her culture innately, so it remained to Didi and me to describe, using the leverage of perspective, what it was about Aama and the Gurung that distinguished them from, and connected them to, Americans. I compared notes with Didi.

"It seems that right and wrong is too often determined by school-teachers, therapists, lawyers, and courts," I said. "It's from these hired specialists that we learn the rules, or else face the consequences."

"And by comparison," Didi said, "Himalayan villagers face constraints that are both taught and sanctioned entirely by their religion, family, and community. That's one powerful modifier of behavior, and it costs their society relatively little. Whether they call it that or not, all of their actions reflect an understanding of karma."

Much could be explained by the principle of karma, the irrefutable law of cause and effect. The aggregate of one's actions, and the merit and demerit that result from them, determine the quality of one's present life. But they also reach beyond the boundaries of this lifetime, into the next and subsequent lives. Whether it does or not in this lifetime, eventually Karma ripens.

Didi and I agreed that we were unsure of our qualifications to interpret and referee American values. But I turned toward Aama and muddled along anyway.

"Our family structure in America has been dismantled over the past hundred years," I told her, wondering if it had more simply deteriorated from neglect. "Our community and extended family were the first to go"—if these had ever been fully established within our Western pioneering culture of expansion—"and now even the nuclear family is threatened." But I was unable to tell Aama why. Somehow, our legal and welfare system has become the surrogate family and community. By its own insidious momentum, or by default, the government has been conscripted to pick up the pieces.

Aama smiled at my sincerity and appeared relieved that I thought about matters other than money and driving around and hoarding things. During my discourse her mood had changed, as it often would. She looked ready for sleep.

We crawled beneath a single large quilt outfitted with a skylight of stars. While Aama chanted her evening prayer, I scanned my own hazy, drifting image of America for a sign of sacredness, for a testament to a shared respect for the land and its people. Uncertain of how to express it, I slid over, faced Didi in the darkness, and made a quiet pledge. If a sense of the spiritual, or even sincere religious devotion existed in America, we would at least try to find it, somewhere amid the swirl of distractions. I was reluctant to mention this resolve to Aama, predicting that she would ridicule my ignorance of not knowing where to look, of having to search for something that for her is part of the landscape we inhabit and the air we all breathe.

I had been raised a Sunday school Protestant, and retained only a child's storybook view of biblical events. But Didi had grown up in a traditional Catholic family and might know where to begin looking. She reflected for a moment, sighed and whispered something about a good idea, then told me to roll over and get some sleep. I lay on my back and worked systematically around the canopy of sky directly above, trying to organize groups of stars. When I returned to the original groups they looked different, they had dispersed and re-aligned with other stars. Astrologers were right: The stars knew. They knew as much as we about our karma and where our journey would lead us.

Didi and I awoke at sunrise. Invigorated by the damp Northwest air, we threw on sweaters and started the camping stove to brew coffee. Feeling a cold draft infiltrate an untucked corner of the quilt, Aama clasped and anchored its corners under her and around her, in case someone might try to roll her over and force in frigid air. Silver hairs strayed from under the quilt onto the Tibetan carpet.

"Is my daughter-in-law up yet?" The quilt muffled her mock-scolding voice. "Tell her to get up! The sun is rising. Time to plaster the floors and porch with fresh cow dung and clay. Then start the fire, put water on for tea, and parch some corn. After that, start the midmorning rice so that we can grab our digging tools and go off to work! You'll have to get water before anything else. . . ." She hesi-tated, then warily peeked out to see if her morning invocation of mother-in-law cheer had transformed our forest camp into a bustling village in the Himalayas.

"Okay, where do we go today?" She threw back the quilt. "I'm up. What's there to see? Let's go!"

Browsing at a roadside tourist information stand, I picked up a bro-chure inspirationally titled "The Promise and The Dream: The Sanc-tuary of Our Sorrowful Mother," promoting a religious retreat out-side of Portland called the Grotto. There, Servite friars and sisters had converted fifty-eight acres of Northwest woods into a Catholic garden, a sanctuary from the surrounding suburbs. The grounds were arrayed with shrines, chapels, statuary, and the stations of the cross. Didi drove while I translated some of the brochure's contents for Aama, describing how the Servites, the Order of Servants of

Mary, are seeking to alleviate the suffering in the world around them by emulating the compassion shown in Mary's service to Jesus. Aama quickly deduced that this was a holy place and that we were about do something worthwhile, for a change.

"If I had known we would be making offerings today, I would have bathed and fasted when I awoke this morning. A religious pilgrim should do this in preparation for an appearance before the deities. I haven't even swallowed my saliva." With her right thumb she began counting up and down the finger joints of the same hand. "We'll need rice, incense, candles, matches, flowers . . . and fresh cow dung. Can you get some cow dung?"

"I don't think we'll find any nearby." I was aware that a small amount of cow manure would be helpful in propitiating Bhagwan, and glanced purposefully toward the margins of the parking lot in a token quest. Cow dung fertilizes the Gurung's fields, cooks their food, and, mixed with clay, plasters their floors. It is a by-product— or product, rather—of Laxmi, the goddess of wealth, and the benevolent source of milk and butter. Aama reminded us of the cows, very small ones, she thought, that we had seen from a distance through the windows of our speeding car. Manure would likely be found on the pasture side of the freeway fence, but we had long ago exited. And I was uncertain how to explain myself if caught removing a cow pie. In Oregon, passersby would assume we were hunting hallucinogenic mushrooms.

Didi spotted the sign for the Grotto, and we turned out of the suburbs into a forested area. I had called a Portland friend, an M.D. who directed a clinic in Kathmandu, and he joined us in the parking lot. Aama knew him as Doctor Sah'b, though he had not seen her as a patient. He was in Portland on home leave. He didn't have any manure, either.

Aama coached us as she organized the ritual objects. "There are lots of flowers right over there. Didi, you pick some of those—no, wait, I'll pick them. You could be having your period. It would be ideal if a virgin girl gathered them."

"Aama, we can't pick these flowers," Didi objected, pleased with Aama's devotion but concerned that she might get us in trouble. "There's a sign there that says so."

"What do you mean we can't pick these flowers? Last night we had to pay to sleep outdoors with no food and now we can't pick flowers? *Kaha hunchha*," she muttered, the Nepali equivalent of "Enough is enough, already."

"If we remove them, other people won't be able to see them and enjoy them," Didi maintained, as if quoting the reasoning behind the Grotto policy. "They look beautiful where they are, don't you think, colorful and cheerful there in the flower bed?"

"Of course they look beautiful, that's why we need to pick them —for offerings." She looked at each of us in turn. "Flowers aren't made by people, by our hands; they don't come into existence because we say they should, they are made by Bhagwan. Everything we see is made by Bhagwan. How can *people* tell you to not pick flowers? I don't understand everything!"

She strode to the flower bed that stretched the length of a parking lot divider and aggressively picked some pansies, irked at our attempt to interfere with her religious devotion.

The release of air from a hydraulic door diverted our attention to the center of the lot. Passengers in summer clothing issued slowly from a bus with CATHOLIC CHARTERS written in large cursive script on the side. The Pilgrimobile. Most of them looked Latin or Asian; the women wore mantillas and clutched rosaries, the Catholic counterpart of the Hindu-Buddhist *mala,* the string of 108 rudraksha seeds carried by most older people on tour of Asian holy sites.

Didi said that Mexicans and Filipinos probably constitute most of the devout Catholics of our generation who still embrace the prospect of acquiring merit through pilgrimage. A few of them, their eyes adjusting to the crisp Northwest sunlight, idly watched Aama pick flowers. I tried to envision how her flower collecting could be legally restricted. People committing quasi-illegalities seem to be caught more often if they are secretive or nervous. Self-confidently, Aama picked all the flowers we would need.

She handed the bouquet to Doctor Sah'b. "I'm going to take my shoes off here," she demonstrated. "You can't wear belts or shoes into a temple or shrine, or to a pilgrimage site—not if they're made of cow leather. There's leather in these new shoes of mine, isn't there?"

We removed our shoes and socks, stowed them in the car, and walked reverently toward the Grotto along a meandering paved trail overgrown with temperate forest flora: rhododendrons, Oregon grape, bracken fern, and salal. The air was saturated with the damp fragrance of Douglas fir needles and rotting bark, censers of the Pacific Northwest. Aama's toes broadened and, like fingers, explored each step. Catholic pilgrims ambled behind us while others returned toward the buses, looking approvingly at Aama as perhaps another Catholic from an old country somewhere in South or Central America, or Asia. One woman asked how old she was. When Doctor Sah'b said eighty-four, she said that she had guessed her age at over one hundred. I told Aama that the woman who was speaking and the other Asian-looking people were fellow pilgrims.

"They don't exactly look like pilgrims. They aren't carrying candles or incense or flowers, and they're wearing shoes. Maybe they are lost and unaware that this is a sacred place—or maybe they believed the story about not picking the flowers. Anyway, they will gain merit simply by having come here," she said sympathetically.

Flaring the fingers of her free hand, she motioned toward the undergrowth like a weekend gardener proposing a new landscaping effect. "Now don't go off into the bushes here and pee. The grounds around a shrine are holy and the trail to it should be respected. You must approach a holy place with a clean mind and body—and an empty stomach. You knew you were coming to a sacred site, but you ate beforehand anyway, didn't you? Did Doctor Sah'b eat, also?"

I didn't need to be reminded of the fast-food designer pizza that

Didi and I had eaten, ravenously hungry, from a drive-in on the four-lane access road that Didi generically named Burger King Drive. "If your stomach is empty," continued Aama, "you have more respect. By not eating you are showing the deities that you are willing to feed them before feeding yourself." She hadn't eaten anything. I was sluggish already, and now I felt self-conscious and sacrilegious, too. As Aama's dharma son, I knew better. I wondered whether I should act as if this were my country or as if it were Aama's. It was beginning to feel like hers.

She stepped from the trail to the edge of a narrow stream that flowed across the garden sanctuary. Bent nearly double at the waist, she splashed water onto her feet and began to wash them, rubbing vigorously behind the ankles and between the toes with the tips of her fingers. She glanced about briefly for a rounded stone, as would be left near the village spring to clean off caked field dirt, but she saw only shrubbery and moist duff. She stood up; from beneath the sarong her wrinkled and callused feet glistened like modern art objects.

Ethereal background music guided us into a natural amphitheater, an outdoor cathedral graced with pews arranged in placid rows. Turning, we faced the Grotto. A statue of the Virgin Mary holding the dying Christ in her arms—a white marble replica of Michelangelo's Pietà—posed serenely inside a fifty-foot cavern.

Vigil candles, which until recently could be placed randomly around the Grotto, were now confined to a locked cage. The people in the religious accessories shop told us that children had been removing or playing with them, and assured us that any candles lit by the staff, by prior arrangement and by phone if desired, would stay lit for seven days.

But there was no time for rules. Aama, authorized by her own devotion, withdrew the chain that impeded entry to the moss- and lichen-encrusted overhang, the Virgin Mary sanctum. She stood directly below the image, her hands together loosely in the outline of a candle flame, or of a lotus bud moments before it blossoms. Her body seemed infused with a warmth fueled by her proximity to a benevolent deity. Motionless, she mouthed her mantra several times, then turned to us, standing in attendance with her offerings. In a businesslike manner she took the candles and, on tiptoe, stretched to place them on the mantle at the foot of the shrine. Nurturing the match flame carefully—matches are expensive in the village—she lit the candles, positioned them upright on the altar, then lit the incense. Taking two steps backward, she clasped the sticks of incense in her hands prayer-fashion, directed upward as if spouting from the tips of her fingers. She revolved them in front of her face three times in a clockwise direction, tracing smoke spirals. A shaft of sunlight illuminated her wattle and the wrinkles of her hands and face with translucent light.

Doctor Sah'b and Didi and I looked around, awed by the vitality, the raw presence of the moment and the etchinglike image of Aama in the Grotto. She became devotion, an extremity of the Grotto itself, a counterpart of the Virgin Mary sitting peacefully and omnisciently above her, aware of all things yet unconscious of her self. Time seemed to stretch and then stop, as when a vehicle screeches to an attention-riveting standstill to allow a blind person to cross the road. But it was the three of us standing beside her who had been struck and were being transported to a temple in Nepal or India, centuries earlier.

Aama set the incense on the mantle, stood back and slowly bent at the waist, then placed both palms flat on the clean slate floor of the Grotto. She lowered herself to her knees and touched her head to the ground. Twice again she prostrated, reciting a blessing. "We are here in ignorance, yet may all people have the fortune to be informed of this sacred place and be able to appear and make offerings and take blessings. We are all of the same race, the same blood, *o Bhagwan*. Forgive my sins and the sins of all the people of America and the world, and protect us all, *o Bhagwan*. Keep us in peace and happiness. Keep us in health and comfort. May those who have no wealth not miss it and those who have wealth not misuse it. I humbly submit these offerings and appeals in the names of my relatives and ancestors, o *Bhagwan. . . .*"

The tour bus pilgrims stood frozen in ambulatory poses, short-sleeve shirts and dresses hanging slack, entranced by Aama's focused, resolute absorption. Here was an old Hindu woman from Nepal expressing their Catholicism for them, worshiping on behalf of all of us. In the authentic tradition of a pilgrim she had endured suffering, left home in old age, encountered hardship en route, and arrived here, finally and fortuitously, to present herself before the gods and goddesses of a holy shrine. But now she was going further, leaving us momentarily in the world of the vulgar while she touched upon the sacrosanct. The tour bus pilgrims betrayed looks of expectancy, as if wanting to join her. Perhaps she could take them, and all of us, along with her.

"It is an act of Bhagwan that I have been brought here—these deities are in a different form than ours, but they are the same gods," Aama said, trembling lightly, refreshed as from a brisk swim. "Which Bhagwan is it, the one in the cave?" she asked me.

"It's the one that—"

"It doesn't matter," she continued. "Bhagwan is one being, one spirit, appearing in many forms, as many deities. Bhagwan doesn't come to us saying 'I am the deity with this name.' It is only us humans who discriminate among them. If Bhagwan is inside one's soul, then one is able to see him."

A one-hundred foot cliff divided the garden setting into two levels. We moved toward the outdoor elevator that lifts visitors from the Grotto level to the upper garden. I passed through the turnstile, then stretched back to insert a token in the metal slot for Aama. Arms extended in front of her, she tested the arm of the turnstile. It began to rotate, causing the lower bar to swing up and catch her on the leg. She pulled back on the upper bar. I motioned for her to come toward me, not back up. Laughing, she ducked and crawled through the bars in the manner that she would enter a small Hindu shrine. A grounds-keeper watched, smiling, as I took her hand.

Doctor Sah'b held the elevator door for us, then stood near the control panel and questioned in a lofty, sanctimonious tone, "Heaven, Hell, or Purgatory?" We broke into laughter, a release from the transfixing scene of the Grotto. Didi translated Doctor Sah'b's joke for Aama. Aama remarked that we were being silly, and possibly irreverent.

The upper garden was crisscrossed with pathways leading to the stations of the cross, fourteen marble images of saints of the Catholic pantheon, each skirted with a kneeling platform. Aama watched Didi kneel and pray, then synchronized to her. She then led Didi and Doctor Sah'b and me on to the next station, guiding us in prayer and prostrating silently at the base of each statue. The sculpted marble feet were rough, neglected, yet to be smoothed and timeworn like the toes of Michelangelo's St. Peter from generations of Catholic pilgrims' kisses and caresses. The hand of one saint appeared to move, quietly reaching out to touch Aama's head in blessing—or to slap her lightly on the cheek, the Sacrament of Confirmation, an ecclesiastical reminder to sacrifice and suffer for her faith. Aama needed little prompting.

We spotted the outdoor rosary *mala* described in the brochure. Aama singled out Doctor Sah'b as the first in need of absolution, after his elevator comment, and she went over and took his hand. Reciting a mantra in Sanskrit, she towed him where she had seen the other pilgrims plodding, in a clockwise circumambulation of the oversized rosary beads made of fishing net floats strung on a rope around a flower bed. Coming from his Jewish upbringing and being led obediently through a Catholic observance by an elderly Hindu-Buddhist woman half his size, Doctor Sah'b couldn't help but look over at Didi and me and laugh in amazement, marveling at the combination of circumstances that had delivered us to this confluence of time and space.

Aama interrupted the flow of her mantra-blessing. "There. Now look. Doctor Sah'b is laughing." Didi and I grinned involuntarily. She caught us. Chanting distractedly, she continued around the rosary a second time, then stopped and confronted us. "You're all laughing. You don't know how to worship. You just come to watch and to laugh. But Bhagwan hears your laughter."

Our smiles suddenly felt like smirks, and we wiped them off our faces. She had returned us to the present moment, her moment, her ground. Chastened, Doctor Sah'b continued around a third circuit with Aama before she released him. In silence we stood and watched the trees and statuary of the park. Rationalizing that we had really been laughing at ourselves, Doctor Sah'b vowed that it was the last time he would mock anyone's genuine devotion. Witnessing the humility in Aama's face and voice, the three of us were humbled by association.

The descent in the elevator was like a return to earth. When we climbed into the car, Aama asked if there was any more of the delicious-smelling food that Didi and I were eating earlier, and if there might be enough to share with Doctor Sah'b, too.

Chapter 7

Didi with Aama, recovering from her baptism in the Pacific. "This would not have been a bad place to die, here in this ocean, because it is auspicious to have Ganges water on your lips at your time of death."

The taste of marine air along the lower Columbia had whetted our appetites to see the coast. Highway 101 was our route to California.

Placid blueness filled the windshield as the wagon lumbered up a long rise. The white sand shoulder and Scotch broom, combed by the wind, indicated that the ocean lay nearby. The car leveled out at the top of the hill, and I released the accelerator. We rolled to a stop, and the Pacific Ocean filled the front window, coaming to coaming, in wide windscreen magnificence. Didi lowered her window, and moist air laden with sea life and negative ions filled our lungs.

"Aama, this is the ocean," Didi announced as she loosened and shook her hair, aroused by the California-style sense of freedom it represented. "It's the largest ocean of the world, and it stretches partway around the earth."

Aama lifted her chin slightly—the scene seemed to lift it for her— and she stared intently at the horizon.

"We flew over part of this ocean on the airplane, during the night," Didi continued, "but it would take nearly a month, maybe longer, to cross it by boat, traveling night and day. In fact, you could sail a boat across this water to Calcutta and then up the rivers of India and Nepal into the Seti River, right below your village."

Aama's gaze seemed to reach out even farther, toward infinity, a place where she might encounter what this really was, or meant. Slowly her eyes lowered and fixed on the horizontal line where the surf breakers met the beach. Her lips quavered, then her eyes gleamed in peaceful and pious revelation.

"This is Ganges water," she said with a great-grandmother's certainty. She raised her hands prayer-fashion to her forehead and held them there.

Of course. The Ganges River, the sacred artery and crematorium of the Indian subcontinent. It flows into the Bay of Bengal, whose waters are contiguous with the Pacific Ocean. The Ganges, bearer of the offerings, ashes, food, and effluvia of hundreds of millions of people; the bath water and tonic for a nation; the source of life, and the attendant and bearer at death. I envisioned a pilgrim sewing leaves together with toothpick-size strips of bamboo, to fashion a watertight votive lamp. Its twirled cotton wick nourished by cow's butter and its flame dancing tentatively, the pilgrim launches the lamp onto the Ganges River at sunset as a floating prayer to Agni, the god of fire. And after a passage of time, it washes ashore in Oregon.

"The rivers that flow from the four directions come together here." Aama turned to look at me. "You didn't tell me that we would encounter Ganges water," she said, suspecting that it must be widely known but, in America, perhaps restricted information. "Or maybe people here don't care."

I refrained from saying that I had simply forgotten to tell her about the ocean, thinking that she would react critically, as my mother might have. I learned in adolescence that forgetfulness was not an excuse, but rather an admission of blame.

"You have come to this place in as much ignorance as I! Haven't you heard me speak the name of Ganga Sagar when I worship? Ganga Sagar is the island in the middle of the great Ganges Ocean, one of the most sacred of the *tirthas,* the holy bathing sites. You said that we would travel around Amrita, which sounded fine, but you didn't say anything about this." She squinted again toward the horizon. "The island of Ganga Sagar must be out there somewhere."

Our overweight wagon descended in a controlled plummet to the beachfront community of Lincoln City, Oregon. We motored beside hotels and shops crowded onto the ocean side of the road, while Aama leaned forward and back, trying to get a stop-action view of the beach through gaps between the passing buildings. An aggressive onshore breeze whistled through the open crack of the seaside window.

"Here," Aama explained, "you'll find mendicants, yogis and saddhus, those who have renounced everything in order to come and meditate and worship by these shores. There should be ghats near here, where pilgrims come to bathe."

"There are, and I think we're approaching a bathing ghat right now," Didi said.

Aama looked up at a passing condominium complex. "This building must be a dharamsala containing the rooms and shelters for the pilgrims, many of whom would be waiting for death. The funeral ghats should be nearby, too."

At the far end of town, Highway 101 appeared to terminate in the parking area for Lincoln City beach. It was the weekend, and cars in brilliant waxed colors idled back and forth searching for parking slots. I felt a remnant surge of the high school adrenaline and hormones that erupted in carefree abandon every Friday afternoon. There were waves that needed surfing, smooth pristine sand that needed running across, and girls to hold daring but disinterested conversations with.

The beach was scattered with sunbathers, sandcastle builders, people running and dancing and playing Frisbee in swimsuits cut to expose the hips. Kites as big as ultralight aircraft, the kind that have two handles, were being pursued by whistling jet fighter kites with buzzing rainbow-colored streamers. Their operators leaped and leaned and jammed their heels into the sand to anchor them.

"Can I bathe?" Aama asked impatiently. "There should be Nepalese or at least Indians here, because you can always find them bathing in Ganges water. But the pilgrims here are wearing less clothing than we do—they're virtually naked. In our village women are embarrassed to show their legs in front of men, or even their hair, unless it has oil on it and is pulled back tightly. And do we have a bottle to put some of the ocean water in? We know for certain that this is purified water. Who knows where the water that flows out of the tap comes from."

Aama knew where we were. For her, the ocean was a fluid link with Asia. The activity on the beach was no mere recreation, it was a joyous confirmation. We parked the car and got out. Aama gathered her saree into pleats and tucked her head into the wind. "There must be a storm coming!" she shouted above the roaring gusts and distant, rumbling surf.

"It blows like this almost every day," Didi said. "It gathers speed as it crosses the ocean and hits us here, on land." She led Aama toward the surf, which was now at low tide and nearly a half mile offshore. Gradually the sand grew wetter. We waded into the tongues of aerated seawater that were working their way beachward like tendrils of an expanding life-form. A boy standing on a plywood disk glided by us, viewing Aama with casual curiosity. He stepped off and continued to watch us for a moment before picking up the disk.

Spent waves washed over our feet and roiled past us toward shore. Aama bent at the waist and threw three splashes of water into the air. Again burying her hand in the foam, she came up with a pinch of sand, arched her neck and pressed the sand against her throat, then the middle of her forehead. She took another pinch and turned to give us a *tika* blessing. Didi stood facing Aama and placed her hands together, and stooped slightly to receive it on her forehead. I took Aama's sand *tika* next. She wished me peace, many children, and a long life.

From the corner of my eye I could see people coming toward us. The boy on the disk, joined by other children, ran up and halted in front of Aama. Without pausing, she turned and applied sand *tikas* to each of their foreheads. As if born Hindu, the children placed their hands together and bowed respectfully before prancing off along the beach. They must have seen Didi's and my motions.

The waves crashed and resounded like monastery drums, calling us seaward to worship. Aama leaned against our restraining hands, her face drenched in salt spray and the vitality of the breakers, a swirling, seething testament to the presence of the deities. Since we had left Nepal, much of what we had seen was either man-made or impermanent. The Palouse and the Channeled Scablands of eastern Washington had been tilled and settled. Mt. Rainier had been climbed. Even the Columbia River had been tamed by a series of dams. But the ocean surf was enduring and dependable, like the Himalayas.

Didi and I tried to judge how far we could go offshore into the shallow water and at least partially immerse without being swept away by the undertow.

"How do people bathe in this maelstrom?" Aama shouted weakly over the surf. She stopped, awed by the frightening size and power of the waves. "I'll just wash my face this time. And remember, don't try to fight moving water, it's stronger than you are." The Gurkha soldiers must have told her that.

A wave muttered loudly as it washed over our lower legs. Aama bent at the waist and quickly cupped as much of the moving seawater as she could and splashed it over her head. She stretched her face, alternately opening and shutting her eyes, and massaged the salt water into every flattened wrinkle and crack, like oiling a soft leather bag. Splash again, then once more. Done. I took photographs. Aama turned toward the beach. The crest of another roller, the largest yet, collapsed behind her and tumbled over itself until it died out forty yards inland from us. Then it began to return. The undertow gathered speed as Aama gazed down at her feet, now concealed by passing foam. The accelerating flow had created a new frame of reference, like the earth moving, or an escalator. Slowly, as if pulled by an unseen force—the spirit of the great Ganges Ocean, or the gravitational force of the Himalayas themselves—she silently tottered and fell forward, knees straight, facedown into the water, as if releasing herself into a snowdrift. I saw it through the viewfinder of the camera.

Panic. I lunged for her. Fragile. Where to grab her? Long moments passed while I faltered, agonizing, watching the seawater wash over the back of her head. I squatted in the undertow and squeezed her ribs with both hands. The suction of the sand and water anchored her like a piece of waterlogged driftwood. Could I crack her ribs trying to break the suction? Why hadn't we been holding her? For years, her fear of falling down had lived with her like an intimate, cynical friend. Now their relationship was consummated.

I lifted anyway, carefully. Slowly, as if waking from sleep, she gained a hold on the shifting wet sand and lifted her head. Salty gray hair and sandy water streaked across her face. Her mouth sputtered. Alive. I helped her to her feet as Didi ran up and took her arms. Reborn.

"*Haré R-R-Ram,* that water is *s-s-salty*. I got to b-bathe in the

Ganges Ocean, after all," she stammered, soaking wet, shaking, grinning, thrilled at her baptism. One of the children who had taken a *tika* from her ran up and handed her a towel.

As we led her back to the beach she chattered away in an inspired description of the bath. "I had been thinking that it would be ideal to immerse my entire body, if possible. But if you go under and don't come up and then breathe in too much water, you can drown, so I didn't breathe while my head was under. A boy from my natal village nearly drowned in a pond that was dammed up in the stream nearby. The men picked him up and turned him over and pounded on him, and he started to breathe again. Some people take training and learn how to swim, but if you grow up at the edge of water you'll learn just by playing in it. . . ."

Didi took Aama into the public bath house to change her clothes. Inside, a woman was vigorously trying to towel her young daughter's hair as the girl squealed "Okay, Mom . . . Okay, Mom." Similarly, Aama squirmed, laughing, while Didi tried to towel her off. Didi led her from the changing room as she mimicked the young girl, repeating 'Okay-Mom-okay-Mom,' in rhythm with her chattering gums.

The heater warmed the car into a womblike refuge.

"Fate didn't call me to death right then," Aama said. "If you are to live, then regardless of how events turn, you will live. And when your time to die arrives, there is nothing you can do to prolong your life. But remember: If your life is taken in an untimely way, before its predetermined time, we say that your soul will wander aimlessly as a transient spirit between life and the resting place of men's souls. This wandering soul can cause trouble for the relatives, until the end of the person's normal life span."

Aama's words triggered thoughts of my mother. Her death was unexpected, untimely. She died in her sleep from what we had been told was a benign heart murmur.

"But this would not have been a bad place to die, here in the ocean, because it is auspicious to have Ganges water on your lips at your time of death." In addition to being purified, Aama seemed happy to be alive, despite her candid desire to die soon. I guided the car toward the exit.

"Wait," Aama said, holding up her hand as if listening to something. "Go and collect some of the sand and rocks from the ghats where I bathed." I double-parked, left the door open, and ran to the beach, then jogged back to the car with a handful of dried sand and small stones.

"I'll keep these in my attic, where people won't get to them," she said as she wrapped them in a piece of plastic that Didi handed her. "Meanwhile, make sure that Didi doesn't touch these. They will be needed for worship, and would be defiled if a menstruating woman were to handle them."

With a faint smile of resignation, Didi shrugged and continued to softly towel Aama's hair. I told Didi that there were some things that Aama wouldn't let me touch, either, such as the central roof column rising through the floor of her attic. The household protective deity resides within this pillar and on the far side of it. "Anyway," I said, "we're going to California, where it won't be so cold at night when you're sleeping on the porch." But, as we both knew, only Brahmin women would not enter their houses at all during their monthly cycle. The Gurung were more relaxed, never having aspired to the Brahmins' elevated level of purity.

Along the coast our camping routine went smoothly, and Aama's steady narrative enhanced her stream of antics. She was amazed to see sticks that I had broken the night before resurrect into bungee-loaded tent poles. Passing a golf course, she was perplexed that adults would play what must be a children's game; it made more sense when I mentioned that the players sometimes bet money on the outcome.

The saline coolness of the nights enveloped us in thick morning fog, which muffled the sounds of the highway. The passing outlines of madrone and pine trees evoked temples on the ghats of Benares, and where the beach sand disappeared into whiteness, I half expected to see Hindu pilgrims swathed in simple cotton garments bathing in the ocean waters, saluting the morning sun.

We slowed at the outskirts of Florence, Oregon, a town of retirees, many of whom seemed to be sitting in the Ocean Air restaurant. Rays of sunlight nudged through the fog and slowly transformed our window table into a cozy haven. Didi's face grew radiant and sultry, and I looked at her longingly. We had had little chance for privacy, what with Aama situated between us in the tent like a distrusting Victorian-era chaperone and awake most of the night, as well.

The beehive-hairdoed waitress filled our water glasses and brought silverware, napkins, and a maple syrup dispenser. Didi asked her about the route south, and I overheard something about being sure to see some caves.

"What's that thing?" Aama said toward the dispenser.

"It's like molasses, made from sugarcane. We put it on the flat breads they're going to bring us."

Aama poured a drop into her palm and tasted it.

"It's sweet. You can tell the woman that we won't need this much, she can take most of it back."

She turned and rolled her lips inward, forming the seam of a pouch. A woman who appeared as wide as she was tall maneuvered past our table.

"Isn't it hard for a person like that to sleep at night? It looks as if she's wearing a hundred-yard-long sash beneath her blouse. Some people here are so fat that, wherever they go, their stomachs arrive first at their destinations." Most Nepalese could only imagine being overweight, although some villagers have been to India and seen Punjabis, among whom body weight is regarded as a status symbol and sign of health—an understandable ideal in a country that is not immune to famine.

The waitress brought our orders. Aama placed a forkful of pancake on her tongue with deliberation, as if it had been dipped in wine and she were the recipient of the Sacrament of Holy Communion— or *prasad,* the blessed food distributed by the guru, the ingestion of which will cleanse one of impurities. She cleansed two pancakes' and one muffin's worth, and rinsed it all down with orange juice and milk.

She belched proudly as we stepped outside. "Which tastes better, being hungry or being full?" she said in the ironic, inquisitive tone that she reserved for her koanlike proverbs. Her eighty pounds moved toward the car like a reptile that had engorged several times its body weight. Crumbs constellated her velvet blouse, reflecting the embryonic sun. Didi brushed off Aama's clothing and looked thoughtfully at her as a mother might when assessing a child's ability to cross the street alone. She turned to me. "I think we should take a precaution on the outside chance that Aama could become separated from us."

Aama spoke no English beyond "juice" and "bye-bye." On a business card I wrote Ann and Greg's phone number, with a message: "If you find this woman, please call . . ."

"Aama," I said, waiting until I had her attention, "this is a card with Ann-Tori's phone number on it." She had referred to Seattle as "Ann-Tori's" place. "Now, tuck this in your sash, and if you ever lose us you can show it to the people who find you. They will call Ann-Tori, and then we can come and get you."

"Good. I need that. It must be easy to get lost in this country, and no one would understand me if I were." She examined the card from several angles. "You should keep this for me," she said, handing it back. "I don't have a good place to put it, and I want to be sure it doesn't get misplaced. You should keep it with my passport. Oh, and this, too. . . ." She pulled from her sash a handful of coins and gave them to me. "I saw Didi pay for our food, and then you left this pile of money on our table when you went to the bathroom. When you came out, you walked straight out of the restaurant."

Didi ran in to return the tip. The waitress was still laughing, and said that she had seen the whole incident. The elderly people at nearby tables smiled at Didi with what looked like fondness and appreciation.

At an overlook high above the surf, we walked as far as we could toward the ocean. Near the edge of the bluff, Aama and Didi stood like subjects of exotic ethnicity from a Cartier-Bresson photograph— or from a faded poster of the surf, the kind that silhouette androgynous people above a short quote from the Bible or a poem about love. A good place to feel the presence of Bhagwan. Three haystack rock outcrops protruded from the ocean like a sculpted portrait of the trinity: Father, Son, and Holy Spirit. Brahma the Creator, Vishnu the Preserver, and Shiva the Destroyer. "These are God," an educated Brahmin had told me. "G-O-D: 'G' is for Generator, because Brahma is the great creator, the one who generated our universe. 'O' is for Operator, because Vishnu maintains and preserves all of us. And 'D' is for Destroyer—Shiva, of course. This is God."

"Those rocks were put there by Bhagwan, in an earlier era," Aama said, sweeping her hand in a large brushstroke. "What do people really know about these things? We can't understand how Bhagwan makes all of this; we can only learn how to say his name. Look at what springs from the ocean: conch shells and cowries, pearls and gems, fish and water. Even cows and elephants originally came from the ocean, the texts say." She turned to me and added mysteriously, "People have gone off to search for the source of the ocean, but no one has ever found it and returned."

The entrance to the Sea Lion Caves perched on a nearby bluff. We walked through the gift shop and proceeded with other tourists to a shelterlike enclosure. Inside was an elevator that delivered us two hundred feet underground.

The doors opened into a darkened chamber a few feet above sea level, adjacent to the caves. Aama stepped up to a lighted panel that described the larger cave and the sea lions, and she passed her hands over it and touched her forehead to it. The panel claimed that the figures of both a native Indian maiden and the Goddess of Liberty can be recognized in the rock features of the cave, if the lighting is right. No further clarification was provided for the two women, frozen beyond the reach of each others' arms in eternal, unrequited love, a metaphor of the split personality of America's history.

Aama moved to the viewing portal and followed the blurred flight paths of pigeon guillemots across the ceiling of the reverberating cavern. Steller's sea lions rocked back and forth on their perches above the sloshing water, as if posing for a group photo, while barking loudly as if trying to get our attention for the main show. Aama observed them as a biologist would. Or rather, a sociologist. Patiently she counted every sea lion and traced their movements into and out of the cave. As if expecting me to take dictation, she identified the young and the old, the males, the hunters, the females and the young, and interconnected them. These were social, tribal, and kinship groups, and the first and closest view of an extended family she had seen since leaving Nepal. It was a diorama of fellowship and community, a lost civilization at work and play.

Aama felt an affinity to those who had affinity. "They raise and protect each other, they play, they show off and they fight. They are just like people. . . ." Just like *her* people, or Asians in general, I was about to amend. Indeed, the sea lions' family structure resembled that of most peoples and societies of the world, and virtually all humans until a short century or two ago. "We have four clans within the Gurung, you know: Ghale, Ghotane, Lama, and Lamchhane. A Gurung must marry a Gurung, of course, but shouldn't marry within his own clan. . . ." Aama didn't want to leave.

We took the elevator up and exited into sunny brightness. In the gift shop, Aama bypassed the displays of fuzzy and shiny objects and headed toward the shell rack, which she had glimpsed on the way in. She perused each bin consecutively and studied every shell.

"Are these conches all left-whorled? You seldom see them, but a right-whorled conch will keep ghosts and evil beings away." I started to ask her more about them, but she moved on, stopping at the cowries, the biggest she had ever seen, the size they must grow on the American side of the great Ganges Ocean. Smaller cowries find their way to Nepal for use as ornaments and as dice in a gambling game.

Aama selected a few and absently handed them to me, then peeked into the next bin, zeroing in on the scallops. Her eyebrows lifted.

"I'll distribute some of these to each of my relatives and neighbors, for votive lamps, but we need to get the right kind. If they are too thin they might break, and if they're too heavy they'll just be extra weight to carry around." The shallow-profiled scallops are said to resemble openly cupped hands, in which these shell lamps are held when offered forth to the deities.

Didi told me that the scallop shells are symbols of St. James and were worn as badges by Christian pilgrims returning from the Holy Land.

"That's what we are," I said as I handed off the shells and some cash to her, "we're pilgrims, except we haven't found the Holy Land yet."

Aama hadn't asked me how much the shells cost, and I didn't tell her. Objects from nature should of course be free, and I was afraid of triggering another Columbia River Gorge campsite scene. As Didi spread the armload of shells on the counter, I tried not to compute their prices, and wondered how much longer we could detour the issue of money, the powerful but silent engine that drives our country. I'll talk about it with Aama in the car, I thought.

Aama had moved to the popcorn vending machine and was pressing her hands and face against the glass, excluding from her vision all but the world of yellow and twisted popped corn, trying to gauge the size of the mountain of snack food.

A three-year-old boy stood beside her, tugging on her skirt. "Hi. Hi," he said. He held up a miniature truck that his mother had purchased for him, then took Aama's hand and motioned her to join him in the cup and plate section. She sat on the floor where he indicated, and he slid the car over to her. She picked it up, her fingers impressed by such a well-made little machine, then rolled it back to him.

Smiling and laughing and talking quietly to each other, neither of them noticed the small crowd that gathered, towering in a wide circle above them. The car skidded sideways under the popcorn machine. The boy withdrew it and then walked toward Aama, aiming for her outstretched hands. Slowly she ran her hands through his hair. He relaxed his arms, tilted his head back onto his shoulders, and rested it there as he settled into the comfort of her fingers. The boy's mother and bystanders stood immobilized, suspended in that protracted, timeless moment.

Aama had cast a spell. The boy looked down at the toy car in his hand and without hesitation presented it to her, a gift from of all of us, it seemed.

"I fall in love with children the minute I see them. Some are afraid of me at first, but others aren't the least bit shy. The little ones who don't yet speak are the first to approach me. When they learn to speak and discover who they are and what their caste is, they will become more cautious. The young ones love me because they haven't yet learned how not to love people."

We moored Aama onto her booster seat. She opened the bag of shells and peered in, as if looking for a surprise or expecting to hear the sound of the ocean. She pulled out a conch.

"Nani," she said, recalling my interest, "this is a left-whorled conch, the only kind that you blow. The right-whorleds are manifestations of Laxmi, so they bring wealth. Krishna and Shiva carry one. Because they are so rare and valuable, Indians sometimes trick people by saying they have a right-whorled, when it is really left-whorled. I kept a right-whorled one in my attic and used it for worship, until it was stolen years ago. The thief must have pulled it through the attic window with a stick—even a child couldn't have crawled between the heavy wooden slats that my husband had secured there. When I told my cousin the shaman about it, he related the story of a poor man who once found a right-whorled conch lying on the ground. The man took it home and locked it in a box, and every day at exactly noon, the conch sounded on its own from inside the box. *Bwaaaahn . . . Bwaaaahn . . .* The man then became very lucky and very rich, and so did his family, until one day his younger brother, overtaken with jealousy and greed, stole that right-whorled conch. The man fell into poverty again, and my cousin heard that the conch in the greedy brother's hands ceased to sound at noon."

I waited for the moral to the story, then felt Aama looking at me. Her mouth remained closed, but the sparkle that came to her eyes revealed the ending. *If something is meant to come to you, it will in its own time,* she had said more than once. *By chasing after it, you only push it beyond reach.* They were words I had too often neglected.

Chapter 8

When Aama momentarily disarmed the cane, I wrested loose her piece of redwood. She passed it to Didi, who hid the contraband inside her shirt, then zipped up the coat. She looked pregnant.

"This looks like the edge of civilization," Didi said. We faced a wall of trees that formed the margin of an old-growth Pacific forest, but we weren't exactly standing in the wilderness. Thirty feet above us, the hinged, mechanical mouth of a giant concrete lumberjack opened and began to speak.

"Hel-lo and wel-come to the Trees of Mystery," the statue's voice said, its deep pitch straining to match the girth of its make-believe lungs. "I'm Paul Bunyan, and this is my ox, Babe. Just come this way to see the 'Wonders of Nature.' " A longhorn ox, painted aquamarine and twenty feet high at the shoulder, stood faithfully beside the lumberjack.

"He's talking, but his mouth isn't moving right," Aama told Didi as we traversed the parking lot toward Paul Bunyan. "I can tell that's no real man, but what did he say, anyway?" Didi grasped Aama's hand and scouted for moving cars. "No, I know what he said, he said, 'How long ago was it, Aama, that you came to Amrita?'—Ha!"

"He said to go behind him there and see some more big trees," Didi told her. "But we have to pay money."

"That's what I thought. How many different ways are there to make money?"

Didi and Aama sat down on a bench near Paul Bunyan's feet. Aama lifted her arm and rotated her hand at the wrist, mocking the creaky, robotic wave of Paul's concrete hand. She must be too small for him to see her, I could hear her thinking, so she added her other hand to the mockery and waved and rotated them both over her head like a one-person fan club. She was trying to signify to Paul Bunyan that she accepted him as real, or to convince him that she was as unreal as he, searching for a common ground of communication—anything to get the statue to continue to talk.

I was restless to move on to the real redwoods. We had become tourists and were losing our ability to resist commercial attractions of questionable value. At our present rate, it would take weeks to reach Didi's house in San Diego. We had just left Oregon, and we could expect California to be one long state of distraction.

"Why do they bother to do such a poor job?" Aama commented. "If they are trying to re-create a giant who actually lived, they should measure the original and copy him exactly. I'm someone who hasn't been anywhere or seen anything. People of Amrita, if anybody, should be able to trick an old lady like me—even the poor yogis who wander up from India into our village can do that."

"We have to go now," Didi told Aama when Paul Bunyan began to repeat himself, although he wasn't speaking from a tape recording. I spotted a curtained window in the adjacent building, a good vantage point for a microphone operator, probably a guy in a closet-like room wearing sunglasses and smoking cigarettes, grinning and chuckling to himself.

"Say bye-bye to the giant timber cutter," Didi said.

"Bye-bye," Aama shouted up at it hoarsely, like David slinging departing ridicule at a slain Goliath. In an aside to herself she said, "Listen to me—saying 'bye-bye' to a big clay statue."

"BYE-BYE" came the slow, staticky response, like a giant masculine windup toy. It nearly scared us. I sneaked another glance at the window and thought I saw the curtain move. Aama and Didi laughed their way into the parking lot, bending over to stabilize themselves on nearby cars. Didi tried to look away from Aama in order to stop laughing—her lungs were hurting—but each time she turned toward her, Aama repeated "bye-bye" like a comedy mantra, bulging and rolling her eyes at Didi. A family of tourists a few parking slots away watched us circumspectly.

Highway 101 continued to wind along the Pacific coast, banking away from the ocean and then toward it again in sweeping arcs, a dramatic prelude to Redwood National Park. Abruptly the car entered the first grove of tall trees.

"What country are we in now?" Aama asked as our eyes adjusted to the tunnellike darkness. Strobes of light burst on the windshield. " '*Mil-ik, mil-ik.*' Bhagwan has a camera and is taking photographs inside the car as we drive along," she interpreted. "*Méro baajay,*" my old man. "In our country we would never see trees like this, because people chop them down as soon as they're big enough to build a house with."

Driving the speed limit through the redwoods felt like running in church. An impatient line of cars congregated behind us until Didi pulled off into a turnout to let them pass. It looked like a good starting place for a hike in the woods.

The needles and duff of the forest floor softened our voices, already quiet and small in awe of the towering redwoods. Aama padded a few steps into the forest, picked up a stick, and waved it about like a lecturer's classroom pointer. She pointed to the outline of a fallen log, long since rotted. "A tree fell down here, and it provides nourishment for new trees to grow from, like fertilizer in our fields. This is another spot that is holy, where you shouldn't defecate just anyplace. Bhagwan has scattered only tree seedlings here, no people seeds. If people were here, this firewood lying around would have been collected."

An aging, deformed redwood stood beside the trail, seeming to express a sinister but charming bitterness at being forever rooted to the ground. Its divided trunk, evidence of an early injury from windstorm or lightning, merged into a single bole about twenty feet up, then strained toward the sunlight. The stabilizing fluting underneath it was hollow. Aama called Didi and me over.

"Okay, let's walk under this tree," she said.

I had seen this before. A tree's roots, its foundation of health, are believed to confer long life and fertility when you walk beneath them, similar to passing under an elephant.

"We'll go through the trunk and circumambulate to the right, three times," Aama explained, "while we chant 'Stomach ailments, go!' You, Didi, because you haven't had any children yet, should chant 'Uterus obstructions, go!' "

Didi looked at me dubiously. Aama grasped my hand and motioned for me to take Didi's. The three of us ducked through and circled the tree as Aama led the chants. Emerging from the third circuit, Aama halted, jerked her cane upward, and snatched the base of it cleverly, like a carnival barker. Wielding the heavy bamboo knot that formed the handle of the cane, she whacked sharply on the trunk. A half-decayed piece of reddish wood that showed from beneath the bark looked as if it might break off, if hit hard enough.

Instinctively Didi and I glanced about for park rangers, picturing federal offenses for all of us. If Aama plans to take this piece of redwood, I was thinking, hopefully she would find something more than her cane to remove it with before the echoing whacks attracted attention. When she momentarily disarmed the cane, I wrested loose the piece of wood and handed it to her. She passed it to Didi, who looked at it as if it were contraband, then hid it inside her shirt and zipped up her coat. She looked pregnant.

"The yellow variety of sandalwood is used to cremate royalty and the very wealthy," Aama explained, "but this looks like red sandalwood, the kind that my cousin the shaman mixes in his medical potions. We can take this piece and test it." We circled around to a footbridge. A park ranger walked by us just as Aama was pointing to Didi's stomach, describing her test.

Didi stashed the wood under the front seat and chauffeured us down the Avenue of the Giants, a grove of the oldest redwoods. As suddenly as it had entered the forest, the road broke into a sunlit clearing, where nature reverted to the dominion and varied purposes of man. Didi saw a sign pointing to an enormous tree and pulled over. The people who owned the tree or ran the concession, or their ancestors, had cut a tunnel-size hole in its trunk in order to take money from those who wanted to witness the indignity up close without having to get out of their cars. Didi paid the fee and aligned our wood-paneled wagon, then slowly nosed it into the tree while I checked the clearance of the wing mirrors. We inched along silently. Near the middle of the tree, Aama exclaimed, *"Car problems, GO!"* I mouthed the invocation along with her, and prayed to St. Christopher, the patron saint of motorists, that it would work. At 130,000 miles, the Country Squire was as old as Aama, in car years.

We got comfortable for a straight shot at San Francisco, which we hoped to reach by nightfall. I drove as Aama spoke in an animated monologue.

"There's not a small amount of land in this country, nor a shortage of landscapes. We've seen trees bigger around than my house, open plains without a twig or a stone, and meadows of grass so tall and thick and green that I want to sharpen my sickle and stroll right into it and cut some. Which is better, living in the city or living in the countryside?" she asked rhetorically. "Most people spend their time in cars, it seems, either moving into or out of the cities."

During her lifetime, Aama had witnessed the rugged, partially forested hillsides of her youth be transformed into intensely farmed habitat for man and his animals. Subsistence farmers of the Himalayas can no longer cultivate the hope that nurtured their forefathers, and which still nurtures the West: the expectation that more bountiful frontiers await each successive generation. While population grows, productivity of the land has remained constant or diminished, and villagers are finding that there simply aren't enough food and resources to go around. Many have joined the migration to increasingly crowded urban areas.

Aama looked up at me. "You didn't realize that I notice these things, did you?"

"Well, no. But have you noticed those?" I said, indicating a herd of sheep grazing in a field directly to the right of the car.

Aama glanced at them and uttered, "Boy, those sheep are moving fast—no, wait, *we're* moving fast, and the sheep are just standing there!" 101 had approached the ocean, and Aama's view strayed beyond the sheep to the sliver of marine blue sky and sea visible through the scattered trees.

"Is this the same shore of the great Ganges Ocean that we bathed in the other day?" When Didi confirmed that it was, Aama said, "The island pilgrimage site of Ganga Sagar is located in the ocean somewhere to the west of Calcutta, so it must be near here. I've heard that yogis and saddhus live there winter and summer, meditating, praying, and doing yoga at the base of a magnificent golden shrine surrounded by ghats. But my Brahmin priest said that, no, Ganga Sagar is little more than a pile of sacred rocks covered over by water every day of the year except one, the first day of our winter month of Magh when the seas open up to receive Hindu pilgrims. You must hurry and bathe and make offerings and return to Calcutta the same day, he said, because the water rises and closes over it. People have been swept away when they tried to stay."

Aama's expression conveyed that this level of risk was not unreasonable. She turned to Didi and then me. "If I had known we would see this ocean, I would have asked my Gurkha relatives about Ganga Sagar. They heard that a group of soldiers found it in their travels around the world by following designs on a piece of paper, and that it can be visited more than one day a year. Can't we go? Pilgrims at the ghats, the people who were bathing way out in the maelstrom, should know the route."

As we coasted heavily into the Eureka city limits, Didi leaned across Aama to check the instrument panel and reminded me that we needed gas. I skipped one station and pulled into the second, a penny cheaper and likely an octane lower.

"You put kerosene—I mean petrol—in the car just yesterday," Aama said.

"That's gone now. The car needs more." I got out, sluggish and careworn from hunger, the heat, and an onerous engine knock.

Salt and sugar from road snacks speckled Aama's hands. Didi held open the metal door to the rest room and Aama stepped over its raised aluminum sill, unsure if it should be walked upon. Didi mixed hot and cold water in the sink, then inverted the gimbaled bottle of blue soap and released a squirt into Aama's hand. Aama brought her hand to her face as if to wash, but instead guided the palmful of blue soap into her mouth, tilted her head back, and gargled noisily. Her mouthwash was also blue, Didi realized. Urgently she explained the difference, then helped Aama wash out her mouth, which had filled instantly with bubbles.

An open wastebasket lined with a white garbage sack sat beside the sink. Aama turned around and backed up to it until she had straddled it, then hiked up her skirt. Didi intercepted her and led her into the stall. The toilet did look similar to the wastebasket.

"I can't do anything for myself," she said to Didi and the tiled wall, listening to her words surround her, still laughing at the mirror and the bubbles in her mouth, laughter that verged on crying. "You have to take me to pee, take me to crap, bathe me and dress me. I'm illiterate, too." About to descend into self-indulgence, she looked up at Didi with a spark of confidence. "But I know things in my own way of knowing them."

I filled the tank and grabbed some groceries, then backed the car around to the rest room side of the service station. Shoving aside the carpets and camping gear, I yanked the spare tire from its well. We could create space for at least one of us to lie down by lashing the tire to the roof, sacrificing aerodynamics and gas mileage for comfort—and gain a more touristic image, as well, though we more likely would be mistaken for dust bowl refugees. Wind resistance from the tire would place an additional load on the pinging engine, so I reminded myself to mix supreme with regular the next time we filled up—another instance of being drawn insidiously into the accelerating cost spiral of life in the West. The more you spend, the more you need to spend in order to maintain or protect whatever it was you purchased.

Aama, Sun Maya, and the other villagers sidestep the money vortex by not even beginning the process. They spend virtually no money, and never travel or act in a manner that demands it. Indeed, among Nepal's hill tribes, saving or investing is associated with selfishness, and wealthy merchants and moneylenders are models for the archetype of greed. For the Gurung, to save is to take a valuable resource out of circulation.

"It was Mrs. Magoo encounters the rest room," Didi said as she watched me heft the tire onto the roof. "We need to keep an eye on this gal."

We took our seats in the car, then Aama said quietly, "Maybe someone in this building knows how to get to Ganga Sagar." When I didn't respond, she added, "We might even find a right-whorled conch on the way there." Her eyes appreciatively surveyed the flat roof that shaded the pumps, as if the station's clean lines and primary colors identified it as a tidy hermitage for great yogis, or a repository of sacred knowledge. It didn't feel like a sacred site, but a place selling gasoline could be considered as a kind of power spot, I deadpanned to Didi.

Intently Aama said, "Go in there now. There must be people there who speak your language and can tell us how to get to the temple in the middle of the ocean."

"Well, I'll ask," I said, "but I don't think they'll know. They're probably not Hindus, and besides, we only have a car, which wouldn't make it. We need a boat."

"A boat could hit rocks and then sink. Maybe there is a bridge. If not, perhaps the people in there would know what sort of arrangements need to be made. For years I have heard about Ganga Sagar from my father and uncle who read to us from the sutras, the thick religious books that describe the battles and dharmic feats of Krishna and the other great deities. I'm only a simple pilgrim who wants to appear before the main temple, light some lamps, leave offerings in the names of my parents and ancestors and deceased brothers and sisters, and then return."

"Didi, do you want to go in and ask the way to Ganga Sagar?" I suggested.

"No. She's *your* dharma mother. You ask." I stepped from the car and headed back to the glassed-in office to buy some gum.

"They said they have no idea," I lied as I climbed back into the car.

From the gas station, the wagon dipped and rocked onto the road like a small boat crossing the wake of a ship. Aama flexed her upper body toward the back and fumbled in the food box.

We were gaining a sense of what she liked: seafood, especially drive-in fish and chips, the kind you chain-feed on, one napkin under the chin and another spread across the legs with hot mustard and tartar sauce in folded wax cups dumped over the whole lap-balanced spread. The kind of food that generates sound effects while you feed, as an aid to digestion. In Aama's case, the sound was a spontaneous

tongue clacking that accompanied hot spices, followed by an explosive sigh.

And box juice. She learned to carefully suck off some of the juice
before grabbing the box outright and squirting a fountain of purple
from the straw. "Did you wring out all the extract from the fruit in
that little box?" she'd ask. V-8 vegetable juice, for the salt. And
tortilla chips. Her poor hearing didn't prevent her from distinguish-
ing from a distance, as the nearly tame Olympic National Park
mountain goats do, the sound of a rustling bag of chips. "What's
that? Do I want any? Not really, but if you're having some anyway. . . ." Her hand would snake into the crinkling bag and take
out exactly three: one for dharma son, one for Didi, and the last for
Aama.

Didi pulled out three granola bars, but she seemed concerned
about something. "I smell gas," she said ominously.

I took a whiff toward the backseat and detected a definite gasoline odor. I tried to imagine other possible sources of it before stopping to check whether I had replaced the gas cap. Gradually I could
picture it sitting on top of the pump at the service station. Retribu-
tion for lying to Aama.

We were forty-some miles south of Eureka, moving fast. I pulled
onto an access road, got out, and stared for a moment at the open
filler pipe. I wondered if I could claim it had fallen off when we
weaved onto the highway, or something.

"*Damn,* I left the gas cap behind," I admitted when I got back in
the car, wanting to initiate my own self-criticism before Didi would
have a chance to launch into me.

"You *always* leave the gas cap behind," she remarked, on cue.
"And you'd have left your testicles there, too, if you weren't carrying
them around in little sacks. Or you might have left me behind, or
Aama."

"*Damn,*" I said forcefully to the steering wheel, ignoring her.

"Why do you always lose things?"

"Look, I'm thinking about other stuff most of the time."

"That's for sure."

Aama was seated between us, I now understood, to keep us from fighting. Relaxed and immovable, she sat peacefully, like a practical-joking Tibetan lama I knew, laughing an impertinent but intimidating body-shaking belly laugh. Words were mere garnishing for the real message, which was communicated through the eyes and face.

"*Gyaaskyap,*" Aama mimicked, then laughed. "Do you know what that means in the Gurung language? I'm not going to tell you because it's dirty. Ha! *Gyaaskyap.*"

"Your adopted son is talking about the stopper for the car's petrol tank, which he lost," Didi said to Aama. She stared at the gravel margin of the highway, then chanted, "St. Anthony, come around, there's something that's lost which can't be found," an optimistic petition.

"Why do you always lose things?" It was now Aama's turn to interrogate me. "You'd lose your body if it wasn't attached to your head." Not déjà vu again. I flashed back to a composite memory of the last several times I had lost something. Just as urgently, I tried to get a grip on it. The Hindu-Catholic guilt patrol had been idle for some time and was ganging up on me here, that's all.

"So what's the big deal? We can easily get another one," I said, first in Nepali, then in English.

"It's wasteful to lose things, and it makes people angry," replied Aama. "You lose something, somebody finds it, you see the thing with the person who found it, and then you accuse them of stealing, which is denied. Everyone becomes bitter. As we say, 'Keep tight your purse's drawstring, so you won't have to accuse friends of stealing.'"

She glowered at me with a face that demanded I look directly at her, the same look my mother used when she wanted to uncover whether I was fibbing. I thought of the white lies I had told her, then wanted to swallow my saliva, but held it for a moment.

Aama scratched her head, hoping her words would sink in. We drove for some time without speaking.

"Now, Malaysia is on the ocean, so isn't the Malaysia camp of the British Army near here somewhere?" She was taking advantage of my chastened condition to test my honesty with a question she didn't think had been adequately answered.

"It's far," Didi said.

"At the rate we've been traveling, we must have passed it by now. Are you sure we won't run across any young Gurungs in the Gurkha regiments?"

"No, I don't think so," Didi said, thankfully reiterating what I had told Aama before.

"If there were any Gurkhas posted in America," I added, "we would certainly go out of our way to see them." Aama remained quiet as she thought about it.

The setting sun gave a majestic bronze glow to the rust-colored framework of the Golden Gate Bridge. Aama napped as we crossed into San Francisco and descended from the viaduct into the Marina district. At a gas station, we called our friend Efale to get directions to her house. Aama awoke and looked around sleepily.

"Why don't we just stay at Ann-Tori's house tonight?" she said in a sour but composed tone of voice.

"What? We're five days from their house—more than a month's walk. What makes you think we can stay there tonight?"

"No, it must be nearby. I recognize this place." She pointed to the gas pumps, promotional signs, and other generic features of the Chevron service station. "We've been here before."

We had stopped twice at a Chevron station on Whidbey Island. "The road we've been traveling looks familiar, too," Aama clarified. "What were you cursed with that makes you drive in circles, lost? Or have you been deceiving me? I've been watching the sun and the moon, which have been changing direction relative to us. Bhagwan ultimately tells me north and south, because both the sun and the moon rise in the east and set in the west." She shot me her penetrating, motherly look. "The sun and the moon don't lie. And when people lie or do anything deceitful, the sun, the moon, and Bhagwan will see it."

And in all likelihood, Aama will, too, I feared. "Americans have put a man on the moon" was all I could think of to say.

"Did the man see Bhagwan there?" Aama rejoined quickly. "A man may have walked on the moon, but did he do anything out of respect for it, to propitiate the deities or sanctify his visit? You say that your people have been to these places, done these things, eaten this food, worn these clothes, grown these crops, and own all this land, but is this how you gauge the value of your human life?"

I felt a tinge of pride mixed with embarrassment when she referred to us as "your people," conferring on Americans a tribal identity, a cohesive social structure that we might not really have, or perhaps deserve.

Efale's house was situated on a hill above an industrial district. With a contagious exuberance she kissed us all on both cheeks while trying to keep her dog from jumping on us. Didi heated some soup while Efale poured wine. I went for the popcorn bowl. Aama peered into the bowl and withdrew a small handful, careful not to disturb the arrangement.

"I become frustrated whenever I see popped corn, because now that my mouth mill is worn smooth, I can't eat it. My upper lip has fallen inward where my upper teeth used to be, so that the two lonely teeth which sit on my bottom jaw collide with my upper lip whenever I eat. And both my lips flap around when I talk, which brings my nose into the act, causing it to bob up and down. It must look funny." She gummed her mouth a few times. "Listen to the way I speak—it's remarkable that people can understand me. Sometimes the opposite of what I mean to say comes out."

I phoned a dentist that Efale knew, to ask about false teeth. I described Aama's mouth for him.

"Dentures probably wouldn't work for her," he said straight-away. He had the voice of a scientist. "People in their eighties are seldom fitted with them for the first time, because once teeth are gone for several years, the bone of the jaw resorbs and there is nothing for the dentures to sit on securely. The patient ends up taking them out most of the time." I explained to Aama why it wouldn't be possible.

She didn't appear disappointed. "You should be planning for other things, anyway, for you and Didi. Why spend money on an old lady?"

Then there was Aama's eyesight. I looked under "Optometrist" in the phone book and circled some numbers to call in the morning.

Didi oriented us on a San Francisco street map that blocked my view through the passenger window, while I tried to discern a pattern to the narrow one-way streets. Aama's eye appointment had been squeezed into a cancellation, and we couldn't afford to be late.

"How do we get on Clay?" I blurted to Didi.

"Hawa jahaaj giroun khoi?" Aama playfully mimicked in my bothered tone of voice, repeating the Nepali phrase for "Where is the airport?" She chuckled a small belly laugh. Traffic had stopped, allowing us more time to fine-tune our navigation system. Aama looked up at the sky—an amateur sun sight might help, I thought—but the sun was eclipsed by a tangle of on-ramps to the Bay Bridge, adventitious aerial shoots of the diurnal citywide gridlock. She focused above us on a delivery truck that was followed by a slow train of cars.

"That truck looks like a mother cow, and the cars behind it are the calves being led to pasture." She paused to listen. "This city makes the same sound as the one at Ann-Tori's house. It sounds like the ocean."

We drove a half block past the optometrist's office before Didi alerted me. I dropped them at the corner, drove another block, and found a multistory parking garage.

I walked casually into the optometrist's office, then drew up short. Something had happened. Aama sat in the waiting room, draped sideways in a chair, engrossed in fluid conversation. She was speaking not in Nepali, but in Gurung. In a chair facing her, a young Asian man sat, enraptured. Aama's mellifluous Tibeto-Burman dialect had elevated both of them and was lightly conveying them along over ridges, across fields, through the pathways of villages and deep into the tall rhododendron forests of the Annapurnas. I looked closer at him; a tear had formed at the corner of his eye. Didi crossed the waiting room and took me aside.

"Yep, he's a Gurkha soldier, and a Gurung. He's posted in London, and flew to the U.S. a few days ago to visit his relatives who run a restaurant here. He's due back in London this weekend. We were barely out of the car and onto the sidewalk when he walked up to Aama and addressed her in Nepali, saying 'Oh, Grandmother,' and then they began speaking in Gurung. He was shaking."

The Gurung recruit was still shaking. Aama, composed and relaxed, continued her running narrative about her relatives and livestock, about fairness and injustice, birth and marriage, poverty and death, and how she was tied to it all, and he, too, of course, by shared culture if not by indirect relation.

He looked at me imploringly, as if seeking affirmation that this was real. I was keen to ask him what village he was from, but Aama had cornered his attention with stories that could only be told in Gurung, stories that had built up pressure and were now bursting into life. He listened, entranced as much by their delivery as their content, springing as they were from this dreamlike manifestation of his own heritage.

Aama's hand grasped the chair while the splayed fingers of her other hand waved freely, reshaping past events.

". . . And then there was my next oldest sister's husband. You wouldn't know him because your village is some distance from ours —two days' walk, is it?—but he was killed in the great war, war number one. Or at least we thought he was killed. On the date the lamas had fixed to perform his funerary ceremonies and purifications, he strolled into the village. He said that he had been captured by the enemy and imprisoned, and then escaped. . . ."

The Gurung man turned to me and spoke. "I look at Aama here and can think only of my own grandmother, she's just like her." His grandmother, too, would wear the tribal dress of Gurung women, a blouse of maroon velvet that ties under the arms. For the past century, bolts of the luxurious fabric have been brought to the villages by Gurkhas returning from foreign lands.

". . . Of course, if we had completed the funerary ceremonies, it would have been inauspicious for him to enter the house again, and even worse for him to find out about the rituals, as another relative once did. That relative disappeared and never came back to the village, resentful that his own funerary ceremonies had shortened his lifespan, as you know can happen in cases like this. . . ."

Homesickness filled the boy's eyes, betraying his regret at having forfeited tradition and family for an anonymous, utilitarian pursuit. But military service for most Gurung, though it generally lasted for seventeen years, was only temporary. The Gurkhas' loyalty to their hills and fidelity to their families while away was seldom questioned; virtually all of them returned.

". . . Then, after oldest sister's husband died, a drunken troublemaker in the village claimed that he was never captured by the enemy at all, but had deserted his platoon, and that was why he had received no pension allotments. How could he respond when he was dead? This made my sister and all of us very angry. . . ."

Aama hadn't noticed me enter the office. She pivoted around finally and saw me, then observed me reproachfully.

"Nani, there are Gurung British Army recruits all over the place. You've been hiding them from me." I looked sheepishly at the Gurung, who had picked up on my quandary. He turned to Aama and assured her that there probably weren't many like him around. But his mere presence had already disproved that notion.

The Gurung boy, as Aama referred to him, wanted us to join him in a traditional lunch of rice, lentil soup, and vegetables at his relatives' apartment. When he phoned them, they were out. Not possible.

"Don't bother about it," Aama consoled. "Your relatives must be very busy, working. They have probably become like the people of Amrita by now. Here, it's not like up in our hills."

The receptionist called "Mrs. Gurung," and Didi held out her hand. Aama's eyes pleaded to be examined some other time. The Gurung boy said that he needed to leave anyway, and I wrote down his phone number. He bowed slightly to Aama and then to Didi and me as he backed out of the office, still facing toward us.

Didi escorted Aama into a small room. The optometrist, an amiable white-haired gentleman, directed Aama to the front of a machine that scans the retina. He peered into one end of the apparatus and clicked a remote switch while Aama stared into the other end.

"She has bilateral cataracts," he said, confirming what we were afraid of. The cataracts hadn't seriously obscured her vision, so glasses would correct her astigmatism. We waited for the lenses to be ground.

"How do you like your glasses?" Didi asked when we stepped out onto the sidewalk.

"Well, I can see far away things better now, but close up things look milky. When I tried on my sister's pair, years ago, they sat on my nose differently, higher up I think. But most important, I now look and feel like the mother of a Gurkha—especially after seeing that Gurung boy. When he called to me on the street, it was as if my own relative was hailing me in a dream."

Chapter 9

"My old man. This is a shop front, isn't it? Is all this food for sale?"

The traffic of Interstate 80 east of San Francisco slowly shouldered by us. Aama thought we were moving in reverse at one point, then became concerned by the football-shape rotating drum of a cement truck in the lane next to us.

"They should strap that load down better; it's rolling around and could fall off," she said, motioning at the window with her head. Several vehicles ahead, ten new cars were stacked at precarious angles on a car-carrier truck. "I see. If there aren't enough people to drive all the cars around, then you have them loaded on trucks so they can be driven from place to place." Hmm. Like science fiction: humans invented by machines as a means of transporting themselves.

Cecilia, an animal trainer and friend, had invited us out to Vallejo to tour Marine World Africa, USA, where she worked in public relations. The grounds were described as a festive, multihabitat safari park, although the billboards beside the freeway could be confused with advertisements for a cable television channel if we hadn't read the wording. The heavy traffic activated my adrenaline, and I drove aggressively until the freeway ramp emptied us into a substantial parking lot.

We met Cecilia on a service road behind the offices, and she showed us the giraffes. A Royal Bengal tiger chained to two trainers padded by; Aama spoke calmly to it and stroked its fur as a child would a kitten.

"I'm impressed by Aama's courage—and her reverence for an animal that eats people in the southern part of Nepal," Cecilia said. She then glanced at her watch and proposed that we head toward the aquatheater for the porpoise and killer whale show, where she had reserved seats for us in front, adjacent to the splash deck.

The outdoor theater was filled nearly to capacity. The children behind us asked their parents impatient questions. The water of the tank heaved and undulated suspensefully.

A man on the public address introduced Yaka, the park's female orca, and we moved our heads around in search of some evidence of her. Eerily, the surface of the tank settled and flattened.

Suddenly, as if she had been waiting for the crowd to blink at the same time, Yaka rose from the depths of the tank and appeared on the splash deck. She faced us genially like an overgrown bathtub toy, her tail arched in the air above her.

The whale slid back into the tank like a christened battleship, amid a revelry of porpoises dancing and flipping in unison, signifying the start of the show.

"These fish have been trained like dogs; they look like they're asking for food. What do they eat?"

"Other fish, smaller ones," I said.

"Does your friend have some fish we can throw them?"

When the porpoise routine was concluded, Yaka came out again and performed slow-motion versions of the porpoises' stunts, including jumping over a rope six feet off the water, tossing a ball, and letting a man ride on her back.

The crowd filed slowly out of the aquatheater. The children were noisier now than they had been before the show started, fashioning accounts of real animals that are even better than the ones on TV. From near the exit, Cecilia worked her way against the flow of people and caught Didi's attention. She mouthed, "Would Aama like to greet the killer whale?"

I told Aama that she had been invited to the edge of the tank to meet the big fish, in person, and touch it.

"Which of the big fish?" Aama asked. There wasn't a lot of time to explain. Didi and Cecilia took her hands and led her to the edge of the tank.

"Where is it?" she said with skeptical curiosity. She rested her forearms on the bulkhead and scanned the surges and reflections on the surface of the pool. The trainer, a whistle pressed tightly between her lips, leaned over the edge and briskly slapped the side of the tank near the water line, a signal that we recognized from our world of television experience as meaning something aquatic would happen shortly.

Like a missile launching from a silo in slow motion, Yaka emerged at the guardrail and stopped, towering above Aama. Treading water with her tail, the whale slipped lower, as if gauging Aama's small stature, and rotated slightly to spy her with her right eyeball. Shocked by the figure appearing so large and so close, Aama stepped back to register its bulk. She wiped a splash of water from her face, then faltered forward, extending her arms toward the mouth of the huge mammal, a sacrificial victim volunteering her body—as a means to gain merit for herself and others—to the wrathful, beckoning goddess Kali, the deity that is fond of blood, especially human. Like a blind person, Aama explored Yaka's mouth, using the whale's lower lip as a handrail to pull herself closer. On tiptoes, she kissed the whale squarely on the front of the upper lip. Then, pressing her forehead to Yaka's lower jaw, she accorded her a blessing, as if communicating with her in a shared language. "May you be healthy, have many children, and live to a hundred years in peace and harmony with others of your race, and all the other fish and animals of the sea. May you not have the misfortune to be eaten by people, and may you please not eat people, but find plenty of smaller fish to feed on. . . ." Slowly Yaka slumped back into the tank. Aama continued to clutch the giant mouth. Her blessing wasn't complete. Didi's and my muscles jerked taut—Aama wasn't relinquishing her grip, she was being pulled forward and was about to go down with the whale. We lunged to grab her just as she released the whale, reluctantly, forfeiting a destiny in a more natural world, Ganga Sagar finally attained. She turned to us and smiled ingenuously.

We climbed into the junior whalemobile and embarked across the oceanlike expanse of parking lot toward the freeway. Aama chuckled to herself as she remarked on the beauty of the tiger and the grace of the long-necked, horselike animals that eat leaves from treetops and which might be trained to collect tree fodder. She then commended the skill and ability of Americans, the people who can implant a reasonable likeness of the breath of life into a giant, mechanical fish.

Didi and I looked at each other, dumbstruck. "Wh-what?" I stammered. "You . . . you mean you thought the big fishlike animal wasn't real, wasn't alive?"

"Uhn-uh. That's a machine," she scoffed self-assuredly, "and I'm proud that I wasn't fooled by a contraption that was designed specifically to trick people."

"But the thing is natural, nature, an animal that swims around in the ocean with other big animals," Didi explained. "It even breathes air, as we do, which is why it's not uncomfortable out of water. And it gives birth to live offspring, just as we do. It doesn't lay eggs."

"Now, don't try to tease me," Aama admonished, both irked and humored by Didi's attempt to dissuade her from something she had experienced for herself. Didi and I shared wide, involuntary smiles of amazement, which made it harder for us to sound convincing. I slipped in behind a truck trailer and quit fighting through traffic in order to listen to Aama's reasoning.

"No fish that size could ever jump that high; those little wings attached to its sides must help it to fly. Even though I'm from the hills, I know fish—we sometimes catch small ones in the stream below the village. And that gigantic machine wasn't slimy like a real fish; it had the rough texture of those paper handkerchiefs you wipe the car windows with. It's probably made of rubber, with springs and metal wires and electricity inside that make it work. Or maybe it's made of dried animal hides stitched together, I couldn't tell for sure."

I knew that contradicting or arguing with her would only inflame her conviction. My mind raced, searching for another angle.

"Okay, if the huge fish is just a machine, then why did you bless it?"

"I did that," she replied matter-of-factly, "just to humor you and all those people watching. The people there who run the thing— they're your friends, aren't they? I didn't want to embarrass you by announcing in front of them that I knew it was only a machine. They wanted us to think it was real, or they wanted me, at least, to think it was real. They must have looked into the crowd and saw that I was the only foreigner there, someone who wouldn't have learned yet what the trick was. Then they called me down."

"But it *is* real," I tried again. "Just believe me." She had believed me when I told her that the earth was spherical.

"Did you feel it? Did you touch it?" she grilled us, looking first at me and then Didi.

"No, but . . ."

"Well, *I* felt it, and I can tell you that it's a machine. If we see one again, I'll show you. Now, don't go and tell your friends that I know their secret. I wasn't even sure whether I should have mentioned this to you."

Didi and I walked up to the corner store to shop for a party that evening. Aama snoozed on the couch, looking like an exhumed peat bog person; I checked her breathing, as a new parent would a sleeping child. She might be blessed with an ability to approach death when she sleeps, or come closer to it than the rest of us by virtue of not clinging to life the way we do. We had hardly seen her sleep other than when she nodded off in the car, because she seldom slept more than four hours a night.

When we returned, Aama was gone. I searched the dining room and TV room, briefly tasting another parents' nightmare. Didi found her sitting on the kitchen floor in front of the refrigerator.

She peered up at us. "I was cold, so I got up to look around for a blanket, then found this big white box made of bone with hot air coming from underneath it. Sometimes the hot air comes and sometimes it doesn't, but the box makes noise just before it comes."

We lifted the groceries onto the kitchen counter. Aama was bored, looking for something to do. Didi set a cutting block on the floor and handed her two large onions from the grocery bag, and a knife. Like a restaurant chef, she went right into them, instantly uplifted by the work assignment. Didi handed me a cold beer, then poured some wine into a coffee mug for Aama and set it on the floor next to her.

Efale came in with more food and booze. Another friend arrived, Well Fed Fred, a Hog Farm commune graduate, world traveler, and Himalayan trek leader known in the mountains as Too Loose To Trek. Fred was fluent in Nepali, and settled his large form on the floor in order to talk with Aama. As usual with strangers, she first wanted to know how many children he had.

"Oh, many, many, of course," he joked. "And why not? Can't you tell by my size that I am a wealthy man?"

Arriving guests migrated toward the floor of the kitchen, attracted by Aama's and Fred's visible feeling of comfort and affluence. A few remained standing in the living room, conversing.

"Call everyone to come in here," Aama said. "Tell them about the warm air that comes from under this box. Those beds with the soft sides on them in the big room aren't for sitting, they're for sleeping."

Music flowed from a stereo system, and more wine and beer bottles were opened. Didi and Efale needed to get into the refrigerator. Aama stood up to allow the door to open, and braced her hands on her knees. She peered in at the volume of brightly lit food overflowing the shelves.

"My old man. This is a shopfront, isn't it? Is all this food for sale?" Indeed, the refrigerator was not much smaller than the few-foot-square cubicles in bazaar towns, in which the shopkeeper can reach any item hanging inside his bear den of merchandise without arising from his straw mat. Aama seemed to be looking for the place where the shopkeeper would sit.

"That food is only for this house," Didi said.

"But your friend lives alone, doesn't she?" Aama reacted. "How could she need all this food? And why did you have to go out and buy more?"

More. A defining word in our culture. I was stumped.

"Well, it's like. . . . It's like your Gurung weddings, where people consume whole porter loads of bread and rice and vegetables, and entire water buffalos."

"Did you sacrifice a buffalo for this evening?" she asked hopefully.

Didi and Efale prodded us toward the living room, to make space in the kitchen for a buffet line. Fred carried some firewood up from the basement.

"What are you doing?" Aama asked. She was on a roll. Nothing was immune from her scrutiny, and the wine emboldened her.

"I'm going to build a fire in this hearth," he told her.

"Why would you want to smoke up a beautiful home like this and blacken all these nice things?"

Fred translated Aama's commentary, and they gradually became the center of attention. As guests worked slowly on their plates of food, Aama used the relative quiet to elaborate on how America worked, just in case we hadn't noticed. Most of us hadn't.

She glanced around at the ashtrays and knickknacks on the tables and bookshelves. "People here leave their beautiful possessions lying around the house, where someone might pick them up and walk off with them. And they keep the doors of their houses closed during the daytime. Wherever we go, it's as if no one were home. The doors should be left open at least around the hours of sunset, so that the gods can return to protect the house."

"Even in L.A.?" one guest asked.

"And somebody parked two cars in that room next to us," she said, pointing at the doorway to the garage. ". . . And you cook your food downstairs, *then go upstairs directly above the kitchen to urinate and crap*. Who knows where it goes after the swirling water takes it away? That white vessel half-filled with water that you sit on looks like a big serving bowl, something from which you might dish out rice for a feast." Fred leaned over to examine his dinner plate and distorted his face in questioning horror.

"Our people may be poor, but we would never do these things." Aama tasted another mouthful of wine and licked her lips, then looked around at each of us. "Who are you? You don't even know who you are."

Fred didn't need to translate the drama carried by her tone. The guests stopped eating and looked at each other. One woman turned down the music. Most of them had suffered and survived various midlife crises or other karmic or legal junctures. Typically, as a result, they had discovered new meaning, were still looking for new direction, or, as Fred described himself, were gloriously facing the existential cream pies that God or Buddha or Bhagwan or whoever pulls from his sleeve when you least expect it.

"Here in America, people can do whatever they want," I said, "which means they have difficulty deciding what to do." Aama looked at me as if that were only part of it.

"You treat your relatives like strangers, and strangers like relatives. Your brothers and sisters are spread all over the place, and I wonder if you even know what relation they are to you. You talk and laugh with someone one moment and then abandon them and pick up with someone else the next—after contacting them on that radio or telephone or whatever it is. You lose your integrity and trustworthiness this way. 'When you raise a cow, she provides food, but when you raise your brother, he provides brotherhood.' And why is it that some couples are married but don't have any children, and other couples have children but they aren't married? And everyone hurries off to work as if their work might not be there for them if they're late. This afternoon by the side of the street, I saw people open up bags made of paper and then remove items of food. Each of them sat alone and read something while they ate. Were they reading about how to eat? I figured as much, because another person was writing with one hand while he put food in his mouth with the other. He must have been writing down the teachings about how to eat, which the others were reading."

Until the recent few centuries in Nepal, reading and writing were limited to religious texts, and the written word itself was considered sacred. Later, when writing was adopted for purposes of government, the sacredness of the written word was conveniently preserved, giving government and now business an uncommon respect.

"Some people are large and some are small, but I've always felt that body size has nothing to do with the size of one's intellect." Well Fed Fred feigned a look of indignance: except in my case, surely.

"And just because you may be literate or rich, it doesn't mean you know how to do things properly. You need wisdom, too. Only a few people know ahead of time what affect their actions will have." Aama was sitting alone at what had become the head of the room, and looked around at each of us. Her voice flowed like a comitragic opera, the strings, French horn, and percussion cascading into each other, while the flourish of a laugh crowned each stanza.

"Somehow, you create what you call productive lives out of books and machines. Machines can talk, they can shout, they can move, and there are even clever ones, huge fish machines that breathe and swim like real animals. . . ."

Efale had heard about our trip to the safari park. While Aama spoke she turned to Didi and suggested that on our way south we stop at the Monterey Bay Aquarium, where marine mammals and possibly whales can be seen swimming around in glass-walled tanks. That should change her mind.

". . . But this must be nothing unusual for you. You can probably make a dead body breathe and speak, too, by opening it up and installing a breathing machine and a talking machine in there like that tape thing you capture voices on. It's funny that you can do this when you don't know how to work with your hands, how to plant or harvest your crops—which is also done by machines. What would you do without them? Machines are your gods. If they weren't, I would have heard people invoking the name of Bhagwan by now, wouldn't I?"

She took a breath, and we breathed along with her. "And when you want to talk to someone, you talk into a machine and hear them speak from it, too. Perhaps it is Bhagwan inside there, and *that's* who all of you are talking to."

Aama had been watching the telephone on the coffee table. Suddenly she leaned toward it with a sense of urgency, as if it were ringing. Coincidentally a phone call was about to come over the line when she lifted the receiver, she sensed, exactly as she had seen happen to me when I had placed a call. Silently the guests watched her.

She picked up the receiver and grasped the speaker with both hands, firmly but awkwardly, and held the earpiece in front of her mouth like a large microphone. Buttressed by the wine, she was equally intimidated by what she clearly expected to be the voice of an important person.

Haltingly but loudly she spoke into the earpiece in Hindi, the language of fashion among returning Gurkhas, the lingo of worldliness. *"Aachhaa, kya baat hai?* Yes, what is it?" She quickly replaced the receiver, as if she may have done something wrong. Without looking up, she could tell that her audience was paralyzed with laughter. Trying to keep a straight face, she played to it. Again she lifted the receiver and spoke into the earpiece. "Hello, Bhagwan? Is that you . . . ? What? I can't hear you. . . . I can't hear anything. . . ." She hung up.

"No, he's not in there," she reported.

The next morning I awoke feeling bedraggled, but randy. Didi roused, and we gazed from the daylight basement at the warehouses that crowded the view of the San Francisco skyline. Aama would have arisen by now from her sleeping nook around the corner from us, I tried to think intelligibly, and she should be puttering about as usual. We heard nothing; the excitement of the night before must have pooped her out, and she was sleeping in. Didi and I lay on our backs enjoying the privacy and quiet and responsible feeling of being parents as much as lovers, during the few moments before the details of life would slap us more fully awake. Didi replayed Fred's rubberized face as he imitated the antics of the villagers, foreign tourists, and government officials he had done character studies of, and Aama's imitation of His Rotund Fredness attempting to mime a thin porter walking up the trail. Simply hunching lower and sucking in his cheeks wasn't quite enough to elicit one.

I felt a surge of desire, heightened by accumulated frustration. Softly I bit Didi on the shoulder. She said that her back was hurting, then rolled to her side. Slipping the covers to our waists, I kneaded my knuckles into her lower back and methodically walked them up her spine. The dimples above both buttocks were open like the still eyes of a wild feline. She sighed quietly, tired and not yet ready for the day. I flared my hands and gently worked them around her shoulders before lightly brushing them across the bulk of a breast and downward over the exaggerated mound of her hips. Mornings, her muscles were tight, and I gave them time to loosen. Ponderously her figure, and her reticence, softened and warmed into fluidity the way modeling clay does with kneading. She turned toward me, and we fell like worn puzzle pieces into each other's arms and legs. "Yoga means union," I murmured to her obscurely in the accent of an Indian pundit.

"Aama is still asleep—can we do this quietly?" she whispered.

"I don't know. Can you?"

The folding bed was still on the castors that I had meant to retract in order to anchor it. The bed began to shuttle back and forth, banging into the basement wall's wood paneling. For lack of other tools, I used my hand as a bumper between the aluminum frame and the wall, which interfered annoyingly with an otherwise pleasant sensation. The springs squeaked and squawked, the frame groaned and the wheels rumbled. We were waking up.

Aama stirred. I tried to hurry up. Noiselessly she padded out from her nook wearing the attire she had slept in, her petticoat and the Tom and Jerry T-shirt that she selected herself from the clothes we had offered her.

"Kray-kray-kray," she chanted softly, as if calling something. "Kray-kray-kray. Where are you? Come on out, you must be hungry." Didi and I froze. Aama apparently didn't see us beneath our mountain range of sheets and quilts and pillows, but she targeted the sound as coming from beneath us. With her hand on the foot of the bed she bent nearly double and inspected under it. "Those chickens must be under here somewhere. . . ." Her words reverberated musically through the springs. "I wonder who let them inside the house, they'll make a mess."

Didi stifled a laugh, and I let go and laughed with her, resigned to the interruption. Unable to hear us, Aama continued to prattle to the chicken sounds. When she stood up, she was startled by the movement of the bed, then heard our laughter. I lifted my head while Didi remained buried beneath the covers, though Aama saw her outline beside me.

"Oh, there you are. Look at you. Yeeehhh. So this is what you two do." Aama sat on the corner of the bed. "Didi should be awake by now. She needs to get up and then step over your feet," she added sarcastically. Aama had became angry one morning when, half asleep, Didi had nearly stepped over her on the way to the bathroom. *Nagnu*, it's called, and is disrespectful if done intentionally because of the defiling energy that emanates in waves from the bottoms of the feet—a symbolic notch below hitting someone on the top of the head with a shoe. I had reminded Didi to never do that, and she said that in America she sometimes forgot, especially in the mornings before coffee. I hadn't been disciplining Didi enough, I could tell from Aama's tone, which was tinged with jealousy that I was paying more attention to Didi than to her.

"I saw Didi step over you once, too," Aama continued. "Her own husband. She just walked over your outstretched legs and carried onward in her rubber sandals, *pitik, pitik, pitik*. We say that this can shorten your life span. Who am I to remark on this, I should ask. If everyone does it here, then I guess it doesn't matter. But it's important to respect one's spouse."

The spouse more than the daughter-in-law, I was about to observe. To Aama, I was a wealthy and intelligent prospect; to not venerate me was a sign of selfishness, or foolishness. At the same time, Aama was dependent on Didi. She was beginning to manipulate Didi and me, and we were easy prey, not having yet weathered the challenge of child rearing. We were parents without parenting skills, parents who were neither married nor divorced.

Didi groaned, then sneaked into her robe and walked off to the bathroom. Aama turned to me and spoke softly.

"Why don't you get a new one?"

"A new what?"

"Wife."

"But we're not married."

"Well, you need to have children in order to have someone to give your inheritance to. To bring happiness into your life, to relax your mind."

"What about Didi? What would she say if I just left her?"

"No, you don't leave her. You just take another wife, as I was telling you earlier. You'll have to get married to Didi first, of course, before you can take a second wife." I was relieved that she didn't think so unfavorably of Didi after all. "A second one will increase your chances of having offspring. The men in our village would keep second spouses more often if they had the money or the land to support them. You simply build separate kitchens for them, which I would think you can afford."

I was faced with enough decisions already—potential mates to choose from, lifestyle choices, work. I didn't even know which country I wanted to live in. No wonder our society was confused, or no wonder I was, at least. I contemplated old girlfriends, then relatively newer ones that I privately hoped were still in holding pattern. No reason not to be, simply because I had been away in Asia; I might call them after our trip, I thought, at least to say hello. In Oregon, when Aama spoke of second wives I had assumed she was joking. Now, except for the legal restrictions in the U.S., it was sounding like a legitimate concept.

Aama looked straight at me. "Now, don't tell Didi that I suggested this."

Didi returned from the bathroom and crawled under the sheets, still wearing her robe. She lay on her back, looking at the ceiling, then spoke to me frankly.

"I overheard Aama say something about marriage. It's embarrassing for her that we're not married, you know, and she's even been covering for us. Didn't you hear her tell the relatives in the village and Fred and the Gurung boy that we're married?" She looked at me severely. "Last night, after you brought Aama down to her sleeping nook and then crashed on us, drunk, I stayed up talking with Efale. You know what she suggested that I do?" She waited for me to prompt her.

Aama stepped into the silence and began speaking. "You two sleep together even though you're not married. A Gurung boy and girl do that only if their parents have agreed that they are to eventually marry. Nowadays, teenagers study in school and then get together on their own, without the consent of their parents. This is what you are doing, but you should be careful for your parents, and each other."

"I have to get up, I need some exercise," I said to Didi and Aama, then slipped out of bed. I threw on sweat pants and a T-shirt to go jogging—as much to escape the heavy discussion I sensed was coming as to burn off the hangover. I could feel Aama's irritation and Didi's frustration as I left the room.

Chapter 10

"My fate granted me this chance to bathe in the holy water of the great Ganges Ocean, in the name of my parents and forefathers."

Half an hour after jogging out onto the sidewalk and up the hill, I returned to Efale's house, cooled off, and indulged in a long shower. The blanket of wet heat boosted the rush of the run into a cleansing euphoria.

As I rebelted my pants, Aama asked where I had gone.

"Running. Like the training the army recruits do."

"I know how you run—you get in your car and drive around to all the places you say you run to."

Didi had packed the car. Efale joined us on the sidewalk and extended a voluptuous good-bye to Didi and me, then embraced Aama. When she stepped back, she held both of Aama's hands between hers, as if warming them.

"You are a very special person, Aama. You're a princess, a queen."

"I guess I must be, because that's exactly how people have been treating me!" Aama said when I translated.

Like a cable car, the wagon labored up Potrero Hill and veered west to Highway 1. Except for a stop at the Monterey Bay Aquarium, there was no agenda and no hurry. And no whales. The aquarium people had said so on the phone. But there were plenty of sea otters visible through the tanks' glass walls. We could show them to Aama and establish that they are related to whales, and are very much alive.

I docked the cruiser behind another out-of-state car and the three of us ambled along Monterey's Cannery Row. At its end, we pressed through the glass doors of the aquarium building and proceeded toward the admission booth.

Aama stopped. Her head tilted up and panned to take in the spacious, echoing, sky-lit atrium. We urged her to come along. Then we saw what she was looking at.

"So there it is," she said quietly, knowing she didn't need to point.

Suspended by cables from the ceiling were two life-size, plastic replicas of killer whales. Beneath them, children craned up at the shiny, sculpted black-and-white forms, giggling.

"That's where they store the giant mechanical fish after they use them in those shows," she said, vindicated. "If they were real fish, people would have cut them up and eaten the meat by now. Look at those kids—even the children here know that it's a trick!"

Didi had already paid the admission. I felt ripped off. On to the next outrageous deception.

"This tank is filled with water from the Ganges Ocean," Didi told Aama as we viewed a condensed marine ecosystem, including one scuba diver. "And that man is washing the windows on the inside of the glass."

"Ha, washing the windows," Aama mocked as she looked from the glass to the fish to the scuba diver. Her veined hands gripped the brass rail, holding onto a world more secure than the fanciful one before us. She looked at the other visitors; some of whom were smiling, and then spoke quietly to herself.

"Is this all a joke or funny show like the theater of dancing and acting out that the unmarried kids do in the village? Should I laugh or be angry? Why did these people come here? And that man smoking a hookah inside the tank should get out of the water if he's done bathing, his clothes are soaking. . . ."

"These are all real, live animals, Aama, with one human," I said.

"Sure they're real—just like those giant fish on the ceiling are real. I don't know about your 'real.' "

At the touch-and-feel gallery, Didi reached into a shallow pool and handed Aama a starfish. An attendant in a maroon vest came over, inverted it for her, and explained that it feeds by moving its miniature tentacles inward to its mouth. Aama listened briefly, then indignantly flung the starfish into the pool.

"Here's a cowrie, Aama," Didi showed her. "An animal lives inside the cowrie shell." It had attached itself to the inside of a clear plastic container. Aama tried to pull it from the plastic.

"What happened here—someone stuck the cowrie onto this pot with glue or something."

"No, it's *alive,* that's the foot it uses to clamp itself onto rocks."

Aama turned the concept over in her mind as she flipped the cowrie and the container back and forth roughly. She looked blurrily at the other intertidal specimens—a sand dollar, clams, and a small abalone—then became mute. Her hand trembled slightly.

When comfortable, Aama would unfold like a sea anemone, absorbing her environment in brilliant display. But when uneasy, she would retract, seeking camouflage. At these times, she viewed the kindest gesture as diabolical or, at best, a frivolous waste. This variety of culture shock, more severe than her moods, swelled like a breaking wave into a sensation of dying and visiting hell, then engulfed her and pulled at her like the undertow, drowning her ability to observe and to respond. *If you go under, just remember not to breathe,* she had said in the Oregon surf. She was adept, we had seen, at following her own advice.

Unsure of which side of the tank we were standing on, she endured graciously in a dimension that was separate from but parallel to that of the people around her leading their dedicated, carefree young lives. But how was it that she was alive, anyway, and what for? Karma and fate had selected her to stay behind in old age, while nearly all of her peers had passed onward. The purpose and the value of this chronic longevity were a mystery to her.

Bhagwan. She didn't simply believe in Bhagwan, she felt him, she was a part of him, a tangible piece of the intangible. My intuition told me that, *a posteriori,* Bhagwan exists. He certainly was attending to her on a level that Didi and I hadn't been. I wondered if we were taking this unseen partner for granted.

We found our way to the street. I asked Didi how the natural world, of all things, and not our impersonal, mechanical world, could trigger culture shock.

"She must feel trapped," Didi said, "somewhere between those two realities. How would you respond in a strange country if you were unsure of what was real and what wasn't? We need our past experience, or divine intervention, maybe, to come like a messenger and help us sort it all out—but they don't always come."

Fortunately, Aama's condition lasted less than an hour, then clicked off, as if the hormones causing her anxiety were fully metabolized. Even from the depth of her indulgences, Aama remained aware that emotions are transitory, like waves on the ocean—one moment a trough, the next a peak, yet always the same water; the turbulence is only on the surface. I was impressed that she handled culture shock better than I had when I first returned to the U.S. after being away for two years. For weeks, I was seized by a painful social paralysis.

As assistant parent for six of her thirteen brothers and sisters—at least one of them cranky at any given moment—Didi knew how to deal with hangups.

"Aama, I just had a bowel movement a few minutes ago," she pronounced in a distracting, sunny tone.

"Really? Good. How long had it been since the last one? That's how I know how long ago something happened, of course. For me, it's been three days now—when we were in the forest of the big trees. Will we see more trees like those?"

"Are you thirsty? I think there's some juice in the car."

Aama pressed her nose against the sliding glass door of our ground level room at the River Inn, near Big Sur. A stream wandered across the motel's wooded backyard.

"Is that water flowing toward the ocean or away from it?" Aama asked.

"Toward the ocean. Why?" I said.

"If you have a calendar, we can find out when Janai Purni, the full moon of August occurs. I should bathe on that day, preferably in streams that form the headwaters of the Ganges."

Through my pre-coffee muddle I seemed to remember that a holy day was approaching. I reached for my briefcase at the foot of the bed and took out a Nepalese calendar, consisting of black and red characters printed on loosely bound sheaves of rice paper. We had missed Janai Purni by about a week, I calculated, but then rechecked it. I wouldn't want to later admit my oversight to Aama. No, it was still one month away. But today was Nag Panchami, the auspicious date to propitiate the *nagas*, the serpent spirits that control the quality and quantity of water. A good day to bathe in the Ganges River, or the great Ganges Ocean. I told Aama about it.

Rustling in her travel bag, she located her airline vanity case. She unzipped it and withdrew her soap-nut seed, one of the few personal items she had brought with her from Nepal. The ocher surface of the thumb-size seed casing was polished like hardwood by the oils from the palm of her hand, and it had been cut across the top and hollowed out. At the temple grounds of Pasupatinath, a priest had refilled the seed with *biphut,* a mixture of ashes from the never-extinguished pyre of ritual offerings. These ashes are a form of *prasad,* a gift of grace blessed for humans by the deities.

She handed the seed to me and asked for some water from the sink—don't turn on the tap, just take a drop from the edge of the spout. I guided a droplet into the depression. She looked into the seed's hollowed-space, nodded okay and dipped in her pinky finger, the only one that would fit. Delicately she lifted her elbow and guided her small finger—like an antenna deployed from her fist—to the apex of the triangle equidistant from both eyes: the third eye of Krishna, the spiritual eye, the *tika* spot. Surprisingly, it left no residue on her forehead. Arching her neck slightly, she pressed more onto her throat, the zone of vulnerability to ghosts.

"It turns white when it dries," she whispered. Her eyes rolled upward and waited there, as if checking her forehead to see if it had. Presently a round, chalky spot appeared. She smiled at the little display of magic she had let us in on. The holy day could begin.

We didn't have to go far to find ritual implements for the Nag Panchami offerings. Adjacent to the inn, a trendy gift shop displayed minerals, medallions, crystals, copper bracelets, and other paraphernalia for attracting and channeling nonmaterial energies. Prismatic colors refracted through the shop's interior, vibrating the aura that money can be an excellent means of accessing mystical powers. The New Age woman who ran the shop had trekked in the Himalayas, and she recognized Aama as Nepalese.

Didi placed candles and incense on the counter. With humility, the woman took the items and pressed them into Aama's hands.

"If she's a true pilgrim, I can't sell her objects that will be used as offerings or as part of a ritual." The woman had done her Hinduism homework. The shop didn't carry vermilion powder, but she opened a small mirrored case containing rouge, and Aama inspected it. Yes, it had the right texture and was close enough to the right color. Tumeric would substitute for saffron. Lawn clippings could symbolize *dubo,* the grass that mice eat, needed because the mouse is the vehicle of Ganesh, the Remover of Obstacles, the portly and charitable elephant-headed god of good fortune.

We stopped for the tumeric, cow's milk, and bananas—deity food, *naga* food. Didi found a book of matches in the glove box, and Aama pulled a scallop shell from her bag of Sea Lion Caves gift shop treasures. At the first oceanside parking area we came to, I stopped the car.

Nag Panchami is observed in July, at the height of the monsoon rains, the season when demons are active and the deities are taking shelter in dry places. The serpentlike *nagas* are the first beneficial gods to emerge, inspiring the others to follow, and they combine forces to intimidate the demons into scampering for their hiding places. The winter months commence from this day, and the monsoon tapers off. The crops can begin to ripen.

On the beach, Aama laid out the offerings and ceremonial items, then sent me with the scallop shell to fetch ocean water. Nearly a dozen picnickers and sunbathers drifted over to watch, but remained standing at a respectful distance, concealing their curiosity behind folded arms.

"No one can find cow manure, or even a few drops of cow urine for a withered-up old lady?" Aama asked, gesturing toward the onlookers. Mustering an everyday sort of air, I squinted up from my crouch and asked the bystanders if any of them might have some cow dung. Nobody moved. "And are there virgin girls here?" Aama added. She looked around hopefully for the young virgins she would need to hand quarters to as blessing, a prescript of the ritual. There was no way to tell, as there usually is in Nepal; Hindu women, once married, streak red powder into the part of their oiled hair. Again I polled the onlookers. Their heads turned, canvassing each other for a proper reaction. A young man and woman exchanged secret smiles. The faces of two men tightened, as if recollecting that in this woman's part of the world, virgins might be used for sacrifice.

An agitated wind made lighting the incense difficult, but Aama was patient, in control. Time is not money, especially when worshiping. Didi lit the candles and placed them upright in the sand. Aama cut a banana across the middle and stuck the severed halves beside the candles, then jabbed sticks of incense into them. One banana section fell over, and Aama righted it, unconcerned by its fresh sprinkling of sand. Then she touched her thumbs to the fingers of each hand, chanting up and down as if counting. Unable to read and having no text, she repeated a short incantation: "Fate has granted me this chance to confer blessings and cast holy water in the name of my parents and their parents, in the manner that they have blessed us. It is the least I can do as their descendant, considering we were unable to reach Ganga Sagar . . ."

That was all for today. The brief bath and offering relaxed and gratified her, and Didi and me, as well, like a meal following a fast. Aama cut the clean half of the banana, the *prasad,* into small sections and passed it around. Two of the bystanders gratefully took pieces but were hesitant to ingest them, as if this could be stronger medicine than they were prepared for. Then Aama unself-consciously walked into the ocean, sat down in a foot of water, and bathed.

In Santa Barbara, our friends Geoff and Janet had cleared their guest bedroom for us. While Didi and Janet reminisced, Geoff and I cracked some beers and hit the TV room. Aama shuffled toward the darkened alcove, drawn by the blue light dancing on the curtains.

She cautiously peeked around the box, keeping her distance as if this, finally, might be a household idol, something that necessitated a sacred radius.

She sat nearly out of view of the screen, but leaned sideways, held her tongue between her teeth and riveted her attention on Louis Rukeyser, who was already well into his wry, facetious recap of the nation's corporate week. She turned to us, then back to the screen, and to us again. She laughed in what sounded like embarrassment.

"Why is that man talking only to me, and not you? He doesn't seem to know that I can't understand him."

The next morning was Sunday. Despite the seductive background hum of southern California hedonism, Didi and I figured that the area's Spanish-Catholic culture must have preserved some level of morality and virtue. When she was in second grade at the convent, Didi said, the students collected $75 to adopt pagan babies overseas, to save their souls. The money might have been better used locally, she reflected.

Over breakfast, Didi explained to Geoff and Janet the nature of our journey: Aama's search for an indication of sacredness or devotion. Janet suggested visiting both the historic Santa Barbara Mission and the Vedanta Center, a Hindu temple and monastery. Geoff advised us not to miss the Cold Springs Tavern, a bikers' hangout in the Santa Ynez mountains above the city. For decades, he said, there has been a kind of pilgrimage there every Sunday.

The Santa Barbara Mission was established in the late 1700s by the Franciscan Order, and the mission's first abbot is buried in the church-yard. As we walked across the chipped slate of the portico, I wondered if "abbot," which is derived from the Middle Eastern word for father, might have some link to *aapa,* the Gurung word for father, or *oppa,* the German. And, in most south Asian languages, the word for mother is a variation of "Aama," similar in turn to many of their words for love.

"This is a different kind of place," Aama said, standing with other tourists in the mission's ancient chapel. "People worship here."

"Early settlers built this temple nearly two hundred years ago," Didi told her.

"Did people build this temple?" Aama asked calmly, then rejoined, "Not exactly. Bhagwan gave it to them and they put it together." Chanting, she took Didi's hand and stepped up to the altar. Her Nepali-Sanskrit prayer reverberated from the high ceiling and harmonized with the ancient Latin and Spanish echoing about faintly in the rafters.

Beautiful and quaint though it was, the mission felt more like a museum than a living church, its spirit compromised by the volume of tourists moving through like dolls on an assembly line, only somewhat curious to view the remnants of their culture. Now the conveyor had jammed. One woman of a skin tone similar to Aama's stepped from the second pew and stood beside her. Together they prayed, and included the other visitors in their supplication.

On the wall near us, a darkened painting seemed to emit a light of its own. A haloed Jesus stood with outstretched arms in invitation: "Come unto me all ye who labor and are burdened, for I will refresh you." His hands evoked Buddha's open-palmed *varada* mudra, the manual symbol of bestowing a boon. Compassion flowed from Jesus' fingers, and the translucent halo behind him matched the aura of spiritual purity commonly shown encircling the head of Buddha and other enlightened beings. Jesus was not someone that Hindus or Buddhists were able to consider as alien.

Outside, Didi asked Aama what she thought of our temple, the church.

"How can I speak about your temples when I'm not sure of your people's intent? The temples alone are nothing without the devotion of the men and women in them." Hearing this, I hoped for the sake of southern California religious traditions that we wouldn't find the Hindu temple to be more active than the Catholic one.

In Janet's car, we switchbacked above Montecito and into the driveway of the Vedanta Society of Southern California. The center was ministered to by a disciple of Swami Vivekenanda, among the first Indians to introduce Eastern mysticism to the West, a century ago. Impeccable landscaping graced a simple, elegant structure skirted by a tile-roofed veranda, appearing more Japanese than Indian. Birds sang in cheerful innocence; I felt we were interlopers disturbing a measured symmetry.

Empowered by our mission, we mounted the broad steps to the temple. A free-standing sign at the entrance requested us to maintain quiet and remove our shoes. Didi whispered that the orderliness led her to suspect that the Vedanta practitioners would recoil at the loud colors, stray cattle, conch shell trumpeting, bell ringing, incense, and smoke from fire offerings of a Hindu temple in India or Nepal—an ambience far too busy for a society busily searching for solace.

The door was ajar, and a gloomy silence emanated from inside. Was the rasp of Aama's Velcro shoes stripping an irreverent sound? A woman in a hand-spun cotton saree came from nowhere and padded up the steps. She faced us inquisitively, and I politely explained that Aama had come from Nepal and would like to light incense and make an offering, if possible.

"We make offerings and light incense on behalf of those who request it, to keep people from approaching the altar all the time—it's usually done that way." Apparently, middlemen must submit your plea, like the Catholics who run Oregon's Grotto.

"Who is she?" Aama asked, admiring the woman's saree. "Is she of your race?"

"Yes, she's a devotee here."

"Did you speak with her in Hindi or in English?"

"English. She said that the Swami is out, but we can go in and meditate."

"Does the Swami wear the sacred *janai* thread? Is he a Brahmin?"

"I think so." I was assuming that he would be of a "twice-born" caste—born first, as all humans have been, into the physical realm.

Later, after undertaking a long trial of purification and fasting, Brahmins are born again into the spiritual world, into their karmic form. To authenticate this, they wear the multistrand cotton *janai* string, enabling them to perform Brahmanical rites upon the death of their parents. Just as the Jewish boy–turned–old–man is buried with the *tallith* prayer shawl presented him at his Bar Mitzvah, the Hindu is cremated with his *janai*.

We tiptoed inside, and our eyes adapted slowly to the musty darkness of a chapel that had succeeded architecturally in creating a kind of perpetual twilight. It may have been intentionally designed— through emulation of the tenebrous silence of a tomb—to nurture after-death experiences. The dankness felt rather soothing, and would make for a pleasant refuge from a hot and hassled work day. Some of the other people present looked as if they were napping.

In the aisle at the back of the hall, Aama prostrated to the dimly lit photograph on the altar: Ramakrishna, the great ecumenical pundit of the late 1800s—not a deity himself, but an attestant to the capacity for humans to achieve sainthood, to realize during this lifetime the presence of God within us. She then lowered herself to the floor and sat cross-legged, perfectly still, her palms together in front of her face. She had slipped naturally into the yoga of devotion to God, Bhakti yoga, one of the practices taught in Vedanta in which everything one does becomes an offering to and exaltation of Bhagwan, allowing one to tap the wellspring of love. When she looked up after several minutes, the rest of us, worldly sorts, made subtle motions to leave. It didn't seem to be the right time for meditation. Friends who meditate would remind me that the timing never seems right, and it is precisely this distraction of not being right that challenges one to develop their practice.

Aama cleared her throat and asked again about the Swami. A man in a pew across from us glanced over at our group. We sneaked outside to the front steps and hastened into our shoes, whispering. Another man in socks came out and with a bewildering seriousness placed the quiet sign near the edge of the veranda so that we could read it again. Formal notification in writing. Aama can be very quiet at times, but not on purpose.

"Hinduism is not so much a religion as a culture," an educated Brahmin had told me. The California Vendantas seemed to have mastered the religion part of it, but had done so in the absence of a readily identifiable culture. Perhaps that was too cynical. All religions, in their essence, are steering us toward the same goal: the realization of God. Vedanta was one of the too-few paths to that goal, a narrow track through the shallow-rooted but overgrown jungle of the modern world.

Before Janet could start her car, she had to open the trunk, which sometimes caused the security alarm to go off. Internal voices, those of the college kid and the playful Tibetan lama, chanted to me that they hoped it would—in a shrill exclamation that, so far this Sunday, we had seen no more than ten people engaged in a devout expression of faith.

We descended into Santa Barbara for soft drinks and to pick up Geoff and the station wagon.

At the house, Aama asked for her bamboo cane. Faintly I recollected laying it on the floor of the transit hall for tours to the Hearst castle, where we had stopped while driving down the coast the day before. We ate lunch in the busy mall-like waiting area but left without seeing the castle. The line was too long, a testament to the public's craving to brush with the wealthy—aloof and lonely though the wealthy may have been. Vivekenanda and Jesus had nothing like that turnout.

"Hey, *Didi,*" I called from the floor of the TV room as I probed under the couch. "What's that St. Anthony jingle you do when something is lost?" I didn't want to tell Aama about the cane right now; we might find it before she asked again.

"*Let's go,*" Didi shouted from the driveway. "We're in the car, waiting for you." I jogged out and made a last check under the front seat before getting in. Geoff was driving. He clunked the transmission into low for the slow climb to San Marcos Pass. Swerving onto the Old Wagon Road, he nosed the mechanical whale into a turnout and switched off the engine.

"Can't we park the car in the shade?" Aama suggested. I relayed this to Geoff. He started the car, mumbled something about people always being smarter than he, and reparked it.

Amps and band equipment were set up outside, and rock and roll buffeted the dense hardwood forest that surrounded the Cold Springs Tavern. We mingled with aging but respectably hip bikers in dress leathers—"fully credentialed," as Didi described them—and with ex-hippies and artists from a nearby ramshackle settlement, a collage of modified vacation cabins called the Trout Club. People approached Didi and Janet, and asked if Aama was a Native American. The women especially wanted to touch her, expressing a mother or daughter instinct in a locale where the mating instinct predominated. Aama extended her hands to each of them.

A blond woman sitting at the picnic table next to us nursed a four-month-old infant. Children, the elderly, the infirm, and others not in their prime of life, I noted, seem to congregate separate from the compulsively young.

"How many children does this lady have?" the young woman asked.

"Only one, but she has four grandchildren and one great-grand-child," Didi answered.

"Does she know what to do when a woman can't conceive? My sister can't."

Didi asked Aama. Aama looked at the woman, pleased to hear of someone who desired to have children.

" 'Such a thing is in the hands of God,' " Didi interpreted for Aama. " 'Remind your sister to say the name of Bhagwan every morning when she bathes, and have a priest perform a ritual. Or she should see one of your doctors. And if she finds a good way to become fertile, be sure to tell my daughter-in-law about it,' " Aama added quickly with a straight face, hoping her words would reach the woman through Didi's translation before Didi realized what she had said.

From her cloth purse Aama fished out a few quarters, then pushed her way through a herd of brawny guys in drinking visors who were standing in ill-formed lines to get beer. She stepped up to one of the microphone stands and dropped the coins on the ground in front of it. The lead singer lifted his chin in thanks, or curiosity. By donating money, Aama had surrendered to their musical appeals and now expected the begging minstrels to move on and sing for coins elsewhere.

But Aama moved on, and wandered past the front of the tavern. She sat down on a bench next to two elderly women who were resting their hands on top of their canes and their chins on their hands, vicariously enjoying the rebellious gathering. They were in the area visiting their sons, they told me. Their silver-gray hair emitted an ephemeral bluish glow that was less a part of the hair itself than the aura around each strand. Aama asked me what kind of fur their hats were made of.

A heavy but muscular middle-age man, one of the sons, walked up and surveyed the bench of old ladies. He was cleanly dressed, but his tattoos and bushy sideburns revealed a past that may have earned him a Harley Ironbutt designation. He turned to me and asked, "Are you with this woman?"

"Yes, I am."

"Where's she from?"

"Nepal."

"Does she have a cane?"

"Uh, no, not exactly. She did, but I lost it. Yesterday. Or today, I guess."

The ex-biker arched sideways at the waist and pulled a thick wallet from the rear pocket of his black Levi's. With his index and middle fingers he selected a $20 bill, slid it out, and extended it to me.

"Here. Buy her a cane."

Privately embarrassed, I passed the bill to Aama and told her that it was a gift, to buy a new cane with. She scanned the bill with the expectation of a teenager who has uncovered a stack of foreign currency in their grandfather's attic. She asked me how much it was worth. I told her that it equaled more than 500 rupees. She looked up at the man and cinched her lips into a tight circle, one of several expressions of gratitude in the absence, for the Nepalese, of a specific notion of thank you. He nodded.

Aama turned to me. "So you really did lose my cane." I fought back a piercing vision of Aama falling down on the road we had just crossed.

"Well, I think we might have left it in that place where we ate yesterday. You haven't missed it, really, have you?"

" 'He who forgets is remembered by others,' " she quoted reprovingly. "You probably lost it along with that stopper for the car, and your head. Now, you're not really going to buy a cane, are you? I can live without a cane a lot better than I can live without the food which that kind of money will buy. *My old man,* people *buy* canes here, and they cost that much? I'll just cut another bamboo stick when I'm back in the village."

"She said thank you very much," I told the man, "and if this is more than needed, she'll use the rest to purchase clothing for her grandchildren." That was a hard one. I'm going to get busted one of these days, I thought, especially because people had been intuiting much of what Aama said. But she would have meant to say something politely thankful, I figured; her look of surprise and appreciation backed me up this time.

"This man must love old people. Maybe he's just showing off his money. Or maybe he's crazy. And what's stamped all over his arms, anyway?"

"She's very grateful," I added flimsily.

Janet walked over and said that we needed to leave for home to prepare dinner. Guests were coming.

"Aama, wave bye-bye to the gentleman." His was the most charitable act of our Sunday.

She turned toward the ex-biker and swept her hand sideways at him, a motion that means "go carefully and stay healthy" among the Gurung, but that Americans read more as *go on, get outta here*. Her simple wave was a startling reminder that a gesture of respect and benediction in one culture could summon a different emotion in our own. I took her hand and rotated it a quarter turn.

"Move your hand here at the wrist, as you were, but upward and downward, not back and forth." I secured her arm at the elbow and articulated her hand at the wrist. She angled her head and watched her hand from the side as she tried it out, like a child watching her own hand puppet. "Right, like that," I encouraged. "Or you can hold your hand still, and wave only your fingers." She tried and mastered it. Then, figuring that a combined movement might be even better, she closed her fingers onto her thumb while she waved her arm, as if trying to snatch a mosquito. She practiced in the car.

"You say 'bye-bye' only when you leave, not when you arrive, right?"

"Right."

"What do you do with your hand when you greet someone?"

"Shake hands."

"Oh, yeah, men do that in our village now, too, the ones who have been to the cities."

Chapter 11

"Call those animals and other creatures over here so I can give them money — the young virgin girls, too. How much do they need?"

$\mathcal{A}$ama observed Janet, who was eating an artichoke.

"An army pensioner in our village planted those once. He got the seed from India, and he called them *Haati-chawk,* a 'bite for an elephant,' but I never knew how you eat them. What if you don't have teeth?"

Didi scraped the meat from a handful of artichoke bracts onto a plate for Aama. Coated in melted butter, there was little doubt Aama would savor the gray-green substance. Butter and calories meant not getting hungry shortly after a meal. Rich food symbolized security and wealth, and its presence on the table accorded Aama a rowdy self-confidence.

"You eat green foliage, raw . . ." With wooden utensils, dinner guests grappled for tomatoes and lettuce from an oversized salad bowl. ". . . the way cows and buffaloes chew grass."

I knew how she felt. My opinion of diet food, I told Didi while poking into an avocado, was the same as a Gurung's: Why pay more for food that furnished less energy? Nepalese farmers mentally calcu-lated the calories of yield per acre for each crop, and their planting regimen maximized this. Vegetables and fruit were tasty and decora-tive, but of limited nutritional value.

"I've noticed that people here eat corn right off its cob, and then leave pieces of the corn behind. And at one place, your friends ate what looked like long white worms. They put the heads or tails of the worms in their mouths and sucked in the rest, the way ducks eat."

It was sounding like the onset of one of her spontaneous rants. I sat back and took a drink of wine.

"Not only that, but people get up in the middle of the meal to serve themselves, defiling the food bowls with hands they've been eating with. At least you're all of the same caste. Do you follow any customs at all when you eat?"

"That's why we serve you first, Aama, so that you won't be contaminated."

"And why don't they serve tea?"

"But you said that you don't drink tea."

"Still, they should serve it."

"You shouldn't criticize us with your mouth full, you know," I said, using her own words of reproach. She looked at me dubiously. I could feel her apprehension about our culture and our motives, but I wasn't sure whether anyone cared, or, in the context of America, whether it mattered. It was summer, and this was California.

"We old people can't help but say whatever comes into our heads

—so be prepared! 'When I get a chance to eat, the food goes in all at once. When I get a chance to speak, the words come out all at once.' "

"That's a nice proverb, Aama." My wine-flavored words came out more obsequious than sincere.

"So who goes around reciting proverbs that aren't nice?"

We both sensed that we may have spoken and drunk too much. Aama stood up, carried her paper plate to the kitchen sink, spun both water taps to full flow, and rinsed the plate off in the aggressive spray. She propped its limp form on the drying rack and returned to her seat. Didi got up to turn off the water while explaining to the guests that, in the Gurung villages that have them, drinking water runs freely from the taps, the way streams flow from the mountains, bountiful and unconfined.

"This straw mat beneath where my plate was has been polluted with food," Aama continued. "Didi, throw this away."

Didi had resumed talking with Janet about Disneyland. Janet wouldn't be able to join us, but the three of us would take her son Jesse. Didi turned to Aama and told her of our plan to visit an extraordinary festival of dancers and games and giant stuffed animals.

"Where is it? Is it many days' travel? . . . It may not be possible to get tickets, though," she added politely, heedful to not directly show that she desired something.

When we took her to bed, her jaw nearly dislocated into the yawn of a satiated lioness.

❖

"Call those people and those animals over here, so I can give them money—the dancing virgin girls, too. How much do they need?" Perched on the curb at the sidelines of the Disneyland parade, Aama dug into her sash. Kids and parents, strollers, shopping bags, and balloons surrounded us. A cartoon-character float in the shape of a jetliner taxied by, dreamlike. Fairy-tale creatures danced on the plane's wings and twirled and high-stepped around its bulbous wheels. Parade music flowed from the trees and buildings. We had to shout to be heard.

"We already paid, Aama, when—"

She cast a splayed handful of change toward the swirling fanfare, then spread her arms as if straining to embrace the scene, or trying to molt and discard her elderly body and plunge into the colors, the motion, the children, the noise.

Gradually the creatures and the music drifted off to the right, and the crowd arose from the curb to wander off.

"Can I get one of those shiny things, to take to my new great-grandson?" Aama asked. A silvered balloon in the shape of a mouse's head was tethered to the hand of a child standing next to her.

"How are you going to get it back to the village?" I asked, bristling at the four-dollar price. I imagined her trying to cram the balloon onto the plane, knowing, thankfully, that it wouldn't survive the day.

"There's the money that the man gave me for the cane," she appealed. I made a mental note to buy her a cane, to keep her from invoking the biker's donation. Didi selected balloons for Aama and Jesse, and we tied them to their wrists.

Ferried along by the crowd, we merged onto Main Street. Didi bought some popcorn from an antique vending cart and handed Aama a bag. Aama tossed into her mouth three or four individual kernels, which landed precisely from almost a foot away. Snow White's seven dwarfs marched by, three steps ahead, two steps back, three ahead, two back, their arms swinging in perfect, absurd rhythm. Aama shook a tempting handful of popcorn at them, as if offering food to animals. Her cheeks were distorted by the mouthful of kernels she had packed into her gums for storage. In comic choreography, the dwarfs piled into each other, back to belly, and drew to a halt. They returned Aama's Namasté at the same moment that a swarm of children converged on them.

In a store on Main Street, a young Disneyland ambassador dressed in a coat and tie and walkie-talkie chatted with Didi and me, while Aama shopped. He leaked official word that Mickey Mouse would be making an appearance shortly. Turning his back to the scene, he leaned toward us and said in a mysterious aside, "This place is weird." His pressed collar resisted his vigorous attempt to loosen it with an index finger.

Aama browsed her way around to us.

"Aama, we're going to meet an animal considered to be an American deity," I said, groping as usual for a sensible translation. "He's like the king of the mouse and animal caste that you saw on TV with Jesse."

Through a forest of balloons and cotton candy, we could see Mickey Mouse in front of the castle, walking and waving like a politician. We pushed forward, and he stopped regally in front of Aama. She tried to clasp his oversized gloved hands in hers, then lifted and lowered his hands with each point of a recited incantation, as if coaching a boxer. She passed her fingers across the surface of his artificial face, feeling each ridge and depression as she spoke, trying to force her blessing through his malleable but impervious rubber skin. "I apologize for coming unprepared, but with humble words I offer my respect and blessings, and pray that your wishes and desires, and those of the children who love you, be fulfilled . . ." Didi and I flinched when she squeezed his nose, hard; the veins on the back of her hand bulged.

Didi pulled Aama to safety. A throng of children were jostling to meet the immense humanoid rodent, having waited all their television-literate lives to be granted a *darshan,* a devotional audience. Here he was, as immortal as the frozen Walt Disney may be, wearing a rubber Trojan-horse mouse suit as a means of charming his way into the hearts of children, to release an arsenal of irresistible consumer products. A giant incarnation of Ganesh's sacred vehicle, the mouse.

In the early seventies, my anthropology professor reminded the

class that "animation" is derived from *anima,* which means soul. He
also said that the inner sanctum of the Magic Kingdom was not
accessible to the simple tourist-type pilgrim and that the interior of
Cinderella's castle—which we weren't allowed to enter—was actually empty. The castle mirrored, however unconscious the motives of
its designers, many destinations of pilgrimage: the arduous trek to
view Shiva's ice phallus in India's Amarnath cave; the Ka'bah, the
building in Mecca containing the sacred black stone toward which
all Muslims turn to pray.

Magnificent and divine though the shells of these sites are, at
their core they are, literally, empty. Indeed, the heart of Tibetan tantric philosophy itself pulses to the concept of emptiness: All phenomena originate in the mind. At the same time, the mind itself has no
independent or verifiable existence. It does exist, the Buddhist sages
teach—as light and cognition, without form, yet ever present. "If you
believe, then it's a god, if you don't, it's merely a stone," Aama had
said. Indeed, the villagers paint colors onto ordinary rocks, which
then become deities. Technically, the paint is not essential.

We strolled the crowded walks and captured on film the mythic
images of more characters from the media of Didi's and my youth.
Something was familiar here, like an emergent memory. The collective unconscious. All humans are linked in pilgrimage, for they are
journeying to the same place. Three steps ahead and two back, I
chuckled, then roused myself. It was fun to imagine, but difficult to
picture, how Disneyland's theology would help in liberating us from
the cyclical existence of birth, death, and rebirth.

The theme park's animated frenzy accelerated as the sun set,
engulfing us in a chaos of music, steamboat whistles, and the clatter
and mutter of the Matterhorn ride and colorful, corpulent Americans. Aama's face drew slowly upward. Escaped balloons and an
aerial tram framed a window of open sky directly above us, revealing
a crescent moon. She placed her hands together and worshiped it
briefly, oblivious to humankind.

The trip back to the car was subdued. I opened the doors to let it cool. Jesse came around the corner of the car, crying. "My balloon went away—and I didn't get to ride on Space Mountain, either." His balloon was a hundred feet above us, heading for outer space. Didi had put Aama's balloon in the car, where it rested smugly on the ceiling.

"Give this one to Jesse," Aama said. "While we are here on earth, we possess something and say 'this is mine.' But after we die, what meaning is there to 'mine'? What is the meaning of 'yours'?"

"We need to buy gifts for Didi's mother—you especially, Nani, because she's your mother-in-law."

"Flowers?" I asked.

"Flowers are good, but you need to give her more than that."

"I could give her the wooden pots we bought in the big forest. She's a gardener and can plant flowers in them."

"Wooden pots for your mother-in-law? Won't that be an insult? What about copper, or a bolt of expensive fabric?" Aama well understood the taste of a newly commissioned mother-in-law. If I were to take her up on her offer of an arranged marriage to a girl in the village, I'd have to pay attention to these things. How could the Gurung be so easygoing yet particular?

"Sometimes we give a shawl to a close relative. When we present it to them, we drape the shawl around their neck and chant, '*Shaaaaaaaai, shaai, shaai, shaai*'—'It has been captured'—meaning their soul has been safely secured within them." Aama twisted sideways in her booster seat, laid her hands on Didi's shoulders, and let go of the *shaais* with soothing, falling tones, like the final gasp of air from a tire.

Didi told me she could feel a lessening of stiffness, as if her tension had been absorbed into Aama's hands, then generously grounded in the earth. "I have an extra pashmina shawl, Aama," she said. "And I think you should give it to her."

Mrs. Thunder met us in the driveway. Her arms bore fresh

scratches from her roses, and her lower legs were horizontally striped from her Weed Whacker. She was followed by a flutter of nieces and nephews. The younger ones took turns holding Aama's hands and touching her dress as they led her toward the sprawling 1950s adobe ranch house. A painting of St. Michael, the archangel and guide for children, hung in the entryway. Cool, old-family-home air wafted from the kitchen and living room, and drafted down the hall.

The long hallway was staggered with bunk rooms and boys' and girls' bathrooms with individual stalls. Three generations of Thunder family photographic history filled the walls, illustrating a partial cross-section of America: engineers, missionaries, businesspeople, students, parents, and grandparents. Mrs. Thunder—Didi told me to call her Genevieve—had kept track of them all, and she reckoned that Didi's grandmother, who passed away in the sixties, now has 147 living descendants. At that geometric rate of reproduction, I calculated, in another one hundred years there could be as many as ten thousand of them.

Aama couldn't always read a photograph, but she innately pictured the matrix of kinship, the lines that form the webs which unite us and catch us when we fall. Didi withdrew the shawl, and Aama presented it to Didi's mother with both hands; it looked like a strand of that web. Genevieve thanked Aama and gave her a small stained glass window that she had made herself. Like Aama, Genevieve was raising a handful of grandchildren, and they each had a new great-grandson.

I envied Didi her mother, and wished that my own could be there with them. I was nineteen when my mother died. Didi's father had died when she was nineteen.

When Didi was a girl, Genevieve spent the late afternoons cooking for the nearly two generations of her fourteen children. They ate in shifts, youngest first, in an octagonal dining room attached to the house like an adobe space pod. A ten-foot-diameter table dominated the dining area. Didi's father had built a lazy Susan into it for circulating the food; when spun, it imparted the unsettling sensation that the pod itself was rotating.

That night, the lazy Susan carried around bits of conversation. In a whisper, someone asked Genevieve if we would be taking Aama to church while we were in San Diego, and that it would be terrible if Didi didn't work on converting her.

"What's Aama saying?" one of Didi's nieces asked in a questioning singsong.

"She says that Mom must need more than two gallons of rice to feed all of us, and that it must cost her a lot."

"Rice costs a lot?"

"Sure, where Aama comes from. Mostly, she eats corn and millet mush."

"What's that?"

"She lives just like the Flintstones!" one nephew exclaimed.

Another nephew, a teenager, strummed an irreverent air guitar riff under the table and said it would be cool to take his Stratocaster to band practice and turn the new students on to some heavy metal. He resembled the young man in the formal portrait that hung behind Didi's seat: her great-grandfather Major George Francis Thunder of the Royal Fusileers, Bombay. While we collected the dishes, Aama studied the painting as if it depicted a member of a lost tribe.

"When my husband and I were in India fifty years ago, I saw white sah'bs, the British, driving about in motorcars without roofs. They led small dogs around on ropes and would even put the dogs into the cars with them. The mem-sah'bs had light-colored hair and wore dresses, not sarees. They walked differently than we did, and would look into each others' faces and laugh loudly, like barking. We were afraid of them, but I only saw them from a distance—from my sitting place in the sun, where the Gurung soldiers polished their leather boots. They buffed them until they shone, reflecting light like the blade of a sharpened knife, and when they walked around, the boots made a *krrik-krrik* sound. . . ."

There weren't enough bedrooms at the family home, so Didi,

Aama, and I would have to stay at Didi's sister Barbara's. Aama
reclined across the backseat of the car. "With all those brothers and
sisters of yours, Didi, your mother's neck and arms should be layered
in gold jewelry. And Nani, you should have been given a seat of
respect; they should have served you bread and alcohol and wrapped
a length of white cloth into a turban about your head, as their new
in-law. . . ."

More like their new outlaw, I thought. I was wary of getting
close to Didi's family, mainly because I wasn't certain I wanted to get
closer to Didi. In the midst of eighteen relatives, at least there was
some anonymity, and her family seemed casual, low pressure.

Especially after her father's death, Didi had told me, none of the
kids got special consideration, and they learned not to ask for it. The
younger girls wore each other's socks and underwear, which were
laundered together and loaded from the dryer into a drawer marked
"Girls." I could see why Didi felt that I was spoiling Aama. Or was
she jealous of Aama receiving individual attention that she never
had?

At Barbara's house, I stared through the sliding glass door at the
underbelly of clouds glowing from the lights from San Diego. Aama
sat upright on the mattress next to us, her legs and waist swaddled
beneath the covers. She spoke to the lifeless television screen as if it
were animated with Didi's sisters' faces.

"*Jeti . . . Maaili . . . Saaili . . . Kaaili . . .*" she enumerated, using the kinship terms that ranked Didi's siblings by age. With
each title, she looked deeper into the whorls on her finger pads, as if
envisioning her own lost kin. "Which one was *Kaaili?* Oh, she's the
one in Hong Kong. Then *Raaili*—that's you, Didi. . . . And *Taaili*
was the one with us in the big forest near Ann-Tori's house. After
that are *Tulo Kaanchi* and *Saano Kaanchi* . . . How many is that?"

"Eight," I said wearily to the darkness.

"But there are nine sisters, aren't there?"

"You remember the brother- and sister-in-laws better than I do,"
I said.

"But how do you call out to someone if you don't know what relation they—oh, yeah, you call them by their names, which you have to distort your mouth to say." She took a breath and spoke quickly, wanting to rectify me on this one. "Okay, I'll tell you how to keep them straight: Your sister's husbands are called *Byena*. They call your sist—I mean their wives' sisters—*Didi*. Your sisters' kids should call your eldest sister *Jyethi Aama*, then *Maaili Aama*—which is Nepali, but in Gurung we say *Maaili Aaji*—for the next, and so on down through *Raaili Aaji*—which is what you are, Didi, to your sisters' children—not *Didi*, because we all know that *Didi* means 'older sister' and that somehow your people gave you the *name* 'Didi' —and then on down to *Kaanchi Aama*. That's so much easier than trying to remember names."

A proper name revealed little. Kinship titles, which varied depending on who was hailing whom, evoked the fabric of lineage. Relatives defining themselves relative to each other.

"I slept poorly," Aama announced in the morning, as usual. The soft mattress lacked the familiar, vivifying discomfort of a simple straw mat. Like most of the elderly, she was sleeping less than she used to, yet had not fully accepted it. It's seldom a good day or a good year for a farmer or a fisherman.

She gamely fought back the covers and pushed herself up onto one arm, then asked me to heat up the hair oil we had bought for her, to massage into her scalp. The Brylcreem sputtered and popped viciously in the tablespoon as I held it over the gas burner. After pouring the Brylcreem into the garbage, I heated some vegetable oil instead, which might have fewer impurities. The night before, she had complained of arthritis and rubbed corn oil on her arms and legs, squealing *"a-wee, shyaa"* in pain when she moved her legs to uncomfortable positions. Old age was like a hangover.

Didi threw on a thin robe and kicked aside my pile of clothes.

"Since you two act as if you're married," Aama said, "shouldn't you wash Nani's feet in the morning, Didi, as a sign of respect?"

Didi laughed, then became serious. "No. In America, wives and girlfriends do what they want to. We're independent." She dug through Aama's travel bag for her sash. Shells, rocks, small gifts, and other found objects randomly strewn about the pieces of clothing fell out. There were more of them than a week earlier.

". . . I worry, Nani," Aama said as she observed Didi, "that you'll tell people about the gifts I've received in Amrita. If those things don't all make it to the village, my son-in-law will ask me where they are, and say that I'm hiding them or that I sold them to make money. Then they will want to see the money. Really. These gifts could become a burden.

> " 'Oh, Herder in your herder's hut,
>   May we have cheese and honey?'
>   'Ma'am I cannot give to all of you,
>   So how can I give to any?' "

"If you're worried about collecting too many things in America, Aama, why don't we discard all this junk?" Didi said emphatically. Aama watched, deflated, as Didi overturned her travel bag. "I'm going to start by washing some of this clothing." As Didi jerked at it, more items clunked to the floor. I told Aama not to worry, and scavenged a box from Barbara's garage to mail the artifacts to Seattle, which would lighten the car. Personally, I was feeling more burdened by family than by things.

Didi was becoming tired of both of us. Annoyed at me, because I wasn't responding to her. Irritated at Aama for needling her about marriage. Didi had become casual nursemaid to the surrogate mother of a nonhusband, and was tired of passively accepting Aama's scolding, sarcasm, and charges of inadequacy. Yet there was little she could do about it, and there probably wouldn't be as long as we were traveling together.

I gave Didi a hug, and we talked briefly. Aama was moody, that was to be expected. At the same time, I reminded her, Aama was highly impressed by her family, especially its size. Aama wouldn't say as much, but Didi had been redeemed, and was now more suitable for formal marriage—the reason why Aama wanted her to wash my feet.

Didi's sisters wouldn't let us leave town before an excursion over the border to Tecate, Mexico, in memory of their unsanctioned weekends of dancing and tequila, away from the convent and U.S. law.

Entering Tecate, we passed a wedding party near the town square, complete with a Cadillac convertible painted in glittered, rainbow colors, done up low-rider fashion. Now this is how people should celebrate, I could see Aama thinking.

The mariachi joint that the sisters frequented was noisy. The odor of spices clung lustily to the velvet oil paintings.

Aama was exhausted. The sisters still wanted to dance. The tavern's parking lot had an attendant, and Didi and I escorted Aama back to Barbara's van, folded out its bed, and tucked her under some blankets. We hoped she would be okay.

Fifteen minutes later, we returned to check on her. She was cowering under the blankets, shaking. Globular tears flowed over the tracks of dried ones. She reenacted what she thought had happened to her.

"I thought I saw something. Bandits may have seen my gold jewelry when I got in the car. All humans don't have the same intentions. My dharma son and Didi are in there drinking, drunk by now, and senseless. Now, finally, I've been abandoned. *What's that?* There's a light on me, and people are looking at me through the window. Oh, Bhagwan, now what? I'll hide under this blanket and make it look like a piled-up rag, nobody under here. I'm trembling. If my breath is to leave me this evening for the last time, then it is the wish of Bhagwan. Now the car is moving. I'm dead. No, I'm crying. They are dragging the car to that forest we drove past and are going to finish me off. Maybe I could take my earrings off and hand them to them, but I'm only able to lie here and say the name of Bhagwan,

O Bhagwan. My granddaughters don't come around to see me as much as they used to, and my relatives are forgetting me. I wonder when my daughter will find out about me and what she will be doing at the moment they tell her . . ."

This was no ordinary, after-dark variety crankiness. Hospital night nurses say that the elderly are "sundowning," I learned later, when they become temporarily disoriented after awakening in a darkened room. Old people seldom like to travel, not because of the difficulty of the journey but because of a generalized fear that they won't return home. The outside, the distant, is threatening, while the home is safe.

"I'm not afraid of anything, except people," Aama said finally. "I've kissed a tiger and a big mechanical fish, crossed bridges over mountain rivers, and have fallen down three times—but haven't died."

I seconded Didi's vow that we wouldn't leave Aama alone again.

Chapter 12

"Nani, this machine needs more coins for it to continue to work."

Sucking fuel like a jet engine, the wagon power-climbed out of the Los Angeles basin and into the San Gabriel Mountains. The traffic thinned and the barren hillsides opened out onto the Mojave Desert, awakening in us an expansive sense of freedom.

"Gambling is like a drug," Aama said as general commentary and warning, recalling what I had told her about Las Vegas the previous night. "It has ruined many of my relatives. Women don't gamble, anyway. Nani, you can go place bets while Didi and I wait in the car. What if someone were to see me? Word would get back to the village, and everyone would point and laugh at me, saying that I turned into a stupid, addicted gambler and threw away what little wealth I've saved for my old age."

To hang out while a bunch of men sat around on straw mats and played cards wouldn't be fun for anyone. But it wasn't likely she'd decline the two free nights at the Las Vegas Hilton that my aunt and uncle had won in a raffle and transferred to us. The food in the casinos was cheap. If we could resist gambling, I said to Didi, Vegas might cost less than camping out. I exited onto the Vegas strip, and as we stood in the lobby of the Hilton, I indulged for a moment in feeling more important than I really was.

We took in a budget buffet at the Tropicana. Afterward, we wandered along the sidewalk and stopped at the corner of The Dunes and Caesar's Palace. As if on a rotisserie, Aama slowly turned to absorb the neon, basking in the waves and pulses of colored light. It was an offering of mythical proportions.

She lifted her hands and placed them together prayer-fashion, then dropped them. Again she lifted them prayerfully and released them, then again, muttering an honorific greeting each time. She had fixated on The Dunes' eighty-foot incandescent column, inset with hundreds of small lights in the ethereal outline of a minaret. The lights went on and off sequentially, moving from the ground to the peak of the minaret in less than a second.

"Those lights are climbing and falling without rest, as if they are saying 'Namasté.' They make everything so colorful, a wonderful petition to the deities. I wonder if the people who make them work invoke the names of the deities each time they turn them on." She spoke in the direction of a limousine that was stopped at the traffic light. "If deities aren't here already, this is the kind of place where they would come to stay." Incandescent or otherwise, Aama had often said that lights should be lit as much as one can afford. The gods, especially Laxmi, the Goddess of Wealth, do not come readily to dark places. Bright lights and idle recreation did make a kind of sense, I thought, after the long passage through the desert. Were it located near a large city, Vegas would be just another theme park, its glaring tackiness an insult to the community rather than this sparkling oasis of imagination and hope.

"Hey, *wait* a minute . . ." The voice of a half-drunk, half-cultured man sputtered behind us on the sidewalk. I turned as he stopped midstride several yards from us. An outstretched arm wavered from the sleeve of his zip-front poplin jacket. "I *know* who that woman is!"

I had written an illustrated book about Aama and her life in the village, by now a few years out of print. Here, in Vegas, was a guy who had read it?

"Hey, *Joe.*" He glanced about for his friend, while his arm remained frozen horizontally. "Check out this woman here. . . . *Joe.* . . . It's *Mother Teresa.*"

He looked in my direction, then screwed in his focus. "Are you with her?" he said suspiciously. Clearly, he expected Mother Teresa's aide to appear holier than I.

"Yes, but—"

"All *right,* that's *great.* What a deal. Does she wanna play the slots?"

Hesitantly I said yes, and asked for his advice; he looked like the kind of guy who would know the town well. Only a moment before, Didi had said she wouldn't mind hitting a casino, out of boredom. Now she stood behind the man, secretly gesturing at me about something not being right. I shrugged.

"Caesar's Palace," the man enunciated, producing a small drop of saliva on his lower lip. "I'll take you. Boy, will she love this!"

Aama asked, "Is this another friend of yours who has arrived here from out of nowhere after you arranged it by telephone? Sometimes I'll get a feeling, too, that a distant relative is coming for a visit, and they usually show up."

"Not this one," Didi said. "But I'll gamble if you will, Aama. Let's give it a try, okay?"

"To have the best luck in gambling, you should carry an amulet containing a piece of your own umbilical cord—the stump part that is left behind when you are born, which dries and falls off—and the placenta from a black cat's birth. I don't know where mine is, but my daughter still has her birth amulet."

That must have meant yes. She spoke like a financial advisor and chaperone, now obliged to see that Didi and I wouldn't get carried away.

We stepped from the sidewalk onto an elevated walkway that paraded us silently past lights and fountains and statuary of Roman gods and goddesses, deities of good fortune, I hoped. Las Vegas, I decided, had been created following the accidental discovery that the human body can convert photons, alcohol, and junk food into an urge to gamble against huge odds.

"Now remember," Aama cautioned, "if I do anything bad here, it will reflect on my family and my tribe. 'Aama went to this kind of place and did this . . .' is what my relatives will say." She wasn't asking us to conceal, but was letting us know that there would be no harm in simply forgetting about anything that would happen next. "We're lucky to be here on a day when there are festivities," she resumed excitedly.

The hall of slot machines at the entrance gave off the energy of a depot at train time. Our guide abruptly wandered off; he was probably a part-time shill for the casino. I changed a ten into a roll of quarters and broke them into my coat pocket. We sat down on three empty stools in front of a line of quarter slots.

Aama watched as I inserted a coin into my slot and pulled the crank. No payoff. "Two or three of these fruits must match in order to win," I told her, indicating the windows with my finger. I dropped a quarter into her machine and showed her how to pull the lever. She reached up and grabbed the arm with both hands, then leaned forward slightly. Forcefully she rocked back and applied all her weight to the arm. The machine shuddered. From beginning to end of the motion, her eyes didn't leave the rolling lemons, oranges, plums, and cherries. One by one, right to left, the items jerked to a stop. No payoff. Still hanging on the arm, she pushed it back up and pulled again, harder. Nothing happened.

"You have to put another coin in the slot each time you pull on the arm—and it doesn't matter if you pull hard or not," Didi told her, taking a break from her own machine.

"So where are the coins?"

I gave her a handful of quarters. Gazing through the fruit-laden windows, she concentrated on a point somewhere inside the machine. After eight tries, a small payoff clinked into the tray. Without expression, she noted that it was about time she won something.

She exhausted the fifteen-odd quarters in her hand.

"Pick up those coins from your tray and use them," Didi told her.

"You can put them back into the machine?" She hesitated, suspecting that to reinsert them might be a kind of monetary incest or autocannibalism. They seemed to work. Another ten-coin payoff and one twenty-coin payoff kept her going, but the reserve in her tray eventually dwindled to nothing. Keeping her eyes targeted on the windows, she ran her fingers along the inside curves of the stainless steel basin like a blind person cleaning the last grains from a rice bowl. Nothing. She leaned over and looked carefully on each side of the machine, then to the floor and under her chair. She sat up and optimistically yanked the lever again. No action.

"This machine needs more money for it to continue to work."

"Does the machine need more money, or do *you* need more?" I asked her.

"The machine needs more."

I reached into my pocket and pulled out another handful of quarters and dumped them into her tray. She turned to me with a grin of revelation.

"There they are. You were hiding them."

"Hiding them? Of course I was hiding them—so that you wouldn't squander them all. These machines eat money, and then feed you back just enough to make you think you're winning."

"But this is prize money that the machine awarded you, isn't it?"

"Money is money—it's the same stuff we take to our bazaar and buy food with. Aama, we've been here only a short while, and do you know how much you've lost? About eight hundred rupees. Think what that could buy in the village."

She sat up straight, motionless. Her gaze seared past the windows and through the back of the slot machine as she retraced her experience of the last few minutes. Finally a series of low chuckles spaced several seconds apart broke her reverie, and she fell into a quiet conversation with herself. "Where have I gotten to, this old lady from the hills taking all this money and putting it into this machine? Is my buffalo in the shed and is she getting enough fodder? Has my house been broken into? My relatives would want me to have fun, I think, and it can't really matter because the women here do it—I saw some. Anyway, I'd never want to gamble in the village, and I'm not using my own money, so it's not really me gambling. But how great it would be to win big! Five hundred rupees is *a lot.*"

Aama looked at me like a naughty child hoping she had a workable excuse. She picked up the single quarter that I tossed into her tray. Slowly, as if a ritual object, she touched it to her forehead for luck, muttered a short mantra, then kissed it. She dropped the quarter in the slot and yanked the lever. A ten-coin payoff. A minute later she scored a fifty-coin payoff, and quietly watched the coins clink into the tray. A fat lady, her favorite spectacle, walked by. She didn't even notice. On a roll.

"Aama, we have to go," Didi said. We were tired, and it was best to leave on an upturn.

"My purse is a real load. How much did we get?" She had discreetly waited to discuss the winnings until we were outside on the sidewalk, in case someone in the casino had seen her unconscionable profit or overheard us talking about it in Nepali. Her arms were folded across her chest, hiding the drawstring purse under her blouse.

"Not that much," I said, detouring the disappointing answer that her bulging pouch held mostly the leftover change from the thirty dollars Didi and I had exchanged.

"How about this?" I proposed. "We'll leave you here, you can use your mantra to work these money machines, and Didi and I will come every day to bring you food and collect your winnings, which will help pay for our trip."

"Well, perhaps," she said sincerely. "I've been lucky in my life so far. I've had no major debt or other money problems. The mantra might help, but it can't be done by force. Gamblers are restless: They say to themselves, 'Money, come!' but how can everyone win at once? For most people, wealth is like the weather. But I won because Bhagwan took pity on an old lady. How could I stay here and take advantage of Bhagwan's pity?"

We entered the elevator of the parking garage across the street to ascend to the cruise wagon's third-floor parking slot.

"Oop, they're weighing us again," she remarked. "After that big dinner, and carrying all these coins, we must weigh much more now."

On our way out of town the next morning, Aama was still grumbling that Didi had jumbled up the quarters that she had squared off into stacks of five on the floor of the hotel room. Aama was counting them, cross-legged in her petticoat and Tom and Jerry T-shirt, when Didi had tried to get her dressed.

Didi looked out the window and suggested that, if we wanted, we could stay another day and get married by a preacher wearing a white suit and cowboy boots in one of the miniature chapels with the false fronts. Aama could witness.

Was she joking, or was this part of her lingering rebellion against the convent? I chose not to respond. At the moment, I was more concerned for the car; the radio said the temperature had climbed to 95 degrees.

The land yacht surged across the mirage of northern Arizona's plateau landscape on an orphaned stretch of Route 66. We passed Kingman and Peach Springs, and arrived at the Grand Canyon.

After viewing the Himalayas, it felt strange to peer downward rather than upward at a massive natural phenomenon, a spectacle created from the absence, not the presence, of matter. Aama held the handrail of the walkway and cautiously approached the abyss.

"Where have I come to? An old woman who hasn't been down to the spring at the edge of her village in months is now seeing *this*. Why didn't you tell me about this place before?" she asked, as she often did. "How could I have ever dreamed this existed?"

Didi and I had given up trying to explain much beforehand. Aama's store of worldly experiences did not contain enough pieces to form coherent pictures. Typically, she dismissed much of what we described by saying "Why would an old lady about to die want to go to those places—I've already seen everything there is to see."

She stared at the ribbon of river at the bottom of the canyon, then turned away, as if the scale were too large to comprehend at once. This *darshan* of Bhagwan, who had shaped this powerful legacy of nature and divinity, was an intimidating sight at close range.

A white-haired woman approached us with a neighborly, inquisitive, but tentative look.

"Excuse me, but may I give this woman a hug?"

"I'll ask her," Didi offered.

Aama fell into a natural embrace. The woman appeared charged, or recharged. Her mouth moved as if she owed us an explanation, but was having trouble finding one that could be expressed concisely. Didi said something to me about an exhilaration hiding and fermenting inside all of us that is spontaneously released at places of grandeur, and that it's contagious. If your lover isn't with you, you have to hug someone. Didi and I hugged, and held each other affectionately. I thought that I would like to return here some time, to climb and explore, or to float the river and dream.

We continued east. In a gas station at Tuba City, Arizona, Aama saw what looked like an Asian—a Tibetan, or maybe even a Gurung, she said.

"These dark-skinned people are the descendants of the original race of people that settled America long before the white people came," I told her. "Many years ago, some of your distant ancestors walked from the Himalayas to America along the northern edge of the great Ganges Ocean. One branch settled on the dry plains, like this grassland you see, and with bows and arrows they hunted a kind of wild oxen that looks like a water buffalo with long hair. Less than two hundred years ago, everywhere we've been since leaving Ann-Tori's house was wilderness, except for the small settlements of your people. They had their own customs and ceremonies and festivals and religion, which were similar in many ways to yours."

At the border of the Navajo Indian Reservation, we passed a roadside Indian souvenir stand and were appealed to by signs that said TURN AROUND—GO BACK and YOU JUST PASSED GOOD INDIANS. The next stand flourished a not entirely authentic teepee. We parked in front, and I told Aama that this was the kind of tent that the American tribe of her people lived in. They could pitch it and collapse it easily, and their horses dragged it around in search of good hunting and food gathering.

Didi got out and perused the line of blankets for sale, then turned to me and mouthed "Tijuana." Aama made a beeline for the teepee. She threw back the door flaps and began talking loudly.

"Do you know my relatives?" she queried in Nepali. "Who are you?" she tried in Gurung. Judging by the angle of her inquiring head, she was talking to someone sitting on the ground. A teenage Navajo boy, appearing to have just awakened, stepped sideways from the teepee. Aama turned to me.

"They've forgotten how to speak our languages. Nani, ask the boy in your language if they know any of our ancestors." I told him of Aama's curiosity, which was obvious. He smiled. "They must have been separated from us for a long time," Aama continued, "so they probably don't know our customs about marriage, either, which means they don't know *who* to marry. In that way they can lose their culture. They probably intermix with you white people, too."

We got back in the car. "Though we may be branches of the same tree," she deduced, "they did whatever they needed to survive here, and in the process became a different people."

". . . That's not all, Aama," I said, wanting to complete our story, our history. "The first white people to arrive in America assumed they had reached India, and they bartered with the American race of your people, whom they called Indians. But they soon realized that this was not India: It was 'Amrita,' the nectar of immortality as you call it, which is how this wild, clean, fertile land must have appeared to them."

At each pause in my narrative Aama provided an "unnh" as punctuation, and her intonation gradually deepened, a signal that she was drifting. *Uuuhnh.* . . . She could follow tributaries of her own stream of consciousness the distance of a full tank of gas, but when others were talking she would nod off if her response was not elicited.

"My Gurung ancestors didn't know how to read or write, otherwise they might have written down when these people split off. Is there someone here who knows more about this?"

There might be. I had been curious about the parallels between the cosmologies of the Tibetans and the Native Americans, especially of the Zuni tribe. Friends in the Southwest urged us to take Aama to meet Grandmother Carolyn Tawangyma, a Hopi elder.

The reddish, lateritic mesa country of the Hopi reservation was littered with boulders. Aama pointed to the horizon ahead of us. "Will we meet up with the clouds over there?"

"We might." On top of Third Mesa, columns of thunder clouds

built into blue-gray spiral volutes. Aama studied a rainbow that was following along beside the car.

"We say that if you go to the end of a rainbow, you'll find a ghost smoking a hookah." We swerved onto a dirt road, and the car jolted and shuddered in the potholes. We had entered a third world within a first.

"*Hoonna, hoonna, hoonna*—'No, no, no,' that's what the car is telling us," she diagnosed. " 'I don't feel good, I don't feel good.' Can't you hear it?" I could, and I worked the steering wheel and gas pedal gently, as if riding an old horse.

Grandmother Carolyn and her daughter and son-in-law had returned home a few moments earlier. Their house emitted the charm of photographs of Native American dwellings of a century earlier, musty and comfortable, shaped around the people in it. To be invited in was to be asked to share a ceremonial robe. Carolyn was placing a pan of biscuits in the oven. She wore a frilled apron.

"It's lucky you caught me," she said, clearly and evenly. "I've been outside all day collecting rabbit brush and gardening. I returned from Geneva only two days ago."

"Geneva, as in Switzerland?" I sounded like an ignorant Anglo.

"Yes, I was there speaking at a peace conference. But whenever I am away, I think of my corn plot and my garden." She spoke as if Geneva were nearby, just as Aama pictured Nepal to be. For both of them, being away from home did not affect the need of their crops for attention.

I told Carolyn of Aama's interest in meeting a Native American and of finding out more about their common ancestry.

"Yes," Carolyn began, "our prophecies foretold that a people will come out of the East to bring an awakening to the West, and if the West understands and accepts their lesson, the entire human family will join hands on a common path. But if we fail, another people will come from where the sun rises in large numbers, and they will fall from the sky like rain. They will have no mercy and will overtake this land in one day; all those who have not entrusted themselves to the Great Spirit will be destroyed: The 'gourd of ashes'—the nuclear bomb—will be dropped."

The Hindus and Buddhists have an uncannily similar prophecy: the cataclysm at the end of the Kali Yug, the black age, the era of destruction. The Kali Yug has already begun.

Carolyn and other Native American leaders had also taken their message of peace to the House of Mica, the United Nations. As she described her efforts there, she showed us the woven winnowing trays and ceremonial baskets she had carefully fashioned from rabbit brush.

"From our ancestors, we have learned that man's prayer is powerful enough to affect the future of life on earth." Carolyn and Aama held the baskets as if they were the physical embodiments of that prayer, textured with permanence, more durable than man's temporal, secular notions. "The Creator teaches us compassion for all life and love for all creation. And the Creator's law cannot be remade, as can the white man's law in what they call democracy."

I translated Carolyn's words for Aama.

"Their religion, their dharma, is similar to ours," Aama said. "This woman is not from our land, yet she can see the different forms of God. What can't Bhagwan do and where can't he go?" She looked at Carolyn and then her daughter. "Just as our hill people don't understand the plains people, your race speaks a different language from the white people. When people can't understand each other, they don't listen and sometimes fear the other. But whether our ancestors are related or not, we are really all one people."

"Yes, Aama, we are all united to creation," Carolyn said. "And now that Tibetan Buddhists have come to visit this country, there has been a closing of the spiritual circle. As awareness of the Tibet issue grows, so docs recognition of the Hopis."

I thought it ironic, and sad, that the Hopis needed Americans' outrage over Chinese-occupied Tibet to attract help to their—or rather, our—situation here.

The Caucasian and Mongoloid races collided not only in North

America, but also in the Himalayas. For centuries, the Brahmins and other Indo-Aryans have coerced the Gurung and other Buddhist and shamanic hill tribes into the mainstream of Hindu culture. The Indo-Aryans are Caucasian; the Gurung, Mongoloid.

Aama became oddly quiet, as if Carolyn were the apparition of a deceased sister. They existed not so much in different cultures as in complementary eras—Aama in the past and present, while Carolyn bridged the past and future. Aama shared Carolyn's concern that "our children are craving the products offered by the doomed culture." The two seemed like grandmothers of a world of adolescents, exalted by their wisdom yet exiled by their age.

Carolyn presented Aama with a kachina doll, for protection and good luck. As we parted, she said, "If you pass through Montana, be sure to look up Chief Austin Two Moons, a brother of the spirit."

We climbed into the car. "When I look at you and Didi next to the split-off branch of my people," Aama said, "you look different. You look so white."

Didi drove, and when we hit smooth pavement at the brink of the mesa a few minutes later, she let gravity bring the car up to seventy miles per hour. We were working our way north, toward Wyoming.

Chapter 13

A cauldron of fire lay dormant within her. "Why did you come here—to simply wander about like sheep and goats? Do you know the deities that are beneath the hot water?"

Well after dark, the Country Squire rolled into the parking lot of a cinder-block motel in Rawlins, Wyoming. Floating in a television-induced trance on a sea of bedding, we fell asleep.

The next day Didi and I traded off driving to Dubois, flooring the wagon. The white noise of the wind and engine heightened the sensation of being mere stationary figures on an immense stage set of sky and sagebrush. Sleep stimuli. Didi napped against a pillow. Aama inclined her head onto the back of the seat and, with half-opened eyes, began to talk softly, narrating.

"When the road is straight like this, it looks as if the car is dividing the road, splitting the world in half, splitting, splitting, and the two halves pass beyond us on either side. We're not moving, but the land on our sides moves . . . this way . . . and . . ." She dozed. For Aama, sleep came only when her tiredness eclipsed her curiosity about life. I was alone with the road.

Delicate, equally spaced cumulus clouds billowed like the fluffy emanations on the margins of Tibetan *thangka* scroll paintings. We were viewing America as an immigrant might, in all its perplexing majesty. We were nomads, Asian-American pilgrims traversing the high, flat dryness of a montane steppe. I envisioned the camels deployed briefly for transport by the U.S. Cavalry over parts of America's West, an undulating and unruly roped-together train of them traversing this ancient vista from left to right, to a destination that at the moment was obscured by the passenger visor.

The visor had begun to sag. The irregular bunches of leaves and flowers and vinelike shoots stashed above it were heading out across the ceiling and now dangled in front of the windscreen. Seedpods barely connected to their stems had dried and opened in the car's warmth, releasing seeds onto our clothing and the upholstery. Aama had rejuvenated the forlorn assortment with matchbooks, chewing gum foil, and pieces of paper, in the manner that she would wad medicinal herbs into paper bulbs and tuck them into the rafters of her porch, between the bamboo laths and the thatch, in case she might need them some day. Rocks and broken shells that hadn't yet found her travel bag sat on the defroster vent at the forward part of the dashboard.

Perhaps, while she slept, I could pull over and throw much of it out. We would need room, anyway, for the new objects she was certain to find.

No, wait. This was something else. It was a formal arrangement of some sort. An altar.

The dashboard and visor had been turned into a shrine to the windscreen—the producer of our visions and the source of our wonder, the medium for viewing the unraveling drama of the landscape and its deities. Something worthy of propitiation. I looked again. Maybe the offerings could be tidied up a bit.

Aama awoke, took the banana that Didi had offered her earlier, and glanced around at the sheeplike clumps of sage and tumbleweed. "This place hasn't heard even the name of rain. When Bhagwan gave humans life, he also gave us land and the means to *continue* to live: soil and water. But this land doesn't have that. People didn't perform the proper rituals or honor the gods, so they were left with this barren, rainless desert. And where do bananas grow around, here, anyway?" she added, taking a bite.

"Well, the surface of the land may have been cursed," I enjoined, "but the earth below us here has been blessed with oil—earth oil— the petrol that we put in the car to make it run."

"I bet it's worth money. And I've heard that it makes good medicine, too. You can rub it on sprains and breaks."

Didi awoke, and she switched on the car radio. Since Seattle we had listened only once, and heard random news clips of an America we weren't sure we had fully returned to. The local news sounded significant but distant, like hearing of turmoil in Africa. She spun the length of the dial before finding a single clear station. The magnetic lilt of a trained but emotional voice urged us to seize the opportunity for salvation.

". . . And NOW, my friends, NOW, and forEVER after, you can REalize . . ."

"—and Namasté to you, too!" Aama blurted, waving the banana peel flippantly at the dashboard, trying to locate where the voice was coming from. "He said something in Gurung, then he said 'Namasté.' I understand what else he's saying, too." We listened.

". . . everlasting salVAtion, everlasting FREEdom, my friends, and to attain this you need only to ACCEPT the Lord Jesus as your savior. . . ."

Aama looked at me quizzically, as if trying to recall my translation of the distorted, excited words of television commercials. "Um, he's saying 'Hurry up and arrive at the place you are going to, in your car, because your food is cooked, your food is ready. . . . GOOD food. . . . FREE food. . . . It's all free!'—that's what he's saying."

"Hey, great," I said. "But did he say where we'd find the place with the free food?"

"No. He forgot to tell us." We broke into a cackle of shared laughter. Not a bad translation of the radio preacher's monologue, Didi commented. He did imply that salvation was nearby, and free, plus he was short on specifics.

"No, wait. . . ." Aama flared her fingers in the direction of the dashboard to clear the air of conversation and better receive the message. The radio jabbered with information about where to send for books, tapes, and salvation accessories.

"Now he's saying that the place with the food is up the road a little bit, on the right . . . or maybe it's on the left. Anyway, he's telling us we're almost there, and to be sure to stop." Didi and I were as hungry as Aama was.

We hitched the car to a parking slot on the main street of Dubois and emptied out onto the town's boardwalk. Shivering from the dismal fall wind and rain, we took a window booth at the Cowboy Café and ordered a lunch of fish burgers, soup, and fries. The aproned waitress dropped off silverware and napkins, three glasses of ice water, and a shallow, woven-plastic basket filled with glassine-wrapped saltine crackers. The air was saturated with the heavy, tantalizing smell of café cooking.

"Do we get to have all of these?" Aama asked, focused on the basket.

"As many as we can eat," Didi told her. Aama looked ready to ask if that meant only the amount we could eat while inside the restaurant, hesitating for fear that Didi might say yes. She tried to open one, replaced it, and tried another. Didi helped. Aama aligned two crackers in her right palm. Anchoring the back of her right hand with the fingers of her left, she used her left thumb as a pestle to grind the crackers into the mortar fashioned from the hollow of her right palm, the way a cowboy prepares snuff. She folded and creased her hand to turn and reposition the broken pieces, then power-thumbed them again. In a spray of spreading fingers and flying crumbs, she launched them into her mouth. Grinning, she looked at us, gumming like an old-timer gnawing venison pulled from a camp-fire.

The food came. Aama counted her French fries and divided them into two piles. She placed one pile on Didi's plate, the other on mine. Too much bread; that went to me. No food could be exchanged after we began, those were the Hindu rules for avoiding contamination, so we should do it carefully now. I was thankful that she had begun to overlook Didi's and my transgression of sharing food.

The napkin that Didi tucked into the top of Aama's blouse stuck out like a starched shirt front. Aama's table manners deteriorated as her hunger level rose. Playing with food seemed to enhance the taste, spicing it with an ingredient of action that children also seem to gain nourishment from. Crumbs gathered on the table and on her clothes and blended with fish sauce into a crust at the corners of her mouth. Her smile testified that this was really why she came to America.

She cleaned her plate, then stretched her mouth partly around the side of her head, flattening the soft leather wrinkles, and patted off the remains of her lunch. Again her eyes settled on the basket of saltines. At the level of the table, she loosened one of the several wraps of her sash and carefully burrowed out a wide pouch. Didi smiled warily. Aama reached toward the plastic basket, purposefully grabbed a handful of saltines, set them on the table in front of her, and began placing them in the waiting nest, lining them up side by side. Her sash bulged as the tray emptied. She folded over the top layer of the sash, tucked it in, looked up furtively at Didi and me, then widened her eyes and pressed her lips outward, proud and im-pressed. Over twenty packages.

"Okay," she said conspiratorially, "let's go."

Didi nodded.

I paid the bill at the counter and walked out ahead into the wind and drizzle to draw the car closer to the café. Didi left a tip on the table, and they slid from the booth. Aama lifted the shawl to her head and twisted it tightly from inside, under her chin. She faced the picture window as she moved, her back to the harried waitress.

The engine was turning over as Aama came around the corner, head down and moving fast, while Didi, laughing, tried to hold her back, afraid she might trip. I leaned across the passenger seat and pushed the door open onto the boardwalk. Hurriedly Aama crawled onto the front seat on hands and knees.

"I've never seen her walk so fast," Didi said. "She was running." Breathing hard, laughing, relieved, Aama nearly collapsed against the front seat, her face flushed with success. At last, she had contributed materially to our journey. She clutched the crinkling treasure beneath her shawl, harboring the saltines as precious fragments of the divine mysteries of our culture.

"Okay, I got them, let's keep moving."

We merged onto Main Street, and the car idled up to a stop sign. A four-wheel-drive sheriff's vehicle carrying two passengers wearing uniforms with shoulder patches and tall monogrammed hats pulled alongside.

"There's the police," I said to Didi, instinctively paranoid. If we were stopped, they would likely find unfastened seat belts, an empty beer bottle or two, and other unforeseen infractions. On a slow day, an out-of-state car would be an easy target for a shake-down.

"What police?" Aama reacted, recognizing the Nepali-English word.

"That car next to us there with the thing on the roof is a police car," I told her, attempting to indicate it covertly with my lips while continuing to look straight ahead.

"Hunh," she said, as if only vaguely curious. She leaned back and from behind my head took another glance at the vehicle. "I wonder where they're going."

"Well, they could be tracking down any number of outlaws," I dead-panned, "but right now they must be out looking for old ladies who take crackers from restaurants." She was prepared for that.

"Okay, if they stop me and try to take me away, uh, you tell them that I'm an old lady, uh, and that I love crackers and biscuits, and that I can't get them in my village. Tell them that when we said this to the people in the restaurant, they laughed and said, 'Take as many as you want—we left them there on your table for you.' . . . Okay?"

Snow and ice were beginning to cover the mountain highways, a different man on the radio announced, but the cruisemobile had already gained momentum for the ascent to Togwotee Pass and the Tetons. Didi urged me either to turn back or to wait for a more favorable advisory. I reminded her that she had grown up driving to the beach, and disregarded her reasonable fear that a loaded suburban wagon could simply slide off the road. The Tetons weren't far, and friends were waiting for us there.

It began to rain and, though we were still well below the pass, a few wet snowflakes appeared. Didi again protested, then folded her arms. I turned on the wipers. Aama followed the wiper blades with her head, laughing, and her hands pitched lightly from side to side, mimicking their motion. Like a child of parents with a problem marriage, she was enacting comic theater, to extract Didi and me from the stew she sensed we were simmering in—striving to restore family harmony and humor, to reunite, to secure a fragile future.

"Whenever it rains, those sticks come out and wipe the windows. Do they somehow know when it's raining and start working by themselves?" she queried. Here was another automatic device, something with a limited but useful intelligence.

"There's a switch. Look." I set my finger on the wiper lever connected to the steering column. "When I pull this branch of this tree downward, the sticks outside stop wiping the windows. When I push it upward, they start wiping again. I have to operate it."

"So that's how that is. Some machines need people in order to run."

We drove on. Aama looked from the steering column to the wipers and back again.

"But you're not running them now."

"Well, I don't have to *continue* to run them. The sticks will keep on wiping until I hit this branch down here again."

"It's probably like the machine inside the giant fish." She scouted the upper part of the windshield for more mechanical wildlife, then fixed on the jiggling water droplets and twisting rivulets, pushed and flattened by wind gusts.

"Some of that water is flowing upward," she voiced quietly, anticipating that this, too, would be explained by one of the countless principles of modern life that contradicted the laws of physics as she knew them.

"The wind blows it upward," I told her.

"Wind doesn't cause water to flow uphill. And there are parts of this window that aren't getting wiped."

From the shoulder of the highway a woman wearing a hard hat signaled us to stop. Stooping to look inside the car, she told us that road crews were blasting up ahead, then directed us to pull over and park behind a long line of vehicles that disappeared around the bend.

"They're exploding bombs to repair the road," I told Aama.

Didi sighed gravely. "There's no sense in hurrying. You're not in college anymore." She said that I could drop her somewhere nearby and she would catch a bus over the pass tomorrow.

I turned off the engine. As we watched water on the windshield flow reluctantly downward, I tried to measure whether her mood would flare into a mutiny. Aama sat stolidly, riding herd on Didi and me as we debated the dangers of driving on snow and ice, and of hurry in general.

" 'Avoid the three evils of yoga,' " I said to Didi, quoting the words of an Indian gentleman I had met on a train platform. " 'Hurry, Worry, and Curry.' " Whenever I was facetious, I could feel a faint pang of regret, knowing that my wisecracks tended to bring more resentment than levity to the situation. Except for the slush on the ground and the rainfall, I would have stepped out to clamber along the adjacent riverbank, to breathe deeply, if only for a moment, and shake off my restlessness and the argument with Didi. I was disappointed that she didn't share my sense of adventure. She was always so cautious and sensible.

" 'In a fight between bulls, the goat gets caught in the middle,' " Aama voiced, reminding us that she was there. "This car has sapped your strength. It has consumed your blood."

The flagwoman motioned for us to proceed. I started the car, and the wipers swung into a lugubrious, robotic rhythm.

"Listen. . . ." Aama cocked her head, attentive. "Now those sticks are saying 'go a-HEAD, go a-HEAD, go a-HEAD.' "

The rain lashed lightly at the windshield as we accelerated. I increased the wiper speed to medium fast. From the corner of my eye I could see Aama nodding, head tilted slightly and mouth puckered, like a retired scout trying to recall semaphore signals or Morse code.

"Umm . . . now they're saying 'I-doop-pa-I-doop-pa-I-doop-pa.' "

"What does that mean?" I asked, presuming she had unearthed another recondite village expression.

"I don't know. Why don't you ask those sticks what they mean when they say that? Ha!" Didi loosened a faint smile, but reserved it for Aama.

A mile beyond the blasting site, the heavy rain grew to a down-pour, sheeting the highway and hammering the roof. I set the wipers to high. The outer tip of one wiper banged against the chrome wind-shield trim with each stroke. Aama interpreted this message clearly.

"Now they're saying 'IT'S-a-BIG-rain-IT'S-a-BIG-rain-IT'S-a-BIG-rain. . . .' " She looked at me and then Didi, who was still smoldering. "But, wait—in Gurung language they are saying something else: 'YOU-two-DON'T-fight-YOU-two-DON'T-fight-YOU-two-DON'T-fight. . . .' "

The guardian deities of the windshield altar had spoken.

"Just as a fire won't burn without stirring the coals, two people who live and work together will inevitably disagree," Aama expounded. At the same time, " 'Couples' fights are like a wheat straw fire, quick to flare up, and quick to expire.' "

"You know, I've been thinking about the words of the Hong Kong psychic," Didi said to me.

Great timing, I thought sarcastically, and said nothing. Just when we were driving into snow was not the right time to get heavy. I shifted into low and turned on the heater—the car's fire, Aama called it—for the first time of the journey. The rain and wet flakes gradually turned to dry snow, which flowed up the windshield and over the roof in a river of endless white confetti. Didi looked out the window. The evergreen trees had receded into gray shadows.

"It comes down thick and just keeps coming, *larrr-ar-ar-ar, larrr-ar-ar-ar-ar,*" Aama said. "Won't it break the window glass? In our village, hail like this would have killed livestock, made fallow our corn fields, and ripped leaves from the trees—leaving them good only for firewood." She looked down at the floorboards and said that she didn't want to watch it anymore.

Didi informed me that there was no traffic coming in the other direction, from over the pass. I continued to follow the vanishing pair of tire tracks set by a car somewhere ahead of us. Then silently our station wagon slid sideways, nearly perpendicular to the road, while keeping its forward momentum. Didi's muscles jerked taut. The car straightened out.

"Were we going to turn off onto another road back there?" Aama asked.

I pulled into the next turnout and shut off the engine, mostly to rest and take a stress-activated leak. The white noise of adrenaline in my head had built to a crescendo.

Didi knew she didn't need to say anything.

Whiteness encircled us. "Let's take a look at the snow," I suggested.

"No, it's just cold, nasty stuff," Aama said. She had seen snow only as dressing on the distant Annapurnas, but a relative of hail was not one to be appreciated.

Didi pulled out a pair of long underwear.

"What are you doing putting these pants on me?" Aama said, startled. "Men wear pants. Where do you climb into them from? How do you urinate?" Aama giggled and squirmed unmanageably as Didi helped her into them.

I scooped up an armful of snow, packed it lightly into a ball, and pegged it at Didi. Aama was surprised to see Didi unfazed by the assault. Didi pegged back.

Aama swung out of the car, picked up a handful of snow near the door, suspiciously, and gauged its weight by jerking her hand up and down. It remained nearly weightless, offering little resistance to motion.

"Abhai. Abhai. Abhai," she uttered softly, the sound of a new thought registering. She then surveyed the countryside. "You can't plant crops here. What can you do with this? It layers the trees like the flaky crust that comes up from the bottom of the pan we cook our millet mush in. Does it leave a white residue everywhere?"

In the car, Aama wiped her hands on a paper towel, then spread it out on the dashboard to dry. At Togowotee Pass, we crossed to the Ganges Ocean side of the Continental Divide and were greeted by blue sky and a panoramic view of the Tetons. Aama was still talking about her encounter with snow, which drifted through the window like insects.

"It's lucky you had these trousers for me to wear."

Despite the freezing temperatures, the roadways of Yellowstone National Park were still crowded with recreational vehicles. We pulled
into a campground at Bridge Bay and crawled into the tent.

After the sun defrosted the tent in the morning, we drove north
through the park. In the Hayden valley, we overlooked a scene of
hundreds of bison grazing in tall prairie grass along the meandering
upper reaches of the Yellowstone River. The distant hills were
fringed with sporadically burned lodgepole pine.

"So this is what happens when man is not around—the animals
increase as they wish, deer walk around like livestock, and the plants
grow tall. It looks planned—as if a hand passed over the scene and
arranged it neatly." In America, the balance of nature did seem to
require the presence of man to protect it from man's presence.

At the Midway Geyser Basin, Aama moved lightly along the
boardwalks, as if her footsteps—even the space displaced by her
body—might disturb the bubbling hot pots. Her voice became rever-
ent.

"The water is going *boolook, boolook*. This is a deity trying to
emerge, but has been unable to get out. What is this place called?"

"Yellowstone."

"*Yatrastan?*" Land of Pilgrimage.

"Uh, yes, like that."

"I thought so. This is obviously a sacred place; these people must
be here to worship."

More than two hundred visitors had gathered on the semicircular
boardwalk skirting Old Faithful. We sat down on the edge and faced
the breastlike limestone fumarole.

Over a period of several minutes, the geyser spurted suggestively,
bubbled, subsided, then spurted again halfheartedly, as if its timing
had been layered with a calculated intrigue to hold the viewers' interest. Finally it reached full height, not with an explosive whoosh and
clamor, but with the gentle swish of a fountain, the amplified sound
of a sheaf of papers sliding off a table. Its cloud of mist drifted

toward the east and dissipated beyond the boardwalk. Aama sat, immersed as if in the geyser itself. She went into prayer.

With a few rebellious spurts, Old Faithful slowly backed into its hole in reverse sequence of its buildup. Before it had receded completely, some of the tourists ran with their children toward the parking lot, hoping to beat the posteruption traffic jam we had been alerted to. Americans' vacations are as short as their attention spans and require continual planning for where to drive to next, and where to find supplies or a phone or more food. The remaining tourists rewound film and rechecked their video equipment, then wandered off. The woman at the visitors' center changed the sign estimating the time of the next eruption.

Aama sat motionless on the edge of the boardwalk, bent forward in prayer to the boiling water, now withdrawn into its underground, sleeping form, though every bit as real and alive as when it presented itself. After several minutes she stood and turned, chanting fervently in Sanskrit. A cauldron of fire lay dormant within her.

"These people, men who look like high-ranking army officers with their red cheeks flushed with blood, and their fat wives and children, they come here and sit and eat their lunch while simply watching this display of God's power and beauty! Why don't I hear anyone saying the name of Bhagwan?

Aama walked with Didi along the evacuated boardwalk. A middle-age couple, the first arrivals for the next eruption, strolled in our direction, rotating their heads about slowly like foreign tourists. They looked at Aama curiously but furtively, not wanting to stare. Aama noticed this, and as they approached she stopped, pulled her hand from Didi's, and stood in front of them. With wide, questioning eyes, she spoke to them in Nepali.

"Why did you come here—to simply wander about like sheep and goats? Do you know the deities that are beneath the hot water? Do you know how or when or why this water came here? Shamans from our village could enter a trance and find the spirits that are causing this to happen; the spirits would enter their bodies and tell them that long ago, such and such mystical events coincided at this place."

The couple froze.

For Aama, this was not an adequate response. "Well, if your ancestors *did* know what was below the ground, this generation shows no indication of that knowledge. It's as if your education and knowledge relieve you from making offerings—and here in a country with such a richness of flowers and fruit to offer, no less. Or did you just come to look at it and then go away?"

The startled pair edged toward the margin of the boardwalk, as if Aama might be performing black magic on them—and as if black magic was something they could believe in.

"May the spirits here bless you, anyway, and all your relatives!" she said loudly, her excited hands amplifying her words. Visibly, she was pushing against a cultural obstruction.

In an echoing silence, we continued along. Aama stepped off the boardwalk and picked up some pebble-size rocks and tucked them into a fold of her sash.

I imagined Hindus managing the phenomena of Yellowstone, allowing the geysers to be swarmed by barefooted, atonement-seeking pilgrims, swamis, ascetics, yogis, saddhus, fakirs, and pundits. And vendors. In the aggregate they might not remove enough geyser water to affect the water table, unless it was aggressively touted throughout the Hindu world. But they might change the shape of the geysers themselves. The pundits would claim, not incorrectly, that the limestone regenerates.

For Aama, Old Faithful and Yellowstone were *prakriti*—primordial nature. As she had said, "Without fail, darkness overtakes the night, and each morning the sun returns. The summer months are always warm. The winter months are always cold." Humans are powerless to change these immutable facts of nature, because the laws of *prakriti* are never broken. Were they to break, were the balance of the universe upset, the Hindus say, the destruction of all life would ensue.

"The seasons demand our timeliness, to plant crops," Aama said, "in the same way that the births of our children sire the necessity for our love. We need two of everything: day and night; cold and hot; rain and sun; men and women; birth and death."

Aama's discourses on *prakriti* also partly answered my recurring question of why we find landscapes and nature beautiful. What is it in our souls that identifies them as such? Literally, *human nature*. Our creature attachment to the physical world resides within our thoughts and genes. This ancestral tie—our dependence upon the physical world—is one expression of primordial nature. The best way to understand this is to experience nature in its undisturbed form, just as meditation is best understood through the practice of sitting.

"The great yogis go into the forest to sit in a blissful state," Aama continued. "But what they learn cannot be communicated directly to us; humans can't impart enlightenment to other humans. Yet there is something that does open us to spiritual understanding, even if we don't study or worship or meditate, and that is *prakriti*, nature, the natural world."

But a Brahmin pundit had told me that *prakriti* refers more directly to the animal instincts of humans and that the negative emotions these generate must be purged through spiritual practice, in order to escape, in our subsequent rebirths, from the animal realm. Only humans can engage in religious practice, and only humans can become enlightened, though an animal rebirth is not unfavorable compared to the numerous Hells and other lower realms, which are characterized by intense agony. Something in the pundit's words reminded me of original sin.

I wondered what I could do with this understanding, or whether I had really gotten it, but I sensed a connection to the Creator's laws that Grandmother Carolyn had spoken of.

The three of us stood watching a new tide of cars ebbing into the parking lot. "Is the earth itself like a deity?" I asked Aama.

"Mother Earth. Sacred places are found on the surface of the earth. Shrines are constructed on a platform of earth. Just as a mother gives milk to a child, the earth provides to us all that we have. Regardless of how much a mother scolds or warns us, the mother's love for the child and the child's love for the mother never dies. We spit on the earth, we piss on her, we crap on her, and we dig in her—in effect insulting her. Yet, without anger, Mother Earth continues to offer forth grains, vegetables, fruit, grass, trees, and animals, for our use. Every kind of person, from the criminal to the highest scholar, is fed by the same earth, without discrimination. *Is that not a deity?"*

"So this hot water is especially sacred," I inferred.

Aama sighed and looked toward the Yellowstone Inn, a small mountain of wooden shingles, then turned back to the fumarole of the geyser. "I don't know, maybe the deities have created this hot water out of anger." This was at least consistent with the native American Indians' view: They avoided the geysers, in which they saw the faces and heard the voices of potentially harmful spirits. "But if Bhagwan was angry," Aama concluded, "why would your country be so wealthy?"

"What should we do at this place, Aama?" Didi asked.

"You should build a shrine here, like the one at Muktinath."

The two sites were similar. Inside one of the temples at Muktinath, located near the crest of the Himalayas, a spring issues from a cleft in the rocks, and an eternal flame of natural gas dances across the surface of the water. Like Old Faithful, Muktinath contains in one place the three primary elements of our universe: earth, water, and fire—the trinity. This is Brahma the Creator, for we are created from the earth, Vishnu the Preserver, for water nurtures and gives life, and Shiva the Destroyer, for fire contains the power to transform the other elements.

Aama became quiet. She was disappointed and weary, and the two feelings fed on each other. No more geysers for her, unless people treated them with respect. At the gift shop she selected a porcelain bell painted with an image of Old Faithful. She would hang it as an offering inside the Shiva temple on the ridge above her village.

Chapter 14

"Somehow these people seem different. They seem like us. They exist and thrive on products created through their own suffering."

The car rolled out of the north entrance of Yatrastan and into Montana. We were feeling breezy and refreshed after a good night's sleep outdoors, though it had taken awhile for Aama to lie down. She had circled around the sleeping bag Didi had rolled out for her, convinced that we had given her a bag without an entrance to it.

Rounding a bend, I indicated for Aama the shoulder of the highway, planted with a thicket of red metal stakes topped with white crosses, placed there by Montanans to mark the spot where people had died in motor vehicle accidents.

"I don't see any bodies," said Aama, craning.

"No, that was where they died some time ago," Didi said. "The bodies were taken elsewhere to be buried or cremated. Maybe two cars ran into each other, or someone fell asleep while driving and went off the road. The white cross is the symbol of our deity—the one you prayed to at the shrine in the big garden with the cave."

"I bet the cars were wrecked, too," Aama added. "What was it in their planetary alignment, I wonder, that guided those people here to die? Their planets failed them . . ."

I pictured celestial, laserlike beams of fate crisscrossing the earth's surface, searching for unsuspecting vehicles to move about like playthings. Crammed amid the other stakes at the unmarked turn, three freshly painted white crosses were positioned together on a single pole, topped by a small wreath. They summoned the image of my frightful experiment of letting Aama hold the steering wheel on a straight stretch of the freeway to Las Vegas. No more tempting the planets on this trip, I decided.

". . . and because they suffered an untimely death, dying before the destined time written on their foreheads, their souls will loiter about, causing trouble."

The Montana air cooled and the grasslands and farm country broadened as we skirted the east slope of the Rockies. The car heaved and settled to the swells of the road. The sky was overcast and quiet.

Forty miles south of Choteau, Didi saw a hand-lettered sign reading VEGETABLES propped beside the road in front of a large spread of farm buildings. I braked to a stop and backed up weaving down the white line. Aama had spotted a cluster of beehives a few miles earlier, and asked whether the farmers collect the honey or just leave it there, and if we could get some. Honey is a *pancha amrit,* one of the five life-giving foods. The car powered up the drive, making a loud crunching sound on the gravel.

The farm structures faced a line of identical, interconnected apartments. Each unit of the rural multiplex was fronted by a square of grass and a single, treelike inverted pyramid clothesline, symmetrically positioned and neatly separated from the next unit's by a narrow cement sidewalk. The grass was either artificial or extremely well cared for.

A bearded man in a white battered cowboy hat was walking between two aluminum utility sheds. He saw our window roll down and veered toward the car. When I asked about the vegetables and if there was any honey, he said they had no honey at the moment, but we could turn left beyond the next cluster of sheds for the vegetables. He wore a black shirt and heavy black trousers. Another two bearded men, dressed identically, walked across a nearby lot.

"Is this farm run by some sort of corporation?" I questioned good-naturedly, wondering whether I might have asked for more information than he wanted to reveal.

"Well, sort of," he answered, with a confidential smile. He spoke with an accent.

Inside a large Quonset hut lined with racks of organic vegetables, the storekeeper told us that they are Hutterites, a sect of Anabaptist collective farmers who had emigrated from Germany and Austria beginning in the late 1800s. There are over twenty-five Hutterite colonies, he said, on the eastern slope of the Montana Rockies. This was the Milford Colony.

The storekeeper, an elder of the colony, went on to explain that they are Mennonites of Tyrolean descent, whereas the Amish are Mennonites of Dutch descent. Oriented to the New Testament, Hutterites view their community as a Noah's Ark safely anchored in a sea of confusion and disarray. They are pacifists and conscientious objectors; during the Vietnam war, boys from the colony were allowed to defer military service by working in the national parks.

I refrained from telling the elder that men of Aama's tribe were renowned for their mercenary service with the Gurkhas—among the most fearless infantry soldiers of modern times.

Women wearing ankle-length tablecloth-print dresses buttoned to the neck walked from shelf to shelf in a stiff but brisk turn-of-the-century gait. Polka dot scarves covered their heads, tightly bound like wimples under their chins. Young boys darted about in acrylic-brimmed stovepipe hats, balanced neatly on their heads as if by magic. One of them pushed a child's wheelbarrow loaded with potatoes.

When they saw Aama, they stopped what they were doing. The teenage girls fell into a semicircle around her, clutching each other. They may have seen an infrequent black person or foreigner, but Aama was new. They stared at her with the concentrated awe of the Tibetan children who stared at me when I had entered their remote valley, the first foreigner they had seen.

"Where is she from?" one asked.

"From Nepal. The Himalayas, north of India."

"Where's that?"

"A long way away, on the other side of the earth," I answered, suddenly feeling as if I were somewhere back in time before Nepal or Asia were widely known by the Western world to exist. Aama could see that the Hutterites were different from the Americans she'd met so far. She looked prepared to offer advice and tell stories of a world she had, by now, traveled more than they.

"Do you drive to Nepal, or take a plane?" the girls asked.

"Plane. It's where Mt. Everest is."

Trying to reckon where each other had come from and where they fit in, Aama and the Hutterites clearly sensed that they were scions of the same rural, farming rootstock—sowed in the same furrow, fertilized with religion and community values. The Milford Colony Hutterites did not speak English as well as Aama spoke her second language, Nepali. Like most Gurung, and Amish, the Hutterites seldom traveled farther afield than a neighboring settlement.

Outsiders are not usually taken on tour, but the young girls were eager to show Aama their communal workplace. Taking her hand, they led us through a white clapboard dining hall to the kitchen, which glistened with immaculate countertops and large stainless steel and enamel appliances, some of them antique, some modern. Aama systematically perused the oversized pots that lined the walls like ornaments. One girl brought her a freshly baked bread roll and handed it to her as if it might explode. Aama took it and appraised it with interest as fifteen children looked on, inspecting and turning the roll along with her. They saw that Aama was as curious about their daily artifacts as they were about her appearance and jewelry. She was an outsider who was an insider.

"Would she like some freshly squeezed grape juice?" one girl ventured, galvanizing three others into a scramble to find some. They returned with a cup. Aama poured it down, her thirsty glugs audible over a roomful of children eager to view the consequence. She smacked her moistened lips and exhaled loudly, smiling.

Careful not to crowd her, they shepherded her to the school-room, after hours, to show off the rows of wrought-iron frame desks with inkwells. Clear, mullioned windows cast a crosshatch pattern on the spitshine-polished hardwood floor. The children took her to the cobbler's workshop and the laundry. Aama was beholding a cultural paradise.

"Even the littlest children look splendid, all lined up, their hair pulled back tightly beneath their hats and scarves. They study and they work, both, and they seem to respect each other. They all live together here with their relatives—they don't need to drive around in cars to find them, or send messages to them on that radio or telephone you talk into."

"The men let their beards grow only after they marry," I told Aama, repeating what the elder had told me. "And the parents select marriage partners, too, just as in Nepal."

Aama fished a Nepalese rupee coin from her drawstring pouch. She handed it to the youngest child in the group, the neatly outfitted toy soldier she had singled out earlier as best behaved. Beaming, he proudly inspected it, then pocketed it.

With a loaf of bread and bags of onions and potatoes, we coasted out the driveway. Aama gnawed on a generous mouthful of bread torn from the loaf, which was moored under her arm like a shoat.

"When we first arrived here, I didn't see anyone. They must have run in and put on those clean costumes when they saw us coming. I can tell that money is not as meaningful for them as it is for you white people. Their work is a kind of worship."

"But they, too, are white people," I demurred.

"Somehow they seem different. They remind me of the Gurung. They exist and thrive on products created through their own suffering."

In Whitefish, we stayed with friends Doug and Karen and their two children. Sunday afternoon, we piled into their van for an outing to Glacier National Park. Aama sat in the back between Teal and Rusty, ages seven and four. As we climbed the Going-to-the-Sun Highway, Aama braided the yarn hair of a vinyl doll, pulling the hair back tightly and then concealing it with her hand to simulate the Hutterite girls. We sang songs, detoured for food, had car trouble, and turned back. It had begun raining, anyway. Near the town of Hungry Horse the kids talked us into stopping at the House of Mystery, situated within "Montana's Only Vortex," which coincidentally had been discovered next to heavily touristed Route 2. Aama appeared immune to the slight dizziness that the rest of us felt inside the Vortex's tilted house. She had never been acculturated to rectangles and level buildings—a prerequisite to being deceived by optical illusions that play with these angles.

The children stamped their shoes boisterously on the doormat as Karen opened the door and flipped on the living room light. Aama looked in, placed her feet together, and pointed her hands prayer-fashion toward the fixture. This was the first light of the evening, the initial offering, a fragment of the energy and brilliance of the gods Parameswor and Agni.

I responded as Aama did when I was with her, having learned

and retained her reaction to the evening's first lamp. But I didn't react that way when she was not nearby. Clearly, immigrants could lose the traditions and nuances of their culture within one generation when not immersed in them, when not reinforced by family and friends. The essence of their customs might survive another generation before succumbing to new interpretations, the written record, or apocryphal accounts. For many educated Asians, including some of the youth of Aama's village, devotion had already become mechanical, enacted more out of deference to family and ancestors than out of inspired visions or reverence for the spiritual realm.

One educated young Gurung described to me the cultural outmigration he made from his village and his return several years later.

"When I was young, I used to look down upon the culture and artifacts of village life, and I wanted desperately to participate in the modern ways of those flocking to the cities. So I joined them. But one day when I was in the United States on scholarship, I went to a nursing home and saw all these old people scattered about watching television and sitting alone, blank, vacant, as if they were waiting for something. Where were their relatives and families? Where was the community and the customs they would need to carry them through their final days? That experience, that single impression changed me. Now I look forward to being with my relatives and the people of my village—when they come to Kathmandu, I am proud to take them to a restaurant, in their traditional dress, and we speak in Gurung. I am going to retire in my village, and bring development projects and do conservation work with the people. The village was where my roots were formed."

Doug and I hopped on their kids' bikes and pedaled off to pick up some take-out Montana Chinese cuisine, something Asian for Aama and a simple alternative to heavy American food for the rest of us. When we returned, Didi and Karen were working in the kitchen. Aama sat alone in the living room, staring at the television—America's latest victim of TV addiction. She didn't acknowledge us. I set down the warm rucksack, then noticed that tears had formed at the corners of her eyes. More tears had filled the loose spaces between her lower eyelids and her eyeballs, creating small reservoirs about to overflow. The muscles of her face revealed a clenched jaw. Homesickness, maybe.

I sat down next to her, my arm behind her on the couch, and asked what had happened. She hesitated, as if withholding bad news. I waited. Again, about to speak, she wavered, then resumed her idle stare at the television screen, flickering with a two-dimensional program.

"You know what happened, and you've been hiding the news from me," she said abruptly.

"No, I don't. What is it?"

"In the village. You know what happened there to Sun Maya. You know that she died."

"What?"

"My daughter, Sun Maya, died," she pronounced again, louder, indignantly, as if it were self-evident. I was stunned.

"I don't know anything about it. How could *you* know about it?" I said. Defensive, trying to comprehend, I looked from Aama to the television, hoping along with her that it might speak to us and extend some guidance. She must have dreamed this during the brief time she had napped. I was tempted to take her vision lightly, but resisted, knowing that it would not dissolve through mere logic. Aama was both decisive and stubborn. When people are upset, I reminded myself, they need to indulge in and accept their fears before gaining sufficient confidence to gradually face them.

"You and Didi heard a few days ago, when we were traveling," she continued. "You received a letter from the village and didn't tell me. Whenever I asked, you said that no letters had come, but I saw you reading a letter with Nepali characters."

Didi overheard us from the doorway. Drawn by Aama's tears and her distant, lonely voice, she came in and sat down.

"Aama, of course Sun Maya is still alive." She comforted her assertively. "Would it be right for your own daughter to die before

you? Where do these ideas come from?" Didi's self-assurance braced
me from slipping further into Aama's reverie.

"You say that so easily, but how do you know?" Aama reacted.
"My right eyelid has been twitching. That confirms that something
bad happened in the village. And I've been having more hiccoughs,
too, which come when someone is thinking about you. I hardly ever
get them." Drinking box juice in a moving car might have something
to do with that, I surmised.

I had written three letters to her relatives, but received no reply,
as partly expected. They may have been short of rupees when they
arrived at the post office a half-hour walk from the village, not anticipating that stamps for a letter to America cost part of a day's wages.
Nothing in the village happens on time, anyway, especially mail delivery and loan repayment. Aama may have seen my stunted handwriting on a letter to be sent *to* the village. She found my curiosity
disingenuous.

On the other hand, I believed she could have sensed this news,
somehow, if in fact it had occurred. Eighteen years earlier I had
experienced a premonition of my own mother's unexpected death.
Within an hour of the time she died, a vivid telepathic dispatch, a
message sent by misaligned planets, perhaps, told me that something
was not right. I was a sophomore in college, bicycling from the bo-
tanical museum to my room in a small cooperative house. One look
at the building's barren visage drenched me in a wave of discomfort,
of disavowal that I lived there. As if by reflex, I bypassed my room
and pedaled on, rolling across town, caroming down back streets
and through commercial districts and suburbs I had never before
seen. Near sunset I tired, dismounted, and chained the bicycle to a
signpost, and began walking, wandering, peering at the houses I
knew must be inhabited but that looked empty and impersonal, even
ominous. When I returned to the rooming house, late, my rational
mind was doing all it could to override an intuition that a message to
call home awaited me. A message did await. My mother had died.
She had passed away before allowing me to say good-bye, to ask her

forgiveness, to be exonerated for my impetuous, selfish youth. There
was no chance to reason or explain, nor even just to talk.

As Aama spoke of Sun Maya, I could feel the presence of my
own mother's wandering, tormented soul. She had died at a young
age and in apparent good health, and she appeared before me now
with a disturbed, anxious look. Aama and the Gurung had told me:
The soul of the victim of an untimely death continues to cause trouble for the living, until shamans can safely guide the wandering spirit
to the resting place of human souls. The dead, especially those who
had not prepared for death, try desperately to cling to the Land of
the Living and to those who remain there.

I gulped, then asked Aama what she wanted to do. Now. Here.
She said that she didn't want to return to Nepal, not to more crying,
not to the firsthand version of this bad news.

Eh, Bhagwan. She sighed. "What an unfavorable day to befall a
mother, the day she is dressed and sent off from the village by her
only daughter, not aware that she is seeing her for the last time. I
didn't call a priest to check the alignment of the planets on the day I
left—I was in a hurry and afraid of what he might say. At my age,
everything becomes inauspicious. But that was a day of ill fortune, I
now realize, not a day to depart on a journey. Sun Maya was getting
thinner. Before I left, I wanted to remind her to not worry about me,
to not hesitate to take on debt in my name to repair the roof, to have
her daughters take care of my livestock, and, most important, to hire
someone to do the work she insists on doing herself."

The outlines of her mouth crumpled and she cried softly. Didi
said that watching Aama made her want to cry, too, and she looked
away.

"Sun Maya has fallen, I'm convinced. Just as Shiva is Shiva and a
burning lamp is a burning lamp, I know what I know. When I have a
sense about something, it often comes true even if it hasn't yet happened."

Could Aama's conviction induce events? I concluded not, in this
case. Intuition can be a powerful and reliable sense, but is not usually

an autonomous force. Aama had wished to see a Gurkha recruit in America, and against all logic there he was, on the sidewalk outside an optometrist's office. Didi and I couldn't help but believe that her faith had actuated his appearance.

Aama said that she wasn't hungry, but she readily accepted a glass of water. Her fatigue made her appear older, and slow. As we led her to Doug and Karen's guest bedroom, she apologized for crying and told us not to go to any trouble for her. We tucked her in and she curled up on one side, then spoke in a monotone about Sun Maya, and herself. It made her lonely to have so few friends her age alive, she said, and sad to know that her good fortune hadn't been equally apportioned to others. Aama cherished life's visceral radiance and indelible sacredness, yet she clung to a bitterness at the cards that fate had dealt her and her relatives. Now, through her living image of a deceased Sun Maya, she was tasting the imminence of her own passing, which heightened the sanctity and impermanence of all she saw. Much had come and gone, not all of it favorable, not all of it adverse, and more would come, but before long it would all be gone.

Her mouth moved slowly as her eyes traced the spiral stitching of the quilt. She sleepily reviewed her memories and loneliness, like a biographer wistfully and in detail recounting a tragic life. Gradually she detached herself, transferring her anger and blame to her son-in-law, which I took to be a good sign.

". . . My roof leaks badly, though my scoundrel son-in-law could repair it in one day if he didn't drink continuously. When Sun Maya was alive he had to respect his mother-in-law, but now he can say to me whatever he wants. He may even try to blame me. And when she was ill and not producing children, the scoundrel said that he was planning to take a new, younger wife. Certainly, I told him, a new wife might agree to live with him—if he were a decent man. Seven months ago he borrowed the silver bracelets I had stored in my trunk and put them up as collateral for a loan. I'll never see those again. Then he tried to get me to sell my house, but he didn't mention where he would put me—probably in the loft above his live-stock. Just as birds look for a roost at dusk, the sun is setting on my life and I need a place to rest. One day out of the blue, a relative asked me why I was trying to sell my house. I looked straight at him and said, 'I'm going to die in this house.' I said nothing more, be-cause I don't like to start arguments, but I was furious. It was my son-in-law, I know. None is as grateful as a dog nor as ungrateful as a son-in-law. He drinks alcohol instead of tea in the morning, and has started chasing after girls his daughters' ages. Men and boys are all of the same mind: No matter where they go, they patrol each side of the path for girls. As we say, 'If you put a dog's tail in a bamboo tube for twelve years, it still won't be straight. . . .' "

Aama's anger had stanched the flow of tears, but two large gem-like drops balanced near the tops of her cheeks, connected to her eyes by moist, parallel tracks.

Teal and Rusty padded into the room to say good night to Aama. She brightened when she saw them, with a look that conveyed *Here rests our hope and our future: They are us.* Teal said that she wanted to take Aama to her school tomorrow. Aama gently passed one hand through Teal's hair. "I would like to hear you count and read," she whispered hoarsely. "Nani," she said to me, "we will need to bring candy for each of the students."

Doug and Karen told me that, months later, parents of children in Teal's class were still phoning the school to find out more about Aama, because their children wouldn't stop talking about her.

❖

The clear Rocky Mountain morning anointed the day with a provi-dential beauty, and we were eager to drive into it. Beneath the carpet of American scenes and events, Aama sensed that there was some-thing yet to be discovered. She wanted to keep moving, as she and her cousin had years ago on their Himalayan pilgrimage, walking morning until evening, restless to see and experience and worship. We pulled out and headed eastbound on Interstate 90.

Our friends Susan and David had invited us to the state of Maine. We had enough time to make it. Our tickets were booked to Kathmandu for a date on the Nepalese calendar that would allow Aama to reach the village before the annual fall Dasain festival, more than two weeks away. Aama thought we might have missed it. She reminded me that our calendar—which the army pensioners use—is different from theirs by fifteen days, so we should add two weeks to the length of time we've been here.

As if taking a daily medicine, Aama painstakingly removed a single Life Saver from its roll, replaced the foil wrapper, then tucked the roll deep within the folds of her waistband.

"Maybe my relatives didn't really write you about Sun Maya, after all," she said unceremoniously. Thankfully, she appeared to have forgotten last night's vision of her daughter. ". . . Because they knew that I wouldn't make it to the village in time for her cremation. They would have been busy sending word to our other relatives. By now her funeral is over and they've all dispersed."

Her face tightened. "Anyway, you didn't tell me which month Sun Maya died in," she added, attempting to steer us into revealing more.

Didi and I said nothing.

"I had a feeling, somehow, that she might die while I was away. When I think of her, I'm using what little strength I have to forge my will like the rocks of the earth. How, when the time comes, will I be able to speak with my relatives, and they with me, without tears falling? Even now, tears are flowing from my tears." She looked at Didi. " 'We mothers carry children ten months, and we nurse them from the ten spouts.' " Nepalese women count ten months of gestation and five small holes on each nipple that milk issues from.

Aama stared at the monotonous eastern Montana highway. Her daughter's life paralleled her own, she believed, and the memory of Sun Maya's youth passed forlornly before her eyes like a eulogy. "She was born a week before the great earthquake of thirty-four, the one that broke off the top of the minaret in Kathmandu and turned many of our houses to rubble. I had gone inside to find some oil to massage her with, and then it hit. The earth and the house shook horribly. I fled to the porch and heard someone shouting to everyone to get away from their houses. Sun Maya's bamboo cradle was swinging on its own beneath the eave where it was suspended; I quickly lifted her out and ran onto the terrace. Now, as I think of her, I can feel that earthquake all over again."

Didi casually reached behind us for the food bag, but Aama caught her. "I know what you're trying to do," Aama growled, "you're trying to shut me up. I eat when it's time to eat and laugh when it's time to laugh—but I don't always sleep when it's time to sleep. My thoughts keep me awake."

"You've never slept much," I pointed out.

"As my health and strength and memory fail, worry comes to take their place. Inside, I'm thinking of the difficulty of life in our village. 'The old woman has twelve sons and a daughter—yet do they go for her to fetch water?' That's what the wife of the village's ex-colonel keeps saying."

In a lilting, singsong monotone, she presented a distress to each of the details on the dashboard, a knob and gauge at a time.

"Aama, we're getting tired of hearing you complain." Didi's forwardness startled me. I was about to disclaim her statement, but she had vented my thoughts, as well. Being called "Nani"—little one—annoyed me, which I wanted to tell Aama, but I couldn't think of another suitable kinship term.

"Uhnn . . ." Aama registered vaguely. She set aside her monologue and appealed to Didi directly. "How can you experience someone else's suffering? You say that you feel sympathy for me when I cry, but can you see inside my soul?

> " 'The basil plant lies far below us,
> The distant ridge looms higher.
> When will we know happiness?
> Just as we expire.' "

While her slow enunciation of "expire" trailed off, Aama turned and shifted her attention to me. "Nani, I haven't told you this, but I overheard you talking with your friends some time ago. One of them was Doctor Sah'b." She paused to let me remember, then signaled that one of her confidentialities was coming next. "From the way you speak and gesture, I can sometimes pick out what you're saying to each other." She waited again, then continued. "You were talking about 'dead body'—what to do with my body if I were to die here, whether to use firewood to cremate me or to bury me in the earth, details like that. And that's when Doctor Sah'b said, 'Feed her good, healthy food, otherwise she could go any minute'—ha! Am I right?"

Partly right, I thought. I tried not to smile.

"I bet Doctor Sah'b might know *when* I'm going to go, too; you've said that doctors in Amrita can transplant hearts and make barren women fertile. If I were to die in Amrita, then that will be why I came here. But what a waste to have brought me all this way. 'We were just showing her around and *now* look what happened to her' is what you'll say. People at home would at least figure that I was lucky to die near my dharma son." Aama's face had brightened. Clearly, the topic of her own mortality was more comforting than dwelling on the death of her daughter.

"My husband's youngest brother is over eighty, and already he's pissing and crapping in his bed. If we go in order, I'll go first." Her eyes looked ahead expectantly as if she were next in line for an arcade amusement. With a laughing sound, she released from her stomach a punctuating "hunh."

"Assuming that I die in the village, my body will be taken to the cremation ridge—at either sunrise or sunset. My eldest nephew will circumambulate my pyre three times, place a cotton wick soaked in mustard oil in my mouth, then light it." She smiled as she spoke, as if she had already witnessed it. "According to our astrology, it is most auspicious to die on the full moon. Evil spirits tend not to stir around the cremation ground in the moonlight. . . ."

I was afraid of the cremation site, if only because the villagers were. Gurung from several villages distant knew me as the white foreigner who slept there, though I had actually spent a single night on the next ridge crest over, a quarter of a mile away. Shortly after moving into Aama's loft, I wanted to escape the crowing and strutting of roosters and the fidgeting water buffalo below me, to sleep under the stars and be awakened by sunrise on the Annapurnas. Aama had alerted me to the cremation site, so I avoided it. The day afterward, villagers regarded me with both awe and concern that I had dared the spirits that only the bravest of lamas and shamans would challenge. I admitted only to Aama that I hadn't slept well, but didn't reveal even to her what had really bothered me: At times throughout the night, my heart palpitated uncontrollably.

My mother had died in her sleep of a heart fibrillation.

". . . And because my husband and I never had a son, a small piece of my property must go to the nephew who performs my death ceremonies. My husband's eldest brother's son will also receive some land. Sun Maya should get some, though my husband's brothers will claim that she'll receive land from her husband's side. . . ." She looked over at me. "Can I leave some land for you, Nani?"

"Aama, a fraction of your few narrow strips of steep, unirrigated terrace, once sharecropped, would yield how much? Maybe a gallon of corn per year? I'm grateful for your thought, but the Kingdom of Nepal doesn't allow foreigners to own land. Anyway, I wouldn't want to live in the village if you weren't there."

"Oh, and I forgot—some of my land will have to be sold to pay for my *arghaun*." More than the cremation ceremonies, the three-day *arghaun* funerary rite is crucial for the proper transmigration of the soul of the deceased to the resting place of human souls. This final ritual may be held as much as a year after death, depending on the alignment of the planets and when enough money has been set aside. "I'm not wealthy, you know," she said, as if I didn't. "So maybe they won't be able to afford an *arghaun* for me at all."

"I'll take care of your *arghaun*, Aama." I caught myself wanting her to know that I would help. At the same time, I was unsure how this offer might imbalance other relatives' obligations. The relatives would probably approach me, anyway.

"I'm already too much in debt to you, Nani. In which new incarnation would I be able to repay you? It's wrong to amass debt in the final days of one's life. Look at the Brahmins—they take precautions to die only while lying on the open ground. If they were on a bed, they would have to carry that bed with them on their shoulders into the next life."

"Well, what should I do?" I said.

"When one's mother dies, you should forgo salt and milk for thirteen days. Also, you can splash some water toward the south as you say my name. You need do nothing more."

Chapter 15

She held up the trampled ears of corn and shook them at Harv. "The grains here are crying—they cry when they are cast aside, telling us to go hungry."

We cruise-controlled Highway 212 through Busby, Montana, without knowing it. Lewis and Clark wouldn't have either, I figured. The landscape was alive with a Plains Indian spirit, pastoral yet struggling. I was imagining the movements and daily lives of the Indians, when Didi spotted a tepee in the drainage of what the map called Rosebud Creek. This one looked authentic; smoke curled from its ear flaps. Didi circled the covered station wagon around and we followed a dirt path to the edge of the stream.

A white man with long braided hair stepped from the oval door and introduced himself as "Yukon." He wore buckskins and rawhide bracelets, and had lived in the tepee, he claimed believably, over the past two eastern Montana winters. He made traditional Indian crafts in the manner taught to him by a Northern Cheyenne elder.

"He doesn't look like someone from the split-off branch of our people," Aama said. "He looks like you."

"I don't think so," I said, though I did see a resemblance. "This man prefers the life of the American branch of your people to our race's way of life—just as I came to your village to live like the Gurung."

"Have you met Chief Two Moons?" Yukon asked. The name rang a bell. "Two Moons lives in the house on the bench there, above the crick. He's driving the pickup that's pulling up to the house right now."

A broad-faced Indian with weathered features eased out of his truck and squinted over at Aama as if she were a long-lost relative, returned to visit the tribe but gone weird on him, altered by time into a cultural subspecies. I explained who we were.

"You must come in." Compulsory Asian hospitality had made it over the land bridge intact. Austin Two Moons settled into his well-worn armchair. "The Creator played a part in bringing you here to visit. I'm happy for you."

"Aama has said, too, that it was her Creator, her deities, who delivered her to America," I offered.

"Well, they certainly introduced us." His wife, Hilda, said that he was the great-grandson of the Northern Cheyenne chief who presided at the battle of the Little Bighorn. I told them that we had just seen the battlefield site.

"There's been a lot of misinterpretation," Two Moons said compellingly, his voice raising in volume. "It was Custer who was attacking, not the Indians. All those books over there at the National Monument center give the wrong damn story." He spoke in articulated, whittled tones, a reggae sound, English words spoken through his tribal language.

"Whether you are rich, poor, educated, uneducated—we all share the same earth, for we are the same people," Two Moons continued. "I want to see unity for all peoples, and that can happen if we pray together."

"When we cut our flesh, the same blood flows," Aama concurred. "People living in Tibet are called Tibetans and people living in Nepal are called Nepalese. And during the time of our ancestors, people took different religions and split into different races and castes, but these are only names. Each tribe feels it is better than the others, but how can humans say this about themselves when it is not humans who created life? Brahma created life."

When I finished translating, Aama spoke to me privately. "What about their daughters? Will they marry with your people? That's what some Gurung want to do nowadays, too." She looked inquisitively about the small house, at the carpeting, the television, and the modest kitchen. "They seem to be doing pretty well. More of our people should have come over that bridge you talked about, to settle here."

Didi had been browsing through a photo album on the table next to the couch. She slid it onto my lap and pointed to a picture of Two Moons sitting with Grandmother Carolyn Tawangyma. Of course. He was the Montana elder Carolyn had suggested we seek out. We had no address or until now even a memory for him, yet had encountered him minutes before driving off the lower right corner of the Montana map.

Hilda presented Aama with a ceremonial shawl and a protective medallion necklace. "This is our way of giving thanks in this world," she said. "By giving a gift to another, we are giving thanks to the Creator."

Aama stopped me in the open doorway of the car. "This branch of our people views the world as we do. Nani, did your white ances-

tors know anything about religion or the origin of the universe? I'm
wondering, because I notice that you've become interested in our
religion. What's wrong with your own?"

We angled south to catch the freeway and put on some miles across
the Midwest. An amber square of sunset reflected from the wing
mirror onto Didi's face, then traversed toward Aama. *Eh, Bhagwan.*
Aama lifted her hands and prayed to the wing mirror. Bhagwan is
everywhere.

I squeaked some farts that sounded like a distant volley of can-
non fire.

"Okay, no more junk food for us," Didi said. She hadn't grown
used to the American custom of never stopping for a square meal
when on the road.

Aama said, "You're just like the frogs that start croaking at sunset, *twaarnt, twaarnt.* You then lean over and go *pu-tut-tut-tut-tut,
phoossa.* What can I do? Both of you, one on each side of me, farting
as if I weren't here. No awkwardness, no embarrassment, and no
control. When I was younger, I wouldn't think of farting in front of
men, even my husband, but especially not in front of my mother-in-
law. Here you defile each other by stepping over each other's legs, so
I guess farting isn't a big thing."

Several minutes passed. "Do you smell a fart?" Aama asked.

"No, why?"

"I was just wondering if you might have."

After night fell, we stopped to gas up in Wall, South Dakota,
then rejoined the freeway. I locked the speed on seventy as Aama
talked about the village. Like an old phonograph, the stories transported us into the past, her hands moving as if her memory was
stored in them. Describing a small box, her fingers curved around its
imaginary edges as she set it down carefully. We could see the package, its contents, the shelf in the village where she was placing it, and
feel its weight.

She turned to me in the midst of a story. "Okay, what are we waiting for? Let's go."

" 'Let's go'? Let's go where?"

"Wherever we're going to tonight."

"We *are* going. Did you think we were standing still?" The rhythmic passage of roadside reflectors and the headlights of an occasional west-bound truck were the only signs of motion. A large bug was caught immobilized in the headlights, then liquefied on the windshield. I opened the driver's door a crack. Rushing air invaded our quiet environment.

"*Achhaa*. It's windy out there. How long have we been moving?"

"Over an hour."

"Haven't you seen the vehicles going in the other direction?" I said.

"I thought they were moving while we were just sitting here."

We drove all night through the warm loneliness of the Midwest, and in the morning arrived outside Chicago at a farm managed by Harvey, a friend. Much of the year's corn crop was being plowed under, due to toxic levels of nitrogen. Aama looked out the window and muttered an occasional, blunt "Unh," one farmer's reaction to another farmer's handiwork.

When we stopped at the edge of the harvest, Aama slipped out and waded into the standing corn; the kernels had dried sufficiently, and there was work to be done. She began breaking off ears. Both arms moved independently, swimming to the ears that her eyes guided her to, and she threw the unshucked ears behind her without looking. They landed in a compact pile.

She carried armloads of ears to the harvested margin of the field, then squatted amid them and began shucking with sharp, jerking motions.

She paused. Odd ears of corn lay scattered about the open field, ears the harvester had missed. Many had been trampled. She picked up a soil-coated ear, then another, each one seeming to mock the care with which the Gurung gathered their crops. Grain was their sustenance, one step removed from the blood flowing in their veins. She held up the neglected ears and shook them at Harv.

"The grains here are crying—they cry when they are cast aside, telling us to go hungry. We must forgo eating a quantity of grain equivalent to what we waste."

We threw the ears Aama had shucked into the back of the pickup, then drove beside the tractor. At the barn, Harv backed the tractor around and delivered a trailer of feed grain to a line of bellowing cattle.

"Your cows are fat from eating grain, and your people are fat from eating your fat cows," Aama deduced. "Can't you take this corn to a mill and at least have it ground into a coarse flour? Think of the food it would produce, for people. Now, after all this, in the evening you'll go to the store, buy a different food, take it home, cook it, chew it, swallow it, and then go to sleep."

I could tell that we were back in the land of cities. The gas pump at a large mini-mart didn't work. I first had to pay for it by placing money in a metal drawer beneath a heavy pane of glass. We drove through Chicago, continuing east.

"Where's that smoke coming from?" Aama stopped and squinted, afraid she might not get a chance to study it further. Mist roiled upward from the barely visible rim of Niagara Falls.

"That's water vapor, like fog," Didi told her.

A handrail and a line of tourists guided us toward a loading dock. To negotiate the steep stairs, Aama grabbed the rail and turned nearly backward to downclimb the way she does from the boles of her larger fodder trees. We boarded the antique passenger vessel, *Maid of the Mist,* and ascended the wide metal companionway to the top deck. The boat rocked torpidly.

"We need to wear this?" Aama questioned as Didi helped her disappear into the rubber folds of a raincoat. She turned her head to speak again, but the rain hood remained stationary, facing forward like a suit of armor several times too large. Laughing into the hood, she tried to pull it back with her hand, which was also buried in the raincoat. "So how can that water over there get us wet way over here?"

The *Maid of the Mist* drifted from the float, and the background resonance of the falls grew into a drum roll of white sound. We entered an encircling fortress of noise and tumultuous aerated water. Aama became silent. "A moment ago the water was in the river below us. Now, like deities wrestling, it's alongside us, above us, ready to come down on top of us—swirling, steaming, boiling water everywhere. Aah! We're being cooked by the gods, and they're stirring the pot! The flash floods that race down the gullies near our village are nothing compared to this. It's like a dream sent from the afterworld. The gods are here, too, like at the boiling and shooting water place, Yatrastan. . . ."

The boat rose and crested on the foaming swells at the foot of the falls, heeled to the side and retreated, then rose upon them again. Aama leaned over the rail of the top deck like a mortal trying to press her head against the gates of heaven. In an excited little-girl voice she shouted to Didi, who had corraled her into a protective hug against the rail, to open a button of her raincoat. Aama's cold fingers faltered as she retrieved her money pouch and pulled from it a handful of money: some modern Nepalese aluminum coins, an old copper paisa coin, and quarters from the Las Vegas slots. Shivering from the wetness—a short, eccentric crone drowning in her raincoat—Aama flung the coins with a smart backhand into the deity-blessed mist. She then put her forehead to the rail in a brief rejoicing prayer. We could feel a deliverance, as if a delinquent loan had been repaid.

"Not a single person has their hands together!" she exclaimed, trying to alert the other passengers to this occasion for prayer. "But I did hear a man on that radio say "Namasté"—he must have been welcoming us to this sacred place." Over the public address, a crew member had repeated an announcement: *"No smoking* in the passenger cabin."

"If this place, and Yatrastan, have never been praised and propitiated, will your children and grandchildren ever learn to honor and respect them?

" *'For those who can see, it is sandalwood,*
  For those who cannot, merely wood;
  For those who can grasp them, these words are profound,
  To those who cannot: Beware of loose ground!' "

Our suburban wagon left the New York tollway and swung north toward the Adirondacks. The hardwoods on the hillside above us vaunted their early fall colors like fireworks.

Aama extended a hand toward the passenger window, turned her wrist slowly, and drew her gnarled fingers in to touch her thumb, as if grasping. Didi and I looked at her curiously.

"Those fruits look so good and so ripe that I want to reach out and pick them. They must be apples, the kind that make a juicy, crunching, saliva-producing noise, *kwom, kwom,* when people with teeth bite into them." Her mouth rounded into an enveloping expression.

"Those aren't fruit, Aama, they're leaves. Old summer leaves turn that color when it freezes at night, and then they fall off."

Breezing by the landing of a logging operation, Didi braked to a stop so Aama could study the movement of a grapple loader. The grapple's claws, operated by a man sitting in a glassed-in cabin, selected the trunk of a mature white pine and cantilevered it onto a long platform. There, a robotic chain saw bucked it to logging truck length. The grapple then swung the log to the side and released it into a pile and repeated the process with mesmerizing regularity. Aama fidgeted, a signal to get out of the car.

"What kind of work is that?" she said sarcastically, verging on agitation. It was the hump hour of the day, the middle of the afternoon, a frustrating time to watch people, fat ones, getting so much work done while sitting down—stacking more wood in a minute than she collected and burned in her fire pit in a year. "You Americans have found your god." Her face flushed with apprehension; she tugged on Didi's arm, then mine. "Go ahead, worship this thing with the crab's claw that throws logs around as if they were sticks. Do a ritual for it. Do a ritual *on it,*" she said emphatically. With her palms on the smalls of our backs, she pushed Didi and me toward the loader. "Make offerings of money."

Why not? I thought for a moment. Aama might not have known that in Kathmandu during the Dasain festival, cab drivers open the hoods of their Japanese cars and sacrifice chickens to their engine blocks. Simultaneously, at the airport, ladders and stairways are set up to elevate the Royal Nepal Airlines' Brahmin priest to the noses of the jets, onto which the priest squirts blood from a freshly beheaded goat. The bleeding carcass is then dragged on the tarmac to encircle each plane in a protective ring of sacrificial serum.

"We make offerings of kerosene and oil to our machines. That's what keeps them running," I told Aama, half serious. She looked at me, interested.

"Oil is fine as an offering—it is used to keep lamps burning. And these machines are made out of metal, which is expensive and must be mined from the earth and forged into this shape. Machines are wealth, a form of the goddess Laxmi." She watched another log hit the pile, then spoke as if to someone else. "From the times of our forefathers it must have been determined that this is how the world would be at this place and time. Could they ever have guessed it? Especially the machine we saw that cleans the streets, the one with lips that eat up everything in front of it, *ja-rar-rar-rar-rar.*"

"So, what do you think?" I asked her. "Are machines good or bad?"

"Why wouldn't they be good? Good for those who have them.

You couldn't live without them, it seems, so you should worship them."

As we traversed central Maine toward our friends' house, Aama was winding down from an intense honey rush. That morning in Plainfield, Vermont, we had come across a covered bridge and an overgrown cemetery named after my family. Considering Aama's obsession with kin and her respect for ancestors, I figured she might enjoy a brief search for my roots. As we drove slowly over the bridge, I told her that it had been named after one of my relatives, several generations gone.

"Aren't there any farmers around here who have honey?" she asked, ignoring the bridge and the value of my ancestors, as I had often done to hers, though I usually feigned some interest. The maple syrup that saturated our morning pancakes had only inflamed her sweet tooth. Sustenance takes precedence over kin.

Curiously, living near the cemetery was a young organic farmer whom I had met in Nepal several years earlier. The young man and his wife showed Aama how honey could be extracted in a kind of centrifuge, without damaging the combs. As the collection bowl filled, she scooped up rounded handsful, licking the honey as it oozed between her fingers and migrated to her elbow. She ate just under a quart, launching her mood into an upward climb that was now leveling out.

David, an artist and building contractor, and his wife, Susan, a physician, had built their rural house by hand. Aama asked indignantly why they would build such a big house when they will most likely end up divorcing like everyone else, one of them to go off this way and the other that way, leaving the children behind.

"Not these friends," I said, fairly confidently. I outlined the branches of their family tree for Aama, an exercise that had been mildly uncomfortable for some other friends.

Susan had been to Nepal with David, and she told their son Matthiah, age six, that the Nepalese move their heads differently when they answer a question. If they are answering "no," they will shake their head right and left as we do, but to say "yes," they waggle it as if trying to free their nose from being stuck. Matthiah practiced, tottering his head like a car's rear-window hula doll.

"Are you Nepalese?" Aama asked, leaning forward and widening her eyes in curious interrogation. He waggled yes, and said that he wanted to show her his vegetable garden.

They waded out and set their wicker baskets among the beans and squash and potatoes. The two began digging, and Aama's hands moved underground as if they could see, or hear. She deftly passed her thumb over the skin of each potato she uncovered, to release the loose dirt. Didi and Susan could hear them talking to each other softly in their own languages.

Aama began another row. "You have sandy soil here, which is good for potatoes, but I see signs of rot. The spoiled part can be cut off and returned to the garden for fertilizer."

"Aama, I've already dug the potatoes from that bed," Matthiah told her in English.

"That's fine, I'm just scavenging. People often miss some the first time through," she said in Nepali.

"Okay." He noticed uneasily that she was finding quite a few more.

"If these turnips go any longer they won't taste very good," Aama said to the next row. After an hour in the garden, Matthiah returned to the house with the first load of full baskets.

"You know, Mom," he announced, "I can understand everything Aama says." Aama was still in the garden, digging, and the two of them watched her. "When the wind blows and the flowers and grass wave back and forth, Mom, my friends and I, we see them waving to us. Is Aama like us kids—does she see the flowers waving to her, too?"

David leaned in the kitchen window and told us that Stevie, their neighbor the dairy farmer, had told him that we were welcome to watch the evening milking.

We had seen enough of farms, I thought, but I went out to the garden to ask Aama. She said definitely. Cows are sacred, and dairy cows wouldn't be the kind that people ate.

Aama was surprised at Stevie's faded coveralls and mannerisms of familiarity—not at all like an overweight *sahu,* an owner, someone who should have adopted the regal bearing of one who derives his livelihood from assets such as cows. Stevie turned sideways to the barn door, grabbed its wood frame, and leaned heavily. It slid open with a slow rumble, and we stepped into the milking parlor, a drafty hall supported by metal trusses that carried a network of electrical and plumbing lines. Holsteins plodded single file into the far end of the shed like laborers returning from lunch break. Aama looked at them, especially their udders, admiringly.

"One of these cows produces from fifty to one hundred pints of milk a day," I interpreted after conferring with Stevie.

"You mean a whole herd of cows."

"No, one cow."

"One cow? What do you feed them?"

"Grain and green grass. These are the same race but a different caste from the beef cows, which don't give much milk."

"Well, any cow will dry up if you don't milk her regularly."

Stevie and his son went to work attaching clusters of glovelike cups to the teats of cows. Milk streamed from each cluster into a pumping device, and from there through clear tubing to the ceiling where it merged with other lines into an artery of milk that flowed out of the milking parlor. The cows stood facing the walls, nosing about in their feed, which was delivered by another semiautomatic device.

"These machines are milking the cows," Aama said, affirming what her eyes were seeing. "How did people learn to do this? What kind of place is this where machines milk the cows, where farmers take milk without invoking Laxmi? Cows *are* Laxmi, the Goddess of Wealth, the mother of all living things. People may drink their mothers' milk as children, but they all drink cows' milk throughout their lives. You must have gotten it backward somehow—machines may be your gods, but that doesn't mean that you worship them *instead of the cows!* We must bear with us a measure of humility when we milk them, treating them as if they were people. Also, they should not be milked in the daytime, only in the mornings and before dusk."

"These cows produce so much milk that they need to be milked in the daytime, to release the pressure. And they come into the milking barn voluntarily," I argued, trying to determine what it was that I needed to defend.

"Laxmi grazes the grass of the forest by day and, with almost no care on our part, look what she produces: milk to drink, butter for lamps and for cooking, urine for medicine and rituals. And manure for fertilizer and for mixing with clay to plaster our floors, which protects our houses from snakes. Oxen plow our fields, and by hanging onto a cow's tail at death we are saved from being dragged to Hell. No part of the cow goes to waste."

Intensity congealed in Aama's eyes, which dared me to not avert my gaze. Her fingers tensed into an open grip as if trying to squeeze an explanation from me, and only one would do.

She sees something that I can't see. She is telling me something that I can't understand. If people living at the poverty line could forfeit eating beef, while their cows consume scarce resources, they must have something to teach us. I could feel our selfishness as a culture, and even more so as an individual.

"What does she think?" Stevie asked hesitantly. I had told him earlier about life in Nepal's hills, and he had laughed and shook his head at the marvel of having no technology beyond hand tools. Now David and he could see that something wasn't right. I had been hoping that Aama might confer on us something from native lore, a wise word about sacred animals and the earth. Instead, her eyes sternly confronted us, as if we were mortifyingly blasé pathologists. I translated loosely while trying to provide some context.

"You think the way I do things is funny," Aama said. "Like insane people you stand back and laugh and talk, yet you do this to your cows. Bhagwan must not know that this is going on. Why did you bring me to this place? I thought we were going to see only good things."

The dividing line between the wonderful and terrible had begun to blur. Aama's lower lip trembled, then her whole body vibrated as if the urine-soaked slab floor were conducting a cold chill. Aama's emotional foundation had been uprooted and moved, and was yet to be replanted. I felt embarrassed. Had we sinned by bringing her here? The tips of her fingers lightly touched the hip of the cow nearest her. The cow's rump twitched. She then raised her fingers to her forehead to take blessing from the animal, and—out of empathy for its disregarded condition—to impart a blessing to it, as well.

She rooted herself against the wall of the milking parlor, shaking and speechless, as if brought to witness a torture yet helpless to intercede. The raised blood vessels on the backs of her hands flowed like turgid monsoon rivulets. She stared at a section of the wall's rough cement plaster, not wanting to dignify the milking by looking at it. Nothing made sense. It was a living Hell.

Gradually her trembling stopped. As if a fever had broken, she stood within an encompassing aura of quiet that radiated from her, protecting her.

We stepped outside. "These people are religious, too, Aama. They go to their temple to worship once a week," I speculated. I spoke softly to her, trying to appeal to her sense of dharma. "Aama, milking in this manner is the only way they can make a living. Dairy farmers don't make a lot of money. Milk is cheap here."

"How could milk be cheap?" she asked. "If you kill all your cows, milk should be scarce." For Hindus, slaughtering cows was a sin that assured countless rebirths in the animal realm, and in the realms below that. "Do many people go to watch them being slaughtered?"

"No, I don't think people are allowed to."

"I wouldn't think so," she said, relieved that we hadn't made a macabre spectacle of it. "So, what do they do with the hide and the intestines and the bones?" she continued haltingly, as if speaking of human organs.

"They use the bones to make fertilizer or glue, or something, and the intestines might be used to make food for pet dogs. The best pieces of meat are sold for the highest price, to a restaurant, maybe, where rich people go to eat."

Aama was uncomfortable with the image. "What if my relatives were to see me here, a witness to sin near my time of death? They say we become like a deity at age eighty-four, which doesn't mean that we are immune to sacrilege or that we are protected from defilement, but rather that we must be especially careful to avoid it—we must remain *choko*, pure. It is certain that we are now in the Kali Yug," she added with solemn resignation.

A shiver crawled up my spine. The Kali Yug, the Age of Kali, the Goddess of Destruction, the wrathful, feminine manifestation of Shiva. According to the Brahmin priests, we have entered the final of the four great ages, or *yugs*, the era of darkness, defilement, and misery. The priests taught that during the originating Satya Yug, the Age of Truth, which lasted more than a million and a half years, humans lived long lives, in a harmonious, near-enlightenment state of bliss. But during the subsequent eras, humans devolved spiritually. Over the two million years of the Treta Yug and the Dwapar Yug, knowledge, purity, and devotion flourished, but humans gradually, almost imperceptibly, succumbed to greed and carnal temptations.

At the beginning of the 432,000-year Kali Yug, the waters of a great flood rose, and Vishnu himself was said to captain an arklike vessel that rescued a number of great sages—and their wisdom. Since this flood, which coincides remarkably with the account of the biblical Deluge, spiritual principles have been progressively compromised such that, at the end of the Kali Yug, people will begin to eat the flesh of their own kind. A wholesale collapse of civilization will follow. We are now approaching year 5100 of this age, dating its debut alongside the earliest records of advanced civilizations.

I pictured indigent, white-bearded philosophers in robes carrying signboards unnervingly predicting the world's demise—a not-inaccurate picture of an orthodox Brahmin priest, or mendicant saddhu. I tended to believe them; I hadn't seen enough scientific or common-sensical evidence to convince me that the end might not be near. I wondered how, judging by the growth in the world's population and the decline of its environment, we would survive the Kali Yug's remaining 425,000 years.

Treating cows with disrespect is one of the sacrilegious activities in the Kali Yug. As we stood on the gravel road near the barn, Aama enumerated on her fingers some of the other forewarnings from the scriptures. "They say that during this *yug,* only a few people will engage in dharma; children won't obey their parents; caste distinctions will fall; men and women will wear the same clothes; boys will grow long hair and girls will cut theirs; iron will replace brass, copper, silver, and gold, for pots and other things; vegetables will grow to a large size; men will shave their mustaches; and women, instead of wearing gold and jewelry and oil in their hair as we do, will let their undecorated hair hang loose. . . . I have seen all of this begin to happen."

Aama had seen enough.

The walk back to Susan and David's house was funereal. Dilatorily Aama removed her glasses and set them gently on a table, then watched them for a moment to assure that they would be safe. Bending at the waist, she placed both hands flat on the floor, shifted her weight forward, and slowly lowered herself. She looked up at the intersection of the wall and the ceiling, and scratched the top of her head. She exhibited all the features of old age.

Aama then lapsed into a recollection that we couldn't follow, about someone giving money to someone else, which had something to do with her; she wasn't sure she liked it, but didn't know what it was she didn't like. She was drifting. Her perception of time had been stretched, broken perhaps. It had become difficult to distinguish what happened this morning from what happened two weeks or two years ago.

"What are you upset about?" Didi said. "Susan and I have cooked dinner for us, and we've been waiting for you."

"Why would you prepare food for a person who isn't hungry?" She spoke as if we, and especially her dharma son, had betrayed her. I recalled the guilt of letting my own mother down when she had supported me.

Our pilgrimage was ending in sacrilege.

Susan brought a small plate of food for Aama, and David, Susan, and I sat with her on the wooden floor, taking me back to when the three of us had sat together in the hours after my mother's death. David was my college roommate, the one who had relayed the message to phone home. On the wooden floor of our college room, David and Susan had held me, crying, long into that night. I had felt as if I were a part of that floor.

"Here in Amrita, I've seen good and bad, and I've cried and I've laughed," Aama said weakly, too tired to provide an inflection to her words. "I've eaten all kinds of food and have seen every kind of people. When I can't understand things, I become frustrated. But if I say anything harmful, please know that it is not meant in anger."

Susan scooted a cushion beneath Aama and unfolded a blanket for her. *Haré Om, Ram Ram Ram,* Aama sighed soothingly, a sound of acceptance and of integration, as if saying "That's the way that is, and will be." She fell asleep before she could complete her evening mantra.

I looked at Didi, then at Susan and David.

Aama was ready to go home.

While we were in the milking parlor, Didi and Susan had been talking. That night, Didi was only partly interested in my account of the
milking, as if she already knew about it or as if it were beside the
point. She said that she had a headache, the same headache that she
had had for some time.

Something was changing. Didi looked as she did in the Tokyo
transit lounge: tired and hassled, but projecting a kind of strength. I
wondered what Susan had told her about me, and hoped that Didi
would assume that I wasn't the same guy that Susan knew in college.

Perhaps our relationship wasn't withstanding the American trial.
For now, that was fine with me. I could stay in the U.S. an extra
month to check out other prospects, starting with old girlfriends. If
they didn't pan out, then I would return to Nepal and again think
about Didi. Not feeling entirely honest, I told her that I wanted to
stay in the U.S. for a while, to look for long-term work possibilities. I
asked if she could return to Nepal with Aama. Quietly, as if anticipating that I would ask this, she said that she would.

In the car the next morning, Didi was subdued. "What's wrong?" I
asked, not eager to deal with two moody women.

"My headache hasn't improved."

"Take some aspirin, why don't you?" My logical but not very
soothing answer.

"I did, but aspirin won't help this kind of headache." She looked
ready to speak further, but said nothing.

Chapter 16

Aama finds her daughter Sun Maya alive. "I saw places that were new and strange, and sacred, too, as though I had finally reached heaven. But I'm not ready for heaven. We may eat only millet mush in the village, but I wanted to return."

The rhythm of our energy levels and emotions had synchronized with Aama's. The station wagon was as fatigued as we were, and friends in D.C. bought it from me as a backup vehicle. Our journey was over.

"National Airport," I said to the cab driver.

Facing in a determined homeward direction, Aama climbed ahead of us into the taxi. The cab spun off from the Washington, D.C., Mall and into the freeway's High Occupancy Vehicle lane.

"My relatives must be wondering whether I'll return to the village as I am now, or without my body." Aama sighed. "They'll be surprised to see me, and listening to all my stories will keep them from their work—I'll have to make room for them to stay in my house."

On the plane to Seattle, the three of us leaned back heavily and gazed out the window at the sky and clouds. The stratosphere turned a navy blue as the plane gained altitude. I thought I saw a meteorite, smaller than the real one we saw a few days earlier, though more likely it was a dust mote from weariness. Closing my eyes, I tried to synthesize our drive from Maine down the East Coast. On the Boston Common, we witnessed an argument—what Didi called a "growl-down"—between a Hare Krishna disciple and a Beware of Cults prophet. At night, on the tollways south, crowded viaducts swept us through constellations of buildings and streetlights, emitting the galactic feeling that we were hurtling through them.

The Hall of Meteorites at the Museum of Natural History in Manhattan may have been the last sacred site Aama would visit before returning to Nepal. When I told her that the monolithic, seven-foot-high Arizona meteorite had fallen from the sky, she held her breath for a moment, then murmured her mantra and gently caressed its metallic stone surface. She pressed her forehead to it, threw coins on top of it, and circumambulated it. I looked at the guard, who gave Didi and me a "Hey, anything can happen in New York" shrug.

In the Native American wing, she coveted and critiqued hand tools that spoke of the work and attention and joy that went into making them and using them. Arrested here in time-capsule dioramas was evidence of a culture she could relate to, of a people who shared her view. Where did they go?

In a nearby gallery, a photo taken in India was labeled "Elderly widow devotes her time to going on pilgrimage." I translated the caption for Aama.

"Yes, this is what we should all be doing. But just because they call a woman elderly doesn't mean she was always that way."

Observed from the roof of the World Trade Center, the city shrank to a miniature replica of a future civilization, a caricature of a grand, material world. With her hand, Aama surveyed the skyline, taunting the mosquitolike airplanes that could be grabbed or batted down, or maybe didn't exist at all. "When will there be another festival like the one with the large mouse and dancing animals with big eyes?" she asked, as if Disney characters should leap and swagger from behind the buildings in animated song. On the ground, cars weaved like colored beads through the yellow necklaces of taxis. As Aama's departure approached, she became less, rather than more, certain whether the things we saw were real or man-made. But this was unimportant. She had released herself into the chaos, and everything she saw became equally a part of her.

In Washington, D.C., the Nepalese ambassador to the United States had invited us to meet him in front of the Capitol, near one of the fountains. "Is this shooting water natural, like the erupting spring we saw at Yatrastan?" Aama asked as we waited. "If so, it is an auspicious place for the president of Amrita to live."

Aama bowed a deep Namasté to the ambassador and his wife. They each returned it, and sat with her on a waterfall-like expanse of marble steps. Aama reran segments of our journey for them, as if validating and securing the images for her own memory. In the village way of speech, each sentence contained a random, key word that triggered her next thought.

"In some places the land is crying from lack of water, while other places see great flowing and surging and boiling maelstroms of it. Maybe priests or shamans can be sent out to determine which gods reside in these places, and then you can apprise the president. I'm not sure about the presidents here, though. We saw the faces of four of them carved in stone on top of a mountain, but the third man in line was set back from the others, hiding behind them. People were laughing at him. That's the place where we saw infants being pushed around in one kind of cart while old people were pushed about in another kind.

"Once, we passed a place where my dharma son said an entire city's garbage is dumped. Birds had come to find food, but instead found death: Machines that push the garbage around were trampling these white birds, which lay with their broken wings flapping, *phyat-phyat-phyat-phyat*. And we saw cows with teats bigger than my thumb being treated sinfully, dishonestly, their milk disappearing through tubes.

"And, off the shore of the great Ganges Ocean, we saw people riding on a floating piece of wood, taming the waves like the clever monkey-god, Hanuman. If the log comes away from their feet, they could swallow water and drown, but if they just sat in one place, they probably wouldn't catch any fish."

"Aama," the ambassador said with genuine amazement, "you've seen more of America than I have."

"Is your dharma son feeding you tasty food?" the ambassador's wife asked, clearly expressing a daughter's concern. She spoke loudly, assuming that Aama would be hard of hearing. She was Sun Maya's age.

Aama spoke to her warmly, reassuringly.

"Yes, it's always delicious. Even when I ask for tasteless food, all I get is the tasty kind. People eat rich food here, but they don't do the work that such nourishing food enables one to do.

"Americans are healthy, beautiful, and blessed," Aama continued, "and they apply their minds to make things work in humanlike ways. But why? Spirituality is our only lasting reference, and nature and children our only true wealth, for these are the sources of our creation. To these we must offer our respect and our wonder, and from these we must learn."

Her fingers curled and pointed dramatically, mimicking her

speech as much as emphasizing it. The ambassador and his wife were captivated but tentative. Aama was not like the Nepalese who normally come to Washington, although her views were shared, with variations, by most Nepalese villagers, the bulk of Nepal's population. I was wondering if the Nepalese ambassador would take action on her words, or even consider or remember them. He nodded politely to her while he listened, seeming to ruminate on how he might act as the envoy to bridge this sizable cultural and conceptual gap.

After we said good-bye, Aama looked at me and then Didi.

"When I'm gone, I imagine you'll tell people that I traveled around Amrita and said these things. They will probably all say that I'm just an old woman, and that I made up all this." She turned again to me with a questioning smile. "You didn't tell them that I played those gambling machines, did you?"

The stewardess brought the meal. Didi found Aama's glasses and helped her put them on. Aama had cried the last time she wore them; salty high-tide lines marked the levels of tears that had dammed up behind the lenses like a scuba mask, magnifying the pores of her skin.

When Aama was done, chocolate cake crumbs lay scattered on her clothing. Brownian motion. She had eaten the cake with her hands and wiped much of the frosting on her sash.

"That's messy," Didi said.

"Why does an old lady have to look good?" She removed her glasses and carefully slid them inside the utensils' cellophane wrapper —a nice fit—then buried the package in her sash. "What the inside of our souls looks like is all that's important. You people don't have dharma, so it doesn't matter what you do."

"That's unfair," I countered, resentful of Aama's generalization. Sullen and lonely, she didn't respond. The scenes and events around us had supersaturated her, and she had lost her desire to unearth meaning from them. Less than two days remained until her departure.

Didi slept, and Aama didn't speak again until we reached the baggage carousel in the Seattle airport.

"I have seen places that are new and strange, and sacred, too, as if I have finally reached Heaven. But I'm not ready for Heaven. Though I eat only millet mush in my village, I want to return there."

Didi and I badly needed to use the rest rooms and make phone calls. I led Aama to a chair and told her sit down. She resisted, then didn't want to stand up, either. Like a child in the travel limbo of the backseat of a car, she was neither at home nor had she reached grandmother's house. The points in between were an illogical blur.

"Where is that recording machine of yours that draws out voices and captures them—I want to talk into it. You're not telling people the right things, and before I leave Amrita I want to set them straight." Her unspoken thoughts had ripened.

I turned on the pocket tape recorder and set it beside her. "Speak into this end of it. Didi and I will come back when you're in a better mood." She glanced from the floor to the machine without looking at me, certain that the recorder would preserve her thoughts more accurately and sympathetically than I could.

Didi was talking languidly on a pay phone when I came out of the men's room. I stood beside her and stretched from side to side to loosen my back. Pressing her lips outward, the way Nepalese do, she motioned toward the far end of the baggage lounge.

Aama was holding the tape recorder in front of her like a hand mirror, scowling at it and lecturing to it, while her other hand graphically made a point, *and another thing*–style.

". . . People here think only of this life, not of the next one. We stay up all night performing rituals with butter lamps and drums and incense, but here, people are too busy for these things, too busy making their livelihood from telephones and machines, as if these things might help get them into Heaven."

The baggage hall's impersonal background music attempted to dull and sweeten her reactive words. Dourly she repeated her disappointment that people wake up in the morning and head off without sanctifying their day with prayer, or bathing, or offerings, or purification, or even ceremonial mumblings or perfunctory hand or facial gestures, however abbreviated or vestigial. Aama had wanted to find the spiritual platform from which the day's deeds are launched. We have been granted human form as well as the rising and setting of the sun, she explained, and are thereby obliged to respond with devotion —to keep our perception from melting into an unconscious, unarticulated state.

Her narrative then looped into a kaleidoscope of images of America that arose, shifted, and dissolved like the changing colors of the landscape we had flown over. She spoke of dogs and cats dressed in clothing and funny-looking hats, of cars that rob our blood of the vital energy needed to think and work and pray, of a pile of sand that we couldn't touch, because someone owned it. Then, as if she were commentating live, she spoke of her own death and the division of her property, the breaking up of her life and land into its essential elements.

She was transiting into her final stage of life.

"If I was going to understand it, I would have understood by now. At least, I can take refuge in the knowledge that everything of importance is written in the sacred scriptures. Whoever listens to this should refer to those original texts, in order to find out what I really mean to say."

I heard this when I replayed the tape, several days later.

❈

"Aama, you've put on weight," Ann said when we reached their house on Whidbey Island, more than two months after we had departed. "And your face looks healthy."

"So the doctors think that I might not die while I'm here, after all?"

Ann was a physician. "I don't think you will this trip," she said, laughing.

Her weight gain notwithstanding, Aama appeared weak and

tired. By touching people, she may have absorbed some of their energy, and along with it the malaise of their culture. Many yogis and incarnate lamas, and Jesus, too, had suffered for this reason. Through their compassionate, healing touch, they knowingly took onto themselves the consequences of others' karma.

A letter from the village sat in taunting aloofness on the desk in the entryway. I picked it up despite an impulse to let it sit and "cook." It read like most letters written in formal, Sanskritized Nepali, containing little news but carrying on in circumlocuted praise and blessings. It closed by saying that the relatives, crops, and livestock were fine, and that everyone was thinking of and remembering Aama with hopes that the remainder of her journey would be a safe and favorable one. It was the kind of letter an army recruit would receive from the village, and the kind he would write in reply. It was signed by Sun Maya.

As I read it aloud, Aama stared at the wall. Teardrops protruded from the corners of her eyes. I assumed they were tears of joy.

"Why would anyone write that everything was fine unless something had gone wrong?" she said, as if this were the obvious interpretation. She wasn't able to recognize Sun Maya's handwriting, so I could have been shielding her from bad news.

Didi and Aama were to leave tomorrow for Nepal. Aama would find out soon enough, I figured, and when I arrived there a month later, we would have a reunion and a good laugh in the village.

That evening we packed her gifts and souvenirs into two metal trunks.

"Where did you put the beaded necklace that the split-off branch of our people gave me? And the other two necklaces? I wore them for a few days, and then Didi put them away. Are they with my things? And the sandalwood and the lucky cowries and the other sea bones?"

She was decompensating. The new world was fading like a television picture. If she was to return with anything more than vaporous memories, she needed to verify that her gifts had been compiled, bagged, and packed in her luggage. She removed the shawls and adornments she was wearing, including the blue Velcro sneakers, and placed them in a trunk. The cheap pair of Indian sneakers she had arrived in sat like glass slippers in the box where we had left them. She set them out for the morning. The clock struck midnight.

To reacclimate before her return, Aama asked for cold water to wash her face. As if squeezing out accumulated impurities, her sinuous fingers kneaded the wrinkles and smoothed the lighter-colored creases that had been shaded from the sun. She had beautiful skin, only more of it than she had facial surface for. Tears flowed like the leaky tap of the sink that she leaned over, and in a maudlin monotone she invoked the gods and spoke a final prayer. Her voice, filled with gratitude, acknowledged that she would never return to America. *"Haré Om, Shiva Narayan Narayan,* Hail to *Kaansi, Vishnumati, Bagmati, Pasupatinath, Gujeswori, Muktinath, Narayan Narayan Vishnu, Kailaspati, Baigundanath, Jagganath, Rameswor, Badrinath, Bhairav Kali Mai* and all the gods and goddesses, *Bindhyebasini Kalo Bhairav.* May sin, sacrilege, and suffering be removed, may there be peace, protection, and auspicious alignment of the nine planets for all, *Narayan Narayan Vishnu Bhagwan.* I know the deities to be seated in Heaven and at Kailash; please excuse the sentient beings that are in Hell, *O Bhagwan;* though I may have sinned, my actions and thoughts have had no sinful intention. I have carried with me only the image of Bhagwan, from whom I now ask forgiveness. I have bathed in the great Ganges Ocean and I have traveled the four directions, such that only you, Bhagwan, remain to be seen, which must mean that I am near to seeing you. . . ."

In the morning, we stood outside and watched silently as Aama spoke to Ann and Greg and their children. Her words, muffled by the fir needles blanketing the driveway, reached out across Puget Sound to the Olympics, and from there to Ganga Sagar, the temple in the great Ganges Ocean.

"Though I have come here in ignorance, I give my blessings, byebyes, and namastés to all the people of Amrita. Should I hear news of the relatives and friends I have made, I will feel full though I may not have eaten; for until the moment when my eyes see the light of day for the last time, I will remember and cherish the faces and the deeds of all of you. Having seen you and known you, I will feel love for you as long as I draw breath."

Calmly her attention reentered the orb of the driveway. Light reflected from the water below the bluff, highlighting our faces and the lush darkness of the fir trees, their tops dancing in the wind. I sensed that Aama had gone beyond Ganga Sagar, that she had reached a place of inner peace from where she spoke to all Americans, and from where they could hear and understand her. For an extended, vivid instant, we were all those American people.

I was grateful for her blessing, though a part of me didn't feel entirely worthy of it. She looked up at Didi and Ann, who were holding her hands affectionately. "I am now satisfied that my pilgrimage is complete. This is the extent of what I have to say." They squeezed her hands. The children hugged her.

The three of us drove to the airport. We didn't speak, and in our silence I could hear the uneasy sound of transition, of one-way passage. After witnessing the dairy farm and the East Coast, we could not have driven back to Seattle the way we came. Not during this lifetime. Aama couldn't tell me directly, but on the airplane home she told Didi that she feared she would never see me again, that she would die before I could return to visit. Didi assured her that I would arrive in Nepal within a month and come straight to see her in the village.

Frazzled and jet-lagged, they landed in Kathmandu. Aama's only thought was to reunite with her grandchildren, the chicks to whom she was the mother hen, and to meet her obligations for the Dasain festival. And to deal with what she believed to be the death of her daughter.

In an empty Fanta bottle, she collected water from the Bagmati River, dirtier than the Ganges but almost as holy. She asked Didi if she could also take some juice or wine from Amrita. Didi prepared a box of nourishment from the West, like a final communion.

Aama's bare feet were tired but confident on the familiar pathways to her village. Approaching her house, she slowed to put on her glasses, the indispensable symbol of a woman returning from her son's post with the Gurkha regiments. Didi tried to take them from her to clean them, but Aama said the dingy glass would help hide her tears. Mumbling, her head angled downward, Aama stepped into the doorway of her house.

Sun Maya sat on the wooden block at the fire pit, cooking fried breads for visiting relatives. Briefly startled, Aama halted. Her face lit up, transfigured. Sun Maya looked as startled, and happy, as she.

The village appeared as it did when Aama left, except that all of her chickens were dead—confirming her intuition that something close to her had died.

Relatives assembled on the veranda to hear Aama's exuberant, disjointed tales of giant mechanical fish, gambling appliances, crab's-claw machines that move logs, shooting hot-water deities, long underwear, sacrilegious milking devices, and the great Ganges Ocean. As she spoke, children opened her metal trunks. The American artifacts were quietly absorbed into the village.

"My own son, had I given birth to one, wouldn't have done this for me—Nani must be the son I was destined to have. And my daughter-in-law was very helpful, too."

Didi had fulfilled her duty: Her role was now concluded. Her bond with Aama, forged by relation through me, was untied. Didi stayed only briefly before saying good-bye. Aama was reimmersing in the warm current of the village and was being spirited away.

Her American lifestyle soon grew peculiar and distant.

The month I spent pursuing other women in America was futile—a disaster, more accurately—as if I had been wearing a PROCEED WITH

CAUTION sign. En route back to Nepal, I contemplated Didi. Although still unsure that we could work together, I began to see that I owed her more attention and respect than I had given her.

There was no mistaking Kathmandu the night I arrived. When I asked the taxi driver to turn his lights on, he accommodatingly switched on the dome and panel lights. The cab rattled up to Didi's house. Didi gave me a friendly kiss. Then she told me she had made arrangements for me to stay elsewhere. She was seeing someone else.

My breathing stopped. Something seized me around the chest. I recognized the wrenching feeling of being both imprisoned and abandoned from when I was told that my mother had died. I was devastated.

I wanted to ask Didi exactly what had happened, yet couldn't stand for her to tell me. Lamely I proposed that she marry me, though her answer was clearly written on her face and in her movements. I attempted to trivialize my offer, to salvage some pride, since I couldn't withdraw it. "Well, it might be something to think about. We could go back to that country-and-western chapel in Vegas. They might have a Catholic priest—to appease your mother—or maybe we could find a Brahmin at the Trump Taj Mahal in Atlantic City, or something." I could barely speak. Didi smiled at me empathetically, mercifully. There was no going back anywhere.

Days passed, then weeks, and each day I felt I had to speak with her. Whenever I phoned, my stomach was clenched with the autonomic dread that another man would answer, or that she'd tell me she didn't want to speak with me again. I replayed to myself our daily conversations, dwelling upon the words I shouldn't have said or the something more I could have.

When I had felt insecure, I tried to control her with language. I was better than she at manipulating words and meanings. I used them as tools. Words, like money, command power, but I began to see that relationships based on them soon become weak and impoverished.

My inability to function led to even greater insecurity. A brutal, sovereign force had taken hold of me and wouldn't let go, and it allowed me neither work nor relaxation. In my mind I desperately tried to alter circumstances of the past, which had grown into creatures more hideous than could possibly have existed. My blood was flooded with the chemicals of depression, catalyzed and intensified by thoughts that wouldn't stop circling upon themselves. This toxic anxiety was insoluble in hot bath water, or alcohol, or the cerebral fluids of meditation, all of which I fruitlessly tried.

"Suffering is a great teacher," the Tibetan Buddhist lama said, several years earlier when I attended his dharma lectures. He had described the illusory nature of mind and phenomena and the inevitability with which suffering will arise. These teachings made sense, and a residual curiosity about Buddhist philosophy had long chafed at me. But I found the concepts difficult to remember or apply in a practical way to my condition.

I delayed visiting Aama, to avoid the embarrassment of explaining about Didi, but I had to talk to someone. The Tibetan lama lectured around the world and was unlikely to be in attendance at his monastery. After a truncated, tasteless lunch, I purchased a *khatta* silk offering scarf at a stall selling ritual implements. I climbed the three flights of stairs to his quarters, mindful also that few lamas held visiting hours in the afternoon.

One pair of shoes sat outside his door. I removed my own, took a shallow breath and withdrew the canvas door curtain.

Tulku Chyöki Nyima Rimpoche sat alone on the couch in his receiving room. His hands were folded peacefully in his lap. He had been watching the curtain at that very moment.

"Come in," he said cheerfully. He stood up and held out both hands. "I've been waiting for you." I hadn't seen him in five years, but fell into his arms. "*Now* you can see *samsara,* the worldly universe of attachment and suffering. This is an opportunity, a blessing." I had said nothing to him.

Didi had, I realized. This was the lama she had consulted before we went to America with Aama, several months ago. But how could Didi or he know that I would come to see him?

I asked him for a *mo,* a divination, an answer to my simple question of whether Didi and I were compatible and if we would get together again. I was tempted to ask him what advice he had given to her, but knew that his response would be frustratingly oblique.

Rimpoche drew out a string of prayer beads and draped them between his thumbs and index fingers, caressing each bead as it passed his finger pads. Space became narrow and silent. The conversations of people in the next room became distant, yet seemed to continue forever. Rimpoche looked up from studying his rosary. He had an answer.

"Difficult. Difficult." My stomach tightened. "But possible," he added with what I took as a note of optimism. "Life is strange." I well understood the latter statement. He smiled at me and chuckled. "I think westerners suffer more than Asians, which is why they become such good students of Buddhism and Eastern philosophy. Westerners have been raised to expect much in life, and they get lost bouncing back and forth between great hopes and deep despair. In that way, they become anxious of what might befall them next and are usually not ready for it when it does, or doesn't. We Asians don't carry around too many expectations. Look about you: What is there to be hopeful for?"

I felt an urge to cling to his robes, but another visitor had arrived. I thanked him, then humbly bowed and departed.

Standing outside in the glare of the whitewashed monastery, I had to stop and think where I needed to go next, and why. I thought of the Buddhist discipline of retreating to the forest for meditation, which might help me to get my head together, if nothing else.

Rimpoche hadn't relieved me of my depression, I thought selfishly. His words were wise, yet I was unable to accept his evaluation. A translator friend's caveat rang in my ears: *Don't ask for a* mo *unless you are prepared to abide by the answer.* By my reckoning, that meant I needed a second opinion.

The second lama was even less hopeful. It looked bad. The first *mo* had given me a neutral prognosis, I decided, which meant that I could go for two out of three.

I sought out one of the highest lamas living in the Tibetan refugee community, Tulku Urgyen Rimpoche, who had given dharma teachings on specific tantric practices to the Dalai Lama. I begged Rimpoche's Western and Tibetan staff to allow me an audience. Once inside his inner sanctum, I presented a *khatta* scarf to him and sat cross-legged at his feet. Rimpoche smiled, jumbled and shook the beads of his rosary between cupped palms, drew them out, then focused through the bottom half of his bifocals like a scientist through a microscope. I caught myself searching for a pattern in the beads. Was it the way the light reflected off them, their spacing, or texture, or some mystical numeric formula? I looked to his face, scavenging for hope there. I tried to calm myself, to determine what level my tension was occurring on: the physical, psychological, or spiritual? Or was my restless fear a carryover from previous lifetimes? "It can go either way," he announced, then smiled impartially.

Aama said that she knew I was coming. The schoolchildren teased her from the path above her house almost daily, and lately had been shouting that I was on my way down the trail to take her back to America. Today their voices betrayed their own envy of that possibility.

The oral seeds of a new mythology were the only remaining evidence of our odyssey. A few pieces of American artifacts—a broken Mickey Mouse cup and tarnished beads from a necklace—sat in her dusty attic like pottery shards, or litter, the ultimate destiny of Western products regardless of where on the globe they fetch up or what currency of respect they may have had at one time.

Feeling too distracted to wait even for a cup of tea, I announced to Aama that Didi had left me. The words came out louder than I had intended. My heart beat rapidly. I waited for her reaction.

She didn't look up from her fire pit. After several moments, she said matter-of-factly, "I saw it coming."

"What?" I paused to again rewind the past, looking for clues I had missed but that Aama might have spotted. "Why didn't you tell me?"

"You wouldn't have listened."

I could see why the Gurung withhold news about death. Death was the principal emotion I felt whenever I faced the reality of my nonrelationship with Didi, and it was excruciating. Aama turned to me. " 'When a pumpkin grows too big, its own weight breaks it open. When a bamboo grows too tall, its own height pulls it down.' "

"But you saw that on some level I loved Didi, didn't you?" Aama might know better than I whether I did or not, and I wanted to find out. She pushed the corn stalks further under the teapot, then puffed on the fire through her bamboo tube. Again she didn't look up. Her expression said that I might not have asked the right question.

"Why don't you get another one?"

" 'Another one'?" I said self-righteously.

"If you hadn't wanted to find another wife, then why didn't you return to Nepal with Didi and me? I'm fine returning here on my own. But what about Didi?"

"Well, I did try to find another one, I admit. I know now that I shouldn't have, but I guess I wanted to for some reason." I was fumbling, wading in the ignorance of not seeing, one of the afflictions of mind that the lama had spoken of.

" 'Once the stream is crossed, the stick is forgotten.' "

"Okay, but now I'd like to have Didi back," I said even more virtuously.

Aama took a breath, the in-breath of a sigh, the precursor to something I was afraid I wouldn't be ready for. She understood me as deeply as my mother had.

" 'Ram and Laxman went hunting,
And didn't disturb a stone.
They knew that with good karma,
Everything comes on its own.' "

Our conversation wasn't going the way I expected. I was in no mood for her proverbs, which were serving only to invert my statements onto themselves.

"You think this is something you can get by force? You think that you can get it just because you say you want it?" she challenged.

It had always seemed to work that way before, I thought, recalling my relatively happy childhood. Then I recalled what Aama had said about it being better to undergo one's inevitable suffering earlier in life, rather than later.

If I couldn't glean advice from Aama on an easy way to get something that I couldn't have, then maybe I could at least get some sympathy. Aama wasn't forthcoming with that, either. Her voice carried a mother's tone, disappointed that I hadn't grown up yet. I desperately wanted to, I thought, but didn't know how. The physical and professional challenges that I had routinely and proudly set for myself appeared prosaic, compared to the task of taking responsibility for my own salvation. To confront *myself* was something too arduous to consider.

I wanted Aama to somehow resolve Didi for me, to bring her back, to clear the pain. Even more, I wanted her to strengthen and purify me in a way that I mistakenly thought my own mother would have. I was feeling forsaken from all sides, and my assumptions were collapsing around me.

"A husband must sense his wife's hunger," Aama continued, "just as a wife must sense her husband's hunger. They should both understand something: They will never be able to give enough to satisfy their spouse, nor take enough to satisfy their greed. To get along together is like churning butter: The milk must be just the right temperature, and the dashing motion must be executed properly—not too fast or too slow—or the butter won't separate from the milk. You have to have a feel for it." And this, I remarked to myself, from a woman whose marriage was arranged, a woman who had hid in the corn fields on the morning of her wedding day, praying that the parents would take her sister instead.

It pained me to envision Didi's patience during the years we lived together. I continued to hope that our separation was temporary, that it was *my* turn to wait for *her*. But how long could I wait? I paced around Aama's courtyard and along the trails of the village and the bunds of the corn terraces. The place appeared foreign, similar to the day when I first walked into the village and up to the house of the headman, Aama's son-in-law, looking for a place to live. I had left my first home years ago. Now it was time to leave my second home, to shape a new life.

Aama knew this.

Before I departed the village to return to Kathmandu, Aama said she hoped I wouldn't be afraid to keep looking. And to keep looking around me.

My depression continued. In a steady pattern, I delivered gifts to Didi, or sent them to her, or dropped them off. A new motorcycle. Ruby earrings. She resisted, as if struggling with herself, it seemed, but then accepted them. Friends helpfully offered that something from my past was working itself out. *"He subdued the tiger of the jungle, but the tiger of his mind got him,"* Aama's proverb resounded, interminably.

Chapter 17

"And my scoundrel son-in-law will be there, too—standing in front of my funerary plinth, smoking and drinking and carrying on, masquerading as an ex-army officer, embarrassing my daughter . . ."

The warped door was stuck on the sill more tightly than usual, and the knob was loose from forcing it. Leaning my shoulder against it, I contemplated my Westernized, Kathmandu house and lifestyle, designed more for show and entertaining than function.

Nothing worked. I had a full-time handyman just to keep the place operating. He fixed the water pump, replaced electrical fuses, set out candles for the nightly electrical load shedding, fed the mastiff, pleaded with the telecommunications agency to fix the chronically faulty phone line, and transplanted the ornamentals outdoors where they could join the rest of the subtropical vegetation that was overtaking the house and erupting through the brick walkway.

I had had it. Even when they functioned, these amenities hadn't made my life any better than it was in Aama's village—not as good, in fact, consumed as I was by the minutiae of a way of life out of sync with the leisurely, agrarian pace of the country. Desire leads to suffering, the Tibetan lama had said, repeating a well-known Buddhist aphorism. Happiness should be found, therefore, by curtailing one's level of desire.

The sill abruptly released the door and the handle slipped from my hand. The door swung free and banged into the wall. I caught it on the rebound and slowly pushed it closed behind me.

My cook and handyman were talking in the kitchen, rather quietly, it seemed. The house wasn't right, as if there were another presence, or something was missing. I climbed the half flight of stairs to the sitting room, listening, reflecting, feeling a peculiar trepidation. I didn't hear the cook slip behind me up the stairs to the landing.

"You had a phone call," he said from the passageway. His voice startled me. "From some relative of your old Gurung lady. She died. She's dead. Gone."

I didn't turn to see him, but fixated instead on the grains of the wood table, seizing the alternating light and dark strands with my line of sight, trying to look inside them, into the molecular structure of the fiber.

An eye spasm diverted my glance to the window, which looked out on a generic Asian suburb, a neighborhood built on the foundation of its own vitality, sustained by the murmur of building construction and the smell of brick factories and industry. Suddenly it all became meaningless and alien. A wave of powerlessness surged over me.

It's happening again. My mother had done the same thing, she had died without allowing me a chance to speak to her. My mind was prepared for this, from years earlier, but my emotions were not. There was something left I needed from Aama, a further understanding, an ability. And there was something I needed to give her. I needed to tell her that I loved her.

Why did I need to tell her?

Well, because I couldn't, or for some reason didn't, tell my own mother. Maybe she knew that I loved her, anyway. But I should have said so.

No, you can't die now.

Mothers die, I should know well.

Who will preserve me from my wandering mind, from my discursive, malignant, self-indulgent thoughts? Who will be here to remind me to stop taking life too seriously, to relieve me of the burden of my attachments?

Aama had indulged, too. She indulged her memories, and her worries. But all conditions of body and mind are temporary—the lamas and Brahmin priests had said so. And there is a reason for everything.

In the narrow garden, a pottery statue of Maitreya, the Buddha of the Future, gazed unperturbed across a miniature fishpond. The outdoor water tap stood beside it. I opened the valve and cupped my hands beneath the brass spout in the *mudra* of acceptance, the shape of a leaf plate offering laid gently on the Ganges. The water filled my hands like tears, like pure and bountiful nectar. *Amrita,* the elixir of immortality. Water, the semen of Shiva spilling from Kailash to grant life to the plains; a liquid that may freeze or evaporate, but perpetually reverts to liquid, the basic element of human life, incarnation after incarnation. Like life itself, only its form and boundaries change.

As Aama had suggested when we were in Montana, I faced east, lifted my hands, and drained water from my fingertips over my right side, toward the south, then said a prayer. The orchids and bird of paradise inclining toward the pond blossomed into the flowers in the church at my mother's funeral service, vibrant and kinetic, eloquent in their muteness. Like a prayer wheel, the water tap spun closed.

I couldn't remain in the house. Stepping softly, as if palpating the tenuousness of human existence with my feet, as if I were without material form, I left the compound through the metal gate and melded seamlessly into the neighborhood. The crowded suburb felt impersonal and anonymous, similar to many in south Asia that strive, in the twilight between city and country, to lose their identities. Concrete mansions sat like self-important icons between adobe brick houses roofed with thatch or flattened oil drums. Passing laborers, farmers, street vendors, merchants, and mendicants—all seemed cast into the human fray of a fraying civilization. Yet in their own ways, I felt, each had experienced Aama's death before.

Something was tearing me apart. It was not grieving, exactly, but rather a purgatory of anguish and confusion. I cried out to the ground in front of my footsteps what Aama had said about America: *None of this makes sense.* Like her, I was losing the energy to understand or respond. *Eh, Bhagwan. All that we see and know springs from Bhagwan.*

I walked an aimless circuit, then returned to the house and phoned Didi.

I could hear her heart sink.

"I will pray for her. She had a good life and a spiritual soul. Her rebirth will be good. I hope you're taking it well." She hung up. My stomach twisted. My emotions were inciting me to long for an ex-girlfriend to fill my emptiness.

Where had my depression come from, and when the hell would it leave? Why had it been so tenacious—what hidden bond had attached it to me? It. The depression had secured an identity of its own. At night it kept me awake, prodding and clinging to me like a child, surrendering me only reluctantly to an edgy and destitute sleep. In the mornings it greeted me within seconds of awakening, barging into the room like an aggressive, uninvited housekeeper.

I felt a haggard suicidal impulse, then reflected on the ease of dying in a town where it took considerable effort to avoid car accidents, disease, disaster, and revolution. But something dictated that I should live. A source of energy and life was in the midst of preparing me for the unknown, for death itself perhaps, and it would not dismiss me until I understood.

I envisioned the tantric mural found in the porticoes of Buddhist monasteries, of a Mongolian monk chained to a tiger in a dialogue of dance. The monk is masterfully reining in and taming an animal that he is inextricably bound to. In the same way, perseverance in the practice of dharma will allow one to harness the powerful and capricious mind. Taming a tiger must be far easier, I thought.

I had last seen Aama three months earlier. One of her grandnephews posted in Kathmandu with the Nepal Police Band had left a message, and I phoned him. He said that her body had been cremated a few days ago. A relative had called him from the single phone line in the district center and asked him to tell me about it.

During the week preceding her death, Aama had grown even more afraid of falling, and used her cane constantly. She had become forgetful, and her hunger dwindled to nothing. To give the appearance of eating, she squatted as usual on her low stool, the best position for digestion, and ate small amounts. She admitted to a relative that she was merely tasting the food in order to sweeten her mouth and to please her daughter.

Sun Maya knew what was happening. Aama grew weaker, and moved to a straw mat on her veranda where she could look out on the hills she had known since birth.

The Gurung say that at the time of death, all one's ancestors and descendants will parade before them. They must have, Sun Maya later told me, for Aama was audibly reciting their names, and Didi's and mine, moments before she breathed her last fistful of air. On the morning of the auspicious full moon of Magh, Aama passed away.

Magh is the most favorable month to die in, and the best day of Magh to die is the full moon. It was the thirty-second and final evening for the village's annual reading from the legend of Parbati, Shiva's consort, recorded in a volume called the *Swasthani*. Women gather on a veranda to read the concluding chapter of this parable, then fast for purification and as prayer. In fasting, as in meditation, the ego is denied the very food that sustains it.

When dying naturally of old age, too, the elderly often simply stop eating. To abstain from eating becomes a form of ascetic prayer, a release of attachment to the physical world before the ultimate denial of ego—unity with God, in death.

When Aama's breathing stopped, Sun Maya called the lama.

Inside Aama's house, the lama chanted as he washed her body. A relative tied a piece of women's clothing and some fruit and flowers to the end of a long bamboo pole, the *a-lāa*, and erected it beside the peak of the roof to identify her home as a place of mourning. Sun Maya broke her glass bracelets and unfastened her hair, in renunciation of adornment. Aama's three nephews were her closest male kin, and they quietly greeted the other relatives who had begun to gather on Aama's terrace.

With exaggerated formality, Sun Maya's husband, Mani Prasad, organized seating for them. He dispatched his daughters to find additional straw mats, bamboo for fashioning a bier, ritual objects, cloth, and matches for lighting the incense and the funeral pyre. His motions looked practiced, as if he had been waiting for the day when he could have the last word about what would happen to Aama, while publicly demonstrating an appreciation for her that he hadn't displayed while she was alive. Partly as a result of the grief of close relatives, a deceased Gurung's son-in-law traditionally acts as the executor. As usual, Mani Prasad was wearing a hangover conspicuously garnished with a few drinks.

Eldest Nephew presented the lama with a length of hand-spun

cotton cloth for covering Aama's body. Then the nephews carried her from the house and placed her on a short bamboo frame positioned in the middle of her terrace. The lama clipped pieces of her fingernails and a lock of hair and placed them in a small bamboo tube, which he hid in the village. Were witches or ghosts to encounter these symbolic body parts, they could use them to interfere with the transmigration of her soul. Both the lama and the shaman will need them later, to guide her spirit on to Siminasa, the final resting place of the souls of the ancestors.

From the front of the funeral procession, Third Eldest Nephew, a shaman like his father, shot arrows in the cardinal directions to ward evil spirits away from the bier, which was carried by the other two nephews. From the woodpile, the party of relatives selected firewood that Aama had cut only a few weeks before. Now it would be used for her own cremation. They joined the procession, a log each on their right shoulders. When the bier approached the peak of the cremation ridge across from the Shiva shrine, the lama blew a distant, melancholy blast on his conch.

Mani Prasad prepared the funeral pyre, a task not assigned to a relative of Aama's lineage. By participating in his mother-in-law's cremation, he could show gratitude for the wife Aama had given him, while reestablishing his link with the wife's lineage.

The lama sat cross-legged on a mat, then untied a stack of woodblock-printed pages wrapped in cloth. His upper body rocked softly as he droned a sequence of prayers, in Tibetan.

Eldest Nephew placed a cotton wick dipped in mustard oil in Aama's mouth and lit it, then ignited the twigs beneath the pyre. The relatives descended to the village, leaving thorn branches on the trail to keep ghosts from following them, while Mani Prasad and the nephews remained to feed and tend the fire. The sparks that arose from her body carried away, in their flickering traces, her *prana*, her breath of life, the same vital essence that animated the earth from which the Christian God molded mankind. Aama had spoken of what happens next.

"As the body burns, its flesh peels off. Sometimes, by the light of its own flames, the letters that are written on the dead person's forehead become visible. These letters are what defined their destiny, and were recorded there on the day of chainti, *the sixth day after birth. If they are black, it means the person was given a troublesome life, and if red, they had a good life and can expect a good rebirth."*

Sun Maya asked Mani Prasad about the letters. He said that he hadn't bothered to look and that he didn't believe in superstition, anyway.

The sunset expired, but the coals from Aama's pyre smoldered on. The nephews silently raked and folded the fire's subsiding form onto itself. By morning, only ashes remained.

After the cremation, the lama was the first to step into Aama's house. The relatives watched as he chanted and shook a ritually empowered dagger, the *gwiyantar,* which amplifies the tantric energy that surrounds him like an aura, enabling him to chase out the evil spirits that are attracted by death to take lodging inside.

According to the Gurung, Aama's soul would remain in the house for one day. On the second day, it would move to the veranda, then advance to the courtyard on the third. From there, her soul would move to the neighborhood, the village, the fields and forest, at each stage becoming more aware and mobile, like a precocious child.

Each of the first few evenings after her death, villagers came to sit on the porch, to embrace her proximity and her affinity, and offer theirs. A dead person's soul is weak, ignorant of where it is, and therefore vulnerable. The lama also came, to pray for her soul's eventual safe delivery to the final resting place, Siminasa, before entering a favorable reincarnation, hopefully human.

Reincarnation. Intuitively, and logically, it worked. Pundits, priests, lamas, shamans, and their generations of antecedents had been unable actually to capture the soul, or even to fully describe it. Therefore, they questioned, can the soul possess an inherent, tangible form? If it has no form, then is it something that can be created? If a soul cannot be created, *then neither can it be destroyed.* If *matter* can be neither created nor destroyed, I reasoned, it must be especially difficult to create or destroy the nonmaterial. I couldn't imagine trying to prove or disprove reincarnation scientifically, but the concept appeared consistent with scientific thought.

Hinduism and Buddhism, with some variation, describe how the soul transmigrates to inhabit the lives of new sentient beings. For most of us upon death, our karma from previous lives will be added to the karma generated from our merit and demerit of this life, to determine the quality of our next rebirth. Eventually we will all be enlightened, the lamas claim, and escape forever the karmic cycle of birth, death, and rebirth, although this may take nearly countless incarnations.

On the day before Aama's soul was to leave the terrace, the lamas announced—chanting in a way that she would be able to hear —the date of her *arghaun,* the funerary ceremony in which she will be guided to Siminasa. The *arghaun* would take place after six months, during the summer monsoon. Until the time of this ceremony, however, Aama's soul would wander.

❖

Where the footpath intersected the upper limit of the village's fields, a party of children suspended their mixture of play and corn weeding to watch me pass. The older boys spoke furtively with each other and laughed, then one shouted, "Your Aama is away in another village right now, but just go to her house and wait—she'll be back." Rain fell in a delicate but invasive sprinkle that worked its way down the inside of my shirt and dripped the length of my spine, an aggravating complement to the slick red clay of the hillside. The trail had become more slippery after hearing their sarcastic jeers.

I rounded the corner at the point of the ridge. The rhythmic *TUN-a-ku-toe, TUN-a-ku-toe* beat of a tablalike drum sounded from within the village, accompanied by the slow bass of a bigger companion drum, the *dhön-dü,* calling relatives and villagers to

Aama's *arghaun*. This was the first time I would see the village when Aama wasn't there.

Her porch and terrace were packed with people, many of whom I didn't know, spilling over into the surrounding houses and buffalo sheds. Sun Maya was inside. At fifty-eight, she looked older than Aama did when I first arrived in the village; her cheeks were hollow from fatigue and hardship and recurring sickness. Her hair was unplaited for the *arghaun,* and it hung in loose, gray-flecked tangles. So this was why Aama wanted to see American women pull back their free-flowing hair: Wherever she turned, their loose hair was a reminder of death.

Weary but restless, Sun Maya hovered in the kitchen and in the background, helping her daughters prepare tea, busying herself. She nodded at me to follow her, then pushed through the girls interlocked in sitting, squatting, and kneeling positions on the veranda. The normally open porch was darkened by their line of heads pressed against the inside of the thatched eave. Raindrops inflated and hung like tears from the tips of the dangling tendrils of thatch straw. Wisps of steam from the sweat and monsoon mud enhanced the smell of incense and mustard seed hair oil.

Sun Maya cleared a place for me to sit in line with the three nephews, the classificatory sons in the absence of Aama's own. Like the other ex-army relatives who were standing outside, two of the nephews wore dark-colored vests and skirts of white cotton cloth wrapped several times about their waists and secured by British Army ammunition belts. They exchanged news, joked loudly, and retold the stories they had reserved for such gatherings.

With both hands, Sun Maya presented me a tumbler of distilled millet spirits. We spoke about her daughters and whether there would be enough rice to feed the nearly two hundred relatives and guests. I asked her where Bujay was, Aama's elderly cousin who lived in the house below. Bujay died one month after Aama. Each one of Aama's other remaining cousins and in-laws had also passed away; Aama was the last of them to go.

Outside, sonorous chanting and staccato discharges from the lamas' human thighbone trumpets signified that the effigy had been constructed. The nephews adjourned to the terrace and I squeezed onto the veranda.

Instantly upon seeing the effigy, I was transported beyond the crowd and clamor to a morning several years before. Sitting exactly where I now sat, I had watched Aama gaze at the empty courtyard and say that she could see in advance, as clearly as a memory, the people and the colors of the day of her funerary rite.

It will be a tight fit for the lamas and their ritual implements. They will sit on straw mats here at the foot of my veranda, while women with their hair untied circumambulate the plah, *my effigy. The* plah *will be placed in the middle and toward the back of the plinth—which they may fashion from the wooden bed that I sleep on. The plinth will be decorated with butter lamps, rich foods, incense, cloth and flowers. My relatives will weave through it all to present offerings, and my Gurkha pensioner nephews from distant villages will be there, the ones I haven't seen in years. They will stand to the side much of the time except when they are inside drinking and telling stories, or when the lamas or shamans call them out. . . .*

Aama's prophecy seemed to guide the service unfolding before us. In the center of the plinth, Mani Prasad had fabricated the *plah* from a bamboo frame about two feet high, and stretched a white cloth over it. The pair of spectacles that were fitted in San Francisco perched on the effigy above her gold and coral necklace. The fingernails and lock of hair were fastened inside the *plah,* along with a *jantar,* a folded square of paper inscribed with Aama's name and a consecrated mystical design, the pictorial counterpart of a protective mantra. A symbolic shed roof made of bamboo screens decorated with poinsettia bracts covered the *plah* and plinth. Aama's grayhaired second cousins and nieces continued to lavish it with food that she liked, showing her that they had not forgotten her. Sun Maya added to the pile the eggs and half pint of rum I had brought, but first opened the rum bottle—to allow Aama to drink from it.

The nephews and male relatives, the trunk of her family tree, stood with their backs to the sun, protectively shading Aama's effigy. The women cousins tossed back their heads and cried as they circled the plinth, and sang an asynchronous but melodic plea that Aama's wandering spirit come and accept their offerings, then retreat to and reside forever in Siminasa, never to return to the village as a ghost or spirit. After each circuit, they paused to heat their open palms on the rows of butter lamps and redirect their hands toward the *plah,* transferring to it the lamps' warm votive energy.

Bystanders stalled on the trail to peer over the stone wall and down upon the terrace. Aama's effigy had been concealed from direct view, but they could sense that potentially troublesome spirits were being dealt with. Their silent stares expressed contemplation of their own mortality.

. . . And my scoundrel son-in-law will be there, too, smoking and drinking and carrying on, waving his arms, masquerading as an ex-army officer, embarrassing my daughter. . . .

Mani Prasad sat disrespectfully on the edge of the plinth, his back to Aama's effigy, chain-smoking cigarettes that were jammed between the first two fingers of his right hand, which was clenched into a ball. The veins on his temple distended as he sucked with a low whistling sound from the spiral of his fist. He let his hand drop as if he had picked up a rock, inspected and then discarded it. His other hand wrapped loosely around an antique glass bottle, now less than half full of alcohol. Taking a deep swig, he jerked his head to the side and flung a straightened arm mock-threateningly at the nearest relatives, children mostly, those talking too loudly or not sitting in the proper place. This theatrical, alcoholic sense of propriety was his way of compensating for a lack of manners, and prompted some relatives to smile sympathetically as they would at a retarded person, one who couldn't help himself. Mani Prasad had become a caricature of himself, and he savored a contrary pleasure in shocking his own kin. A self-satisfied smile sneaked across his lips whenever someone responded to him with defiance.

"Through Sun Maya, he may get Aama's house after all," Second Eldest Nephew said to me privately. "But, looking at the state of his health right now, he might be following Aama sooner than he thinks." Most of the relatives barely noticed Mani Prasad. Aama's soul would come to inhabit the *plah* anyway.

One of the shamans carefully cracked open a raw egg and poured it into a brass bowl. The unbroken yoke would indicate in which form Aama's soul would return, whether as a bird, mouse, or other animal. The shaman set the bowl on a bamboo mat and spread a dusting of ashes around it, to record footprints. Another shaman suspended a chicken by one foot from a low bamboo archway, to isolate the precise moment when Aama's soul would enter the effigy. He carefully calmed the hen. It hung motionless for several minutes.

Abruptly the hen's wings fluttered vigorously, signifying that Aama's soul had occupied the *plah*. At once, the women wailed. As if melding into a single body, they fell to their knees at the plinth and cast their hands onto the base of the effigy.

Aama was here. She had come to see us in the Land of the Living. My face flushed with shock and bewilderment, which suffused into a glow of awe and affection. She looked as she did sitting next to us on tour in America, quietly watching, ready to speak once she could compose her words or recall a proverb. Her eyes caught me not paying attention, not hearing what she'd been saying. She was happy to be with us.

The relatives may supplicate and attract the soul, but only a psychopomp, a shaman, can guide her onward. The shamans separated into two groups, and both circled counterclockwise with the *plah* between them. They swung their legs in unison, drumming single beats at one-second intervals. Chanting a ballad called the *shyerga,* they described her destination and named the frontiers and dangerous regions they passed with her, making sure she took the correct forks in the trail.

One group of shamans assumed Aama's voice. *"What is happening to me?"* they called in song across the *plah*.

The other group responded in the voice of the shaman guides. "You are dead, you have died."

"How did I die?" Aama's side asked.

"Of old age, after a long, fruitful, spiritual life."

"Why are you doing this arghaun?"

"You have been taken by the God of Death, but we the living have pulled you from his grip and have cleared the way for you to reach Siminasa. You will remain there with your ancestors, or from there you will be reborn."

Christians are undecided about the movement and schedule of the soul, but generally believe that it resides within the body until death, then departs promptly and permanently for Heaven or Hell. Effectively, the soul is retired, and the funeral services neatly conclude the Christian transmigration. I was curious whether death could be such a simple and short process. Village Hindus and Buddhists believe that only great practitioners are able to pass through the after-death state without succumbing to crushing distraction: The light is blinding, the noise deafening, the smell overwhelming, the taste strong, and the touch enervating. Confusion prevails.

Clearly, the nonpractitioner needs guidance after death. This period is most distressing because the soul does not retire easily. It is grasping anxiously for the life it lost, or searching for a new rebirth. Unable to recognize its condition as that of death, the soul can loiter about the village, vulnerable to vagrant spirits, resisting the journey to Siminasa. Only a clever shaman can retrieve such a wandering soul and lead it onward. They say that the soul most onerous to survivors, the one most difficult to escort, is that of a person who has died an untimely death.

Untimely death. I sucked in a short breath. *My mother.* A flood of memories and visions emanated from the *plah,* from Aama's glasses and coral necklace.

My mother was forty-two, in good health. She was unprepared for death, and would not have gone willingly.

Images arose from a dream that over the past two years ran and reran with a vivid and tireless precision. Graphic fragments of it, too visceral for memory, were beginning to fit together into a single, animated vision: In a thickness of suspended time, I wandered through a darkened, foreign house. My movements decelerated, my breath pounded, my speech became paralyzed. There was something malign in each of the rooms. I was drawn to one room in particular, yet couldn't force myself to enter.

I awoke from this dream only after it had been impugned and forgotten, deserted in the conveniently remote world of the subconscious. A vague lethargy and headache were the only vestiges of those long nights.

Now, on the terrace of Aama's house, I became able for the first time to see what was inside the room: my mother's headless body, draped in a black robe. She was hiding, yet searching for me, and jumped out either to startle me or to hold me—my fear rendered me uncertain.

I couldn't halt the vision; it wouldn't retreat. I ran down a list of queries—groping for details, analyzing. Logic and forwardness had always worked for me before. Had I wanted to enter the rooms? Was she an evil or a benign spirit? Had I disappointed or mistreated her or not placated her adequately? Was she here with us now?

I tried to relax, and wait. The lamas pointed their thighbone trumpets skyward, ballooned their cheeks, and blew convulsing, glottal blasts. Halos of smoke from the incense and butter lamps filled the ritual enclosure of the *plah,* anointing Aama's effigy. Hypnotically, the shamans revolved around the plinth.

There she was. My mother. She had taken a place beside Aama and sat a congenial distance from her on the plinth. They had found the pathway, and the shamans were guiding them. They were together.

My mother fixed me with her wry, charming smile. Her face was framed by ageless blond curls. She looked at ease. *You have found me.*

I wanted to suspend her image there, to bundle up the warmth of her face and secure it in an insulated shrine. I could see myself in her features, and recognized her gestures as part of me, the part of me that was love—the love that had been dormant and reclusive, afraid that, if it were expressed, would be taken away, just as she herself had been. This love was the dangerous and powerful force that occupied, along with my mother, the rooms I had been unable to enter.

I glanced at Aama. She returned my look with a glow that said, *Yes. We are who you think. Now you can see, Nani, that I am not different from your mother, and she is not different from me. In death, we are all kin.*

The dead must not linger in the Land of the Living. The shamans halted. They stood up straight, preparing to address Aama's soul formally. They announced to her that they had reached the threshold of Siminasa.

"Aama, please recognize the boundaries: Humans do not go to the land where the ancestors live, so please—do not return to the Land of the Living. Relinquish your desires and your attachment to your daughter, to your adopted son, to your house and livestock, to your wealth, and to your own body, as well, for you no longer have a bodily form to be attached to. This is your resting place. You must stay here while we who are alive now leave you and return. . . ."

"But how will I survive, what will I eat and drink?" her soul asked.

"You will feast on the abundant offerings brought by your descendants and relatives, and their generous gifts of cloth will keep you warm." By now the *plah* was half buried in food, fabric, and bottles of alcohol. The Gurung knew that if their offerings were tasty and plentiful, Aama's soul would remain satisfied, and far from the village.

But the gates to Siminasa were barred. Spirits had blocked Aama's transmigration in order to detain her among the living, to keep her here to wander just as they do. Ghosts and evil spirits can survive only in the physical realm of the village, because only here can they cause misfortune.

Aama's relatives were now obliged, using the coercion of kinship, to break open the gates. Sun Maya and Mani Prasad and the nephews and nieces assembled beside the water buffalo shed. Eldest Nephew lifted a symbolic spear, a long-handled spade of the kind used for scraping the weeds from the risers of rice paddies. He balanced it lightly on his shoulder. The assembly parted. Three yards from him sat the gate to Siminasa, represented by the *taar,* a piece of bamboo that had been whittled flat and etched in charcoal with a geometric design. He aimed and released the spear. It missed.

Mani Prasad retrieved the spear from the muddy pathway and handed it to Aama's next closest male relative. Second Eldest Nephew stood as his brother had in composed relaxation, then released the spear. It struck the *taar* squarely, flipping it from the path to the terrace below, behind Bujay's house.

Like a rogue wave, the relatives converged on Second Eldest Nephew, reaching for his shoulders. The moment their fingers touched him they chanted *shaaaai, shaai, shaai,* in cascading tones, to sanctify and fix the event and protect his soul from escaping, as it can in this vulnerable state. Their arms writhed like serpents around his chest and shoulders as they fastened string necklaces, each with nine knots, reconnecting Second Eldest Nephew to the nine protective planets and the nine elements of his soul.

The gates to Siminasa were now open, and Aama's soul entered, peacefully, of its own will. My mother's soul was with her, and they appeared like sisters. The next moment, they were indistinguishable.

The lamas closed and secured the gates.

For the return trip to the Land of the Living, the shamans changed direction and circled clockwise around the *plah.* Elbows and arms lifted as the women replaited their hair.

After hours of a slow *dum, da-dum* drum beat and occasional conch shell blasts, the tempo quickened. The shamans were reapproaching the village.

Like celebrities, two lamas issued from the buffalo shed wearing dancing robes of magnificent draped velvet patched with colored stripes. Panels painted with icons of the primary deities graced their headdresses. The crowd parted as they swept around the periphery of the plinth, dipping and spinning, flamenco style, lifting and crashing their cymbals in a crescendo that roused the assembly. The nephews removed the offerings and butter lamps from the plinth and set them aside for the shamans and lamas. One of the lamas carefully unfolded the *jantar* inscribed with Aama's name, wrapped her fingernails and hair in the paper, burned them, and kneaded the ashes into a handful of red clay. From the clay he molded a statuette of Avalokitesvara, the Buddha of Compassion, later to be placed at a power spot on the ridge. The main part of the *arghaun* was complete.

The lamas dismantled the effigy and decorations, and heaped them into a pile. In his dirty T-shirt and cotton skirt, Mani Prasad squatted and vainly tried to show his sense of convention by sweeping his hands about in the mud, gathering the loose scraps that should not remain at the site. He worked as if trying to reverse the harmful effects of his behavior, and to show Aama's army pensioner nephews that he had steadfastly remained in the village, keeping the Gurung traditions alive during their years in the outside world. The pensioners looked down at him in humored disdain, relieved that someone would see that no evidence of the *arghaun* remained on the terrace. This was the least Mani Prasad could do for the mother-in-law who had accepted him all these years, the mother-in-law who had loaned him increasing sums of money, some of which had come from her dharma son.

Just look at my daughter now, Aama had said. *Wrinkled. Worried. Shamed.*

Sun Maya and the nephews organized a single-file line of over a hundred relatives. Solitary drum beats at intervals of three seconds set the pace for the departure from the courtyard. The procession snaked past the buffalo shed, ducked beneath the haystack elevated on stilts, and flowed over the stile and onto the trail leading out of the village. Children clung to their mothers' skirts, plainly aware of the presence of spirits.

Seven male relatives carried aloft a ten-yard-long banner of white cloth, fastened between thin bamboo poles. This *gyam-bal* caterpillared along the trail, deflecting evil spirits in the manner of the insubstantial but never challenged "beat" cloth used to direct and control tigers in the jungle.

The trail passed beneath a lone house. Darkened from the forge, the village blacksmith stood with his family on the edge of their corn terrace, looking on in silence. Their memory of Sun Maya's mother filled their faces; the rules of untouchability hadn't precluded her from being close to them.

The caravan meandered up the stone stairway to the brink of the cliff that marks the periphery of the village's fields. This is the place where the clothes of the dead are cast onto thorn bushes, to frustrate witches from taking them for use as the conduits for hexes. Above the horizon's farthest ridge and below the pastel clouds, rain washed across the slash of sunset.

The relatives congregated beside the trail. Sun Maya rolled out the straw mats for Aama's nephews, son-in-law, and me. Nearby, the lamas faced each other and arranged the tangled remains of the effigy into a crude pyramid. One lama ignited it. Sun Maya handed him a brass urn. Chanting, he poured a narrow stream of liquefied butter onto the fire. He handed the urn to Eldest Nephew, who did the same, silhouetted by the layered aura of the fire's flare and the orange-red sunset. The other nephews followed.

Eldest Nephew sat on the mat beside me, then spoke to me quietly. "It's over. This is it. The end. As you make your offering to Aama, say 'Good-bye, Aama.' Give her your farewells and wish her your best."

In the manner of the nephews before me, I took the urn and poured butter onto the effigy's expiring carcass. Tears welled up in my eyes almost instantly. I felt lost and unworthy, but sincere, the man-boy that Aama and my mother both knew me as. I mimed the nephews' words as best I could, but the hollow sound of weakness came forth, a cry for help more than a cry of sorrow. I was trying to let go.

"I make this offering in Aama's name."

Aama. The kinship term for mother. My own mother was Aama, too.

The obsequies were over. The lama cast the smoldering matrix of cloth and bamboo from the trail. It collapsed below, inert, no more vital than the debris and limp flowers that littered the ground beside us. Yet when two passersby approached from around the bend, the lamas waved at them to clamber onto the terrace above where the burning effigy had been. Defeated malevolent spirits still loitered on the trail, gazing down on the effigy like empty-handed predators.

Again I took a seat with the nephews on the line of straw mats. Our positions within the lineage were to be reestablished; we were to be honored as elders.

Sun Maya, as the only daughter, squatted in front of each of us and poured mustard oil into her palms. She rubbed it onto our faces, hair, and necks, and massaged it in lightly. Then she coiled lengths of white cloth into turbans around our heads. The turban felt protective like a helmet, comforting like a bandage.

Slowly we followed the trail to the village. An ordeal had ended. Simply discussing or enduring Aama's and my mother's deaths would not have been sufficient. Death, like life, cannot be explained away by science or simple homilies. For the survivor, death requires an intentional, ritual release, a casting away of kinship equivalent to an *arghaun*. Without it, the cycle of life remains interrupted.

It was among the Gurung that I had come to know Aama, and it was among the Gurung that I would free my attachment to her. And it was here that I had to learn, finally, to let go of my own mother.

By accompanying the soul as it transmigrates, the Gurung reestablish ties with their family, clan members, and Gurung customs and cosmology, while familiarizing themselves with the path that they, too, will follow after death. The Gurung don't say "I think . . ." but rather "we believe," using the tribal and affinal, not the royal, "we." Their religion is not an opinion or a position. It is nothing more than a way of life. And death.

Over the past two years, I had developed a resistance to diversion from my favored state of self-pity. But now I felt a soft sadness. Grief. Slowly, as if this grief were an essential precursor to it, an emotion of anticipation and awakening circulated through my body, and throughout the village.

That night the village was bathed in a steady, cleansing monsoon rain, an auspicious sign after an *arghaun*. On the porch, more than twenty relatives sat talking as they watched silt-laden rivulets swell and consolidate beside the house. Sun Maya's grown daughters brewed tea and poured glasses of alcohol. They were uncharacteristically quiet compared to the children I had laughed and played with on Aama's terrace. Aama's infant great-granddaughter played beside her mother, now grown, a picture I had seen eighteen years and one generation earlier. When that child becomes a woman, the features of the village will not have changed. And she, like her mother, will assume Aama's form.

Sun Maya sat down next to me. She sighed deeply, then smiled. "This *arghaun*, Younger Brother, is the reason that you, too, must have children—to have someone to perform it for you when you die."

It was as if Aama had spoken.

Chapter 18

" 'We come naked, we leave naked—
A life of but two days.' "

The phone rang. It was Didi. For the first time in almost two years, my words sounded strangely free of desire. My perception of her had shrunk; she was a human of normal size and ability. The internal voice that had been urging me to escape to the privacy of my room and to my habitual self-doubts became feeble and remote.

Didi asked how I was and who the woman was that a friend of hers had seen me with yesterday.

"Someone new in town who I met last week. She's working in the health field. Why?" My desire for Didi had cooled to the point where I could touch it.

"Oh, you've sort of been out of circulation for a while. I was glad to hear that something might be happening for you."

I told Didi about Aama's *arghaun*.

"I had something that I forgot to send with you for her *arghaun*," she said. "Why don't you come by and pick it up after work tonight?"

As we sat at Didi's dining room table, it seemed that only a short time had passed since we were together, though it had been more than two years. At the end of the evening, we stood in a long and careful hug, an embrace of hope and sincerity. Our body heat warmed us into sharing a fluid kiss, unlike any kiss I could recall. I felt a germination of trust. We had ripened, independently, and were being plucked from the Peepul tree, the floral incarnation of Vishnu under which men and women are paired for life, and sometimes into death.

She forgot to give me the items she had wanted to return to Aama, a bead necklace, a T-shirt and some more conch shells, left behind with Didi's things when Aama returned to her village. I smiled at the image of Aama's Tom and Jerry T-shirt arranged on the *plah*.

A few days later, I asked Didi about the past and the trip around the U.S.

She looked at me with a penetrating, amused scowl, as if I should know by now what she'd been thinking, and if not, then I wouldn't want to hear. She took time to craft an honest summary of her experience.

"Well, before we left for the States, I went to one of Chyöki Nyima Rimpoche's morning teachings on Buddhist philosophy. Afterward I met with him privately, to ask him about my future with you. He told me, 'Didi, this life of ours is a joke: Everything is illusion. Whether you and your boyfriend get together or separate, it will be all right. If a marriage kind of happiness is meant to come to you, you will be married.' I remember that I went away smiling. Somehow, what he said lightened me up."

"And, on our way to the U.S. with Aama, what did the psychic in Hong Kong say to you?" I interjected.

"Teddi said that her psychic is usually correct. The woman simply looked at the Tarot cards and meditated as I sat there, scared. After several minutes, she said that she was 'spiraling down into it, as if in a funnel,' and that she could plainly see that my association with you was a drain on me. She said, 'Your partner has been causing you pain, and it would be best to *end it*—unless the situation improves dramatically. He may not have the capability to love you, and you need to get out in order to save yourself.' It upset me to hear the psychic say what I had been afraid to admit even to myself."

Could a total stranger see in Didi and me what I had been unable to? Yes, maybe, I decided. Familiarity and an unresolved past had obscured my vision. The same things had obstructed Didi's ability to act.

"So that's why you were so frosty in the Tokyo transit lounge," I offered, realizing that I had said the obvious.

She looked at me with friendly severity. "When you came up to where I was sitting in the lounge, I saw no indication that you wanted to see me in a personal, loving way. You were all wired up, yet blasé, self-absorbed—immature, like a jerk. You said, *What's happening?* and at that moment I realized that I would follow the psychic's instructions. I said to myself, 'Well, I just have to set this thought aside for now and get on the plane.' "

Seldom talkative, Didi was now on a track where each thought found its place in her phrasing, and each phrase its place in her story. "Following our trip, I went to another of Rimpoche's lectures. Afterward he stopped, squeezed my hand, and said, 'I saw your boyfriend, and he talked with me about you.' He winked and added, 'It's karma,' and then turned and walked on. I think that his wink meant different things. After all the pain you caused me, some of that pain had returned to you, as it inevitably will. But it also may have meant that fate and our karmas dictated that we would get together again."

Now it was Didi who was spiraling in. She brushed back her hair with a free hand. "I think you know now that Aama was your surrogate mother. As long as she was alive, you didn't need to resolve your own mother's death. And Aama—because she had no son of her own until you were delivered to her by the gods—wasn't especially keen that you deal with your original mother, either. She may have wanted to keep you as the young son she never had, the son in need of nurturing. You were locked into a second adolescence, this time with Aama, and you didn't want to face the reality that a woman would leave you, as your mother had. And then I left you. And then Aama did. Now, after a lot of anguish, I think you see that none of us took any of our love for you away with us when we went."

Didi fixed herself a drink, then faced me. "Despite all my years of hoping that we would marry, I know now that our marriage wouldn't have worked then."

"You're right," I said quietly. I was looking forward to describing my personal discoveries to Didi, but she had quoted them to me instead.

The emptiness left by Aama's death was indeed meant to be occupied by Didi, but not on my schedule. All along, my love had been drowning in my attachment. Didi had been waiting, in her charitable way, for it to resurface.

In America, I had been hoping to acquire a greater perception, a wisdom perhaps, by seeing our country through Aama's eyes. I expected it to appear before me on the physical landscape. Instead, the envoys of that understanding had been beside me all along, patiently wondering if I would see them and acknowledge their presence: Aama, Didi, and the ghost of my mother. My mother was no longer my mother. Aama's village was no longer my home. The home is the severed heart that is revealed, and reattached, at the culmination of pilgrimage.

The pilgrimage that Aama and Didi had completed was for me a beginning, the start of an inner journey, one that I suspected would be long and difficult. But Aama's cousin, the shaman, had stressed that spiritual merit can be gained by simply undertaking the journey itself, by enduring the inevitable obstacles and suffering that occur en route to a destination that is unknowable in advance.

Didi and I crawled between the sheets, together yet alone, as we are always. Lying on my back, I could hear the melodic rasping of Aama's evening devotional song, sung as she would while peering up at me with her ironic, cautionary smile, seeing through me and beyond me. She was singing also to Didi, to Americans, to her Gurung ancestors and descendants, to all of us, bathing us in love.

> " 'We come naked, we leave naked—
> A life of but two days.
> Earth is our cradle,
> Earth is our cushion,
> And earth is our shroud;
> Yes, this is how it is. . . .' "

Through the opened window, Didi sighted a shooting star. She said that she made a wish. Her expression, light and promising, seemed to include me in its appeal. I told her that the Gurung believe that a falling star is a soul returning to earth, being reborn. It shoots across the sky at the moment it has found the womb of a woman ready to conceive.

Phoebe Thunder Coburn was born to Didi Thunder
and the author on January 2, 1993.

ABOUT THE AUTHOR

Broughton Coburn lived and worked in Nepal and the Himalayas for over seventeen years, initially as a Peace Corps volunteer teacher and later as an overseer of rural development and wildlife conservation efforts for the United Nations, the World Wildlife Fund, and other agencies. A graduate of Harvard, he is a native of Washington State currently living in Wilson, Wyoming.

ALSO BY BROUGHTON COBURN

Nepali Aama

Life Lessons of a Himalayan Woman

In 1973 Broughton Coburn lived and taught school in a subsistence farming village in the foothills of Nepal's Himalayas. It was there that he met and developed a unique friendship with a septuagenarian native widow named Vishnu Maya Gurung, fondly known to her relatives and locals as *Aama* (Mother). When Coburn moved into the hay loft above her water buffalo shed, Aama became his landlady, but she also treated him like the son she never had. Having lost his own mother shortly before he met Aama, Coburn took an instant liking to the sprightly Nepalese woman.

Nepali Aama is Coburn's enchanting account of his experiences living, working and traveling with Aama in Nepal, illustrated with his own photos and Aama's candid, sometimes salty, often hilarious observations on everyday life in the rural third world. By combining Aama's deep-rooted wisdom with his striking black and white photographs, Coburn places the reader in a setting that few have ever experienced. He also offers rare insight into a culture alive with humor, folklore and religion. "Aama and her people were poor and uneducated, but they seemed to possess an uncanny strength grounded in tradition, family, community, and self-sufficiency," he writes. "The values and philosophy that I have learned from Aama, her relatives, and the villagers are life lessons that are valuable in my own country, or wherever I go."

0-38547433-4/$12.95/$17.95 in Canada/photos throughout

ANCHOR BOOKS